MONTALE'S *MESTIERE VILE*

PUBLICATIONS OF THE FOUNDATION FOR ITALIAN STUDIES
UNIVERSITY COLLEGE, DUBLIN

General Editor: John C. Barnes

Dante and the Middle Ages: Literary and Historical Essays, ed. J. C. Barnes and C. Ó Cuilleanáin

Dante Comparisons: Comparative Studies of Dante and: Montale, Foscolo, Tasso, Chaucer, Petrarch, Propertius and Catullus, ed. E. Haywood and B. Jones

Dante Readings, ed. E. Haywood

Dante Soundings: Eight Literary and Historical Essays, ed. D. Nolan

Word and Drama in Dante: Essays on the "Divina Commedia", ed. J. C. Barnes and J. Petrie

J. Petrie, *Petrarch: The Augustan Poets, the Italian Tradition and the "Canzoniere"*

T. O'Neill, *Of Virgin Muses and of Love: A Study of Foscolo's "Dei Sepolcri"*

G. Talbot, *Montale's "Mestiere Vile": The Elective Translations from English of the 1930s and 1940s*

Italian Storytellers: Essays on Italian Narrative Literature, ed. E. Haywood and C. Ó Cuilleanáin

B. Reynolds, *Casalattico and the Italian Community in Ireland*

BELFIELD ITALIAN LIBRARY

Dante Alighieri, *Vita nuova*, ed. J. Petrie and J. Salmons
Lorenzo de' Medici, *Selected Writings*, ed C. Salvadori
Luigi Pirandello, *Il berretto a sonagli*, ed. J. C. Barnes

MONTALE'S *MESTIERE VILE*

The Elective Translations from English of the 1930s and 1940s

GEORGE TALBOT

Published for
The Foundation for Italian Studies
University College, Dublin

IRISH ACADEMIC PRESS · DUBLIN

Publication of this book was assisted by grants from

The University of Hull
The Istituto Italiano di Cultura, Dublin

Printed and bound by Antony Rowe Ltd, Chippenham, England

First published 1995

by

Irish Academic Press Ltd
Kill Lane
Blackrock
County Dublin
Ireland

A catalogue record for this book is available from the British Library

ISBN 0 7165 2526 7

PREFACE

This book has its origins in a dissertation for a doctoral degree in Italian awarded by the University of Dublin. I should like to acknowledge here the thorough and constructive supervision of Dott. Roberto Bertoni and Dr Cormac Ó Cuilleanáin. I should also like to record my gratitude to Prof. Maria Antonietta Grignani of the University of Pavia for her encouragement at an early stage of my research while I was studying in Pavia, and to Mrs C. Salvadori Lonergan, Head of the Italian Department at Trinity College, Dublin, for her continuous encouragement. In the various stages of revision of the monograph I should mention the constructive comments of Prof. F. J. Jones, Neil Vickers, Donncha Ó Croinín, and Jennifer Petrie and Prof. J. C. Barnes of the UCD Foundation for Italian Studies. I am also grateful to Kerry Houston for his technical assistance.

Parts of this book have been presented at conferences, symposia and research seminars. I should like to thank everyone who discussed points arising out of my papers presented at the Dublin Istituto Italiano di Cultura, University College, Cork, the British Comparative Literature Association "Across Europe" conference (University of Warwick, July 1992), the Royal Irish Academy "New World in Literature" symposium (University College, Galway, October 1992) and the Society for Italian Studies Conference (University College and Trinity College, Dublin, July 1993), as well as staff and postgraduate students of Dublin City University.

Finally I wish to express my love and gratitude to my wife Caitríona for her encouragement, patience and support during the period of research by dedicating this book to her.

Hull, 1994

Addio addio crudele,
ti ho dato troppo spago,
se manchi non ti pago,
volgo altrove le vele.
Lascia i pesci in *barile*
e a Camillo al rabarbaro,
per me ha tanto di barba
questo mestiere vile
ma solo traduzioni
mi chiedono i coglioni!

Posthumous poem written by Montale in 1943 and contained in a letter to his sometime "ghost translator", Lucia Rodocanachi. First published in 1983, it is now contained in *Tutte le poesie*, edited by Giorgio Zampa (Milan, Mondadori, 1984).

CONTENTS

INTRODUCTION: HISTORY, THEORY AND CONTEXT

> Il decennio dal '30 al '40 che passerà nella storia della nostra cultura come quello delle traduzioni, non l'abbiamo fatto per ozio né Vittorini né Cecchi né altri. Esso è stato un monumento fatale, e proprio nel suo apparente esotismo e ribellismo è pulsata l'unica vena vitale della nostra recente cultura poetica. L'Italia era estraniata, imbarbarita, calcificata—bisognava scuoterla, decongestionarla e riesporla a tutti i venti primaverili dell'Europa e del mondo. Niente di strano se quest' opera di conquista di testi non poteva esser fatta da burocrati o braccianti letterari, ma ci vollero giovanili entusiasmi e compromissioni. Noi scoprimmo l'Italia—questo il punto—cercando gli uomini e le parole in America, in Russia, in Francia, nella Spagna.[1]
>
> Cesare Pavese

Montale and the Decade of Translations

The Translation Industry

In 1946 Cesare Pavese claimed that the 1930s in Italy would be known in literary history as the decade of translations. In that decade Pavese himself made the first Italian translation of *Moby Dick,* and other Italian writers including Gadda Conti, Montale, Moravia and Vittorini translated American novels and short stories for the home market.

In 1938 Elio Vittorini and the Milanese publisher Valentino Bompiani began exchanging letters on the matter of translating

American literature. Vittorini was soon working for Bompiani as a translator, editor and administrator organizing the Italian translation industry. Vittorini promoted North American prose zealously and enlisted professional writers and translators to make translations. Although Vittorini and Bompiani had to be careful in their choice of texts so as not to incur the disapproval of the state censor, they soon had an impressive list of American titles on the market, including work by William Faulkner, Dorothy Parker and John Steinbeck.

Vittorini's great editorial project was to be a two-volume anthology of North American literature. The anthology was assembled by 1941, all the stories and novellas having been translated by established Italian writers including Pavese and Montale.[2] Vittorini divided the material into nine sections and wrote introductory notes for each section. The censor considered Vittorini's editorial commentary provocative, and the first edition of *Americana* was immediately sequestered.[3] After negotiation with Corrado Pavolini, the minister for "cultura popolare", Bompiani secured a compromise.[4] In 1942 *Americana* was re-issued without Vittorini's commentary and carrying an introduction by Emilio Cecchi.

Cecchi was an older man and a distinguished critic of both Italian and Anglo-American literature. He had made important contributions to prestigious literary journals such as *La ronda*, *Solaria*, *Il Baretti* and *La voce*. Cecchi belonged to Croce's generation, and like Croce he was a liberal opposed to Fascism and baffled by the modern American writing which inspired Vittorini and Pavese. Cecchi's introduction to *Americana* was sober and sensible and had none of the polemic which informed Vittorini's commentary.

For Vittorini translation was in itself a form of political activity because it gave substance to the myth of America. He had written in 1929: "Prezzolini, *La voce*, non insegnavano nulla. Nulla Papini. Nulla Soffici. Essi non hanno fatto la carriera che ci voleva per essere i nostri maestri; né l'opera loro ebbe tanta consistenza da giungere fino a noi con qualche utilità."[5]

Looking beyond the national frontiers Vittorini and Pavese found "una America pensosa e barbarica, felice e rissosa, dissoluta, feconda, greve di tutto il passato del mondo, e insieme giovane innocente."[6] According to Pavese, the translations performed a vital service for the Italian reading public:

> Almeno nel campo della moda e del gusto la nuova mania giovò a perpetuare e alimentare l'opposizione politica, sia pure generica e futile, del pubblico italiano che leggeva. Per molta gente l'incontro con Caldwell, Steinbeck, Saroyan, e perfino col vecchio [Sinclair] Lewis, aperse il primo spiraglio di libertà, il primo sospetto che non tutto nella cultura del mondo finisse coi fasci.[7]

Another young intellectual, Giaime Pintor, described this mythical America as a discovery for which Columbus was not required, because "è scoperta dentro di noi la terra a cui si tende con la stessa speranza e la stessa fiducia dei primi emigrati e di chiunque sia deciso a difendere a prezzo di fatiche e di errori la dignità della condizione umana."[8] The myth of America was thus an ideological deformation of reality or even a form of lay religion whose sacred texts were modern American novels and short stories in translation.

Vittorini worked as a translator but more significantly he organized others into what might be called a translation industry. This consisted of ghost translators who did the primary task of translation.[9] Their crib translations were then sent to established writers who made whatever changes they deemed fit and subsequently received sole credit for translation of the finished product.

Montale as Translator

Montale's first collection of poems, *Ossi di seppia* (1925), had been an instant critical success, but it had not been sufficient to find him a steady job. Living in Florence from 1927, he eventually found employment as director of the Gabinetto Vieusseux. His contract was terminated in December 1938 on the grounds that he was not a member of the Fascist Party. His career as a translator began early in 1939.

Montale belonged quite definitely to the Cecchi faction. His version of the American dream was more complex than those of Pavese, Pintor and Vittorini.[10] His most frenetic activity as a translator is set in the period which runs from 1940 to 1947. As part of the translation industry he became a translator of prose, principally of American novels and short stories: between 1940 and 1947 he translated work by John Steinbeck, Dorothy Parker, Herman

Melville, Eugene O'Neill, Nathaniel Hawthorne, Mark Twain, Francis Bret Harte, Evelyn Scott, F. Scott Fitzgerald, Kay Boyle and William Faulkner.[11] These were all commissioned translations, the commissions coming mainly from Bompiani through Vittorini. Montale almost certainly has these translations in mind when he describes his "sgradita attività di traduttore" in his "Intervista immaginaria".[12]

Yet not all his translations were as uncongenial as one might think from reading the "Intervista". In 1942 he began translating *Green Mansions* by W. H. Hudson, without a publisher's contract. This is an exception to his unwritten rule which was to translate poetry out of interest and novels and memoirs for a living. For his version of *Green Mansions* he worked with Lucia Rodocanachi, who acted as ghost translator. Rodocanachi made a literal translation of the text and sent it to Montale for revision. Given the existence of an uncredited ghost translation between the source text and Montale's final version, it may be objected that the term "translation" is not entirely appropriate as a description of Montale's part in the process.[13]

In any case, Montale was an important presence in the Italian translation industry of the 1930s and 1940s. Although he disdainfully described translation as his "mestiere vile", I suggest in the following pages that his elective translations from English, as opposed to the commissioned ones he undertook to make ends meet, form an important context to his own "original" work of the period. The texts on which I shall base my arguments are the poems collected in the first edition of his *Quaderno di traduzioni* (1948) and *La vita della foresta*, his version of *Green Mansions*, translated in the 1940s but not published until 1987. Montale certainly translated from English before the 1930s and after the 1940s, indeed an enlarged second edition of *Quaderno di traduzioni* came out in 1975; but the 1930s and 1940s are the background against which this monograph is set.

Montale's *Quaderno di traduzioni*

In 1928 T. S. Eliot's *Criterion* had carried an English version of "Arsenio" made by Mario Praz. The following year Montale had published his own version of Eliot's "A Song for Simeon" ("Canto di Simeone"), based on the *Nunc dimittis* (Luke 2. 29–32).[14] During the 1930s he had translated three sonnets by Shakespeare, which are of particular critical interest in that they may be compared with Ungaretti's versions of the same poems, made around the same time.[15] In 1931 *Circoli* carried Montale's translations of six poems by Jorge Guillén under the title "Sei liriche del *Cántico* di Jorge Guillén".[16] Montale's translation of "Billy in the Darbies" ("Billy in catene") closes his translation *La storia di Billy Budd*, which was published as a component of *Americana* (1941 and 1942) and separately in 1942.[17] "Berlina ferma nella notte", Montale's translation of "La Berline arrêtée dans la nuit" by Milosz, appeared in 1943.[18] His version of Emily Dickinson's poem then known as "The Storm" ("Tempesta") was published in 1945.[19] Montale translated two poems from James Joyce's *Pomes Penyeach*, "Watching the Needleboats at San Sabba" ("Guardando i canottieri, a San Sabba", which later became "Guardando i canottieri di San Sabba") and "For a Flower Given to My Daughter" ("Per un fiore dato alla mia bambina").[20] He also translated a poem by Dylan Thomas.[21] His translation of Maragall's "Cant espiritual" ("Il cant espiritual") was published in 1947.[22] And his version of Hopkins's "Pied Beauty" ("Bellezza cangiante", which later became "La bellezza cangiante") was published in 1948.[23]

The *Quaderno di traduzioni* was published in 1948 and contained, along with these previously published translations, Montale's versions of William Blake's "To the Muses" ("Alle muse"), Thomas Hardy's "The Garden Seat" ("Vecchia panchina") and W. B. Yeats's "The Indian to his Love" ("L'indiano all'amata"). A slightly enlarged edition of the *Quaderno di traduzioni* was published in 1975. This included three more Yeats poems ("When you are old and grey and full of sleep" ["Quando tu sarai vecchia"], "After Long Silence" ["Dopo un lungo silenzio"] and "Sailing to Byzantium" ["Verso Bisanzio"]), as well as an adaptation of a poem by Djuna Barnes ("Trasfigurazioni"), a translation of "Hugh Selwyn Mauberley", I. 5, a translation of "The Barbarians" by Constantinos Cavafy ("I barbari") and a Latin translation of Montale's own "La bufera" ("Nimbus") made by Fernando Bandini.

There are partial attempts to assess Montale's activity as a translator in the critical literature, and some of these assessments are both stimulating and convincing. There is as yet, however, no sustained work of criticism which deals with the theoretical and practical difficulties of translation and originality in relation both to Montale's uncommissioned translations from English, and, beyond the limits of translation, to his own poetry.

Montale and Translation Theory

Newmark, following Bühler and Jakobson, distinguishes between three main functions of language: the *expressive*, the *informative* and the *vocative*.[24] A text may include any combination of different language functions, but generally speaking one function will tend to dominate in a given text. According to this theory, the literary texts which will concern us here are texts in which the expressive function dominates. Such texts are open to a number of different methods of translation, and these methods rely (at least implicitly) on different theories of translation.

The Montalian Theory

In a brief essay on the ontology of works of art Montale wrote:

> Chi legge, chi guarda, chi ascolta, modifica, traduce, adatta secondo la propria particolare sensibilità. Sconsolate poesie di Arturo Graf (ma scritte in ottonari) sono finite in libri di lettura per le elementari. Gli antologisti (laureati in lettere) le avevano capite alla rovescia. E non mi stupirei affatto se dal fraintendimento quelle liriche traessero qualche nuova ragione di vita. Pare dunque che l'opera d'arte esista solo per chi l'ha creata, e in quel momento, *non dopo*. Dopo, diventa una traduzione per tutti, anche per l'autore.
>
> Da ciò si potrebbe inferire (ed è stato fatto) che non esiste l'arte ma solo l'esperienza estetica, la quale non ha bisogno di oggetti assoluti ma di rapporti, e che può benissimo crearsi da sé i propri oggetti senza bisogno dei sedicenti "artisti" e delle cosiddette "opere".
>
> Ma qui credo bene di arrestarmi. Non sono nato evidentemente per creare un'estetica nuova, costruttiva.[25]

If Montale accepted this ontology of art (note the "pare") then there are some important corollaries for his own attitude to reading. Reading cannot be merely a passive act, therefore it is in some way creative. If every reading is a re-creation of the text then a written translation (say, text B) of a poem (text A) has a status which is objectively independent of text A. There is an internal relationship between text B and text A but that relationship is essentially an aesthetic experience and as such takes place in the mind of the reader/translator at one specific time. Montale's notion of *translation* here is thus a very broad one and one which gives the reader/translator quite a measure of freedom.

The Benjamin Model

Montale's theory is clearly influenced by Croce's Idealist aesthetics, and thus shares some features with one of the most famous of twentieth-century translation theories, that of Walter Benjamin. Benjamin's introduction to his translation of Baudelaire's *Tableaux parisiens* is well known in translation studies, but it may be useful to summarize his arguments at this point.[26] Benjamin starts from the premiss that literary works (*expressive texts* in Newmark's terminology) have an existence independent of human perception; or, as he puts it, "Kein Gedicht gilt dem Leser, kein Bild dem Beschauer, keine Symphonie der Hörerschaft" (page 50) ["No poem is intended for the reader, no picture for the beholder, no symphony for the listener" (page 69)]. The essential quality of a literary work, he argues, is not the imparting of information. But, given that translation cannot transmit anything except information, translation is doomed to convey the inessential—what he disdainfully describes as "the innacurate transmission of an inessential content" (page 70) ("eine ungenaue Übermittlung eines unwesentlichen Inhalts": page 50). Only the translator who is also a poet, he contends, can reproduce the essential quality of a literary work.

Translation, Benjamin argues, is a mode, and to understand it as such, one must go back to the original and ask two related questions: firstly, will an adequate translation ever be found for it, and secondly, does its nature lend itself to translation? The first is a contingent and uninteresting question; its answer is arbitrary. The second is more profound. Translation, he continues, is an essential quality of certain works. It is an operation effected in the afterlife of a literary work. Thus, he concludes:

> Translations that are more than transmissions of subject-matter come into being when in the course of its survival a work has

> reached the age of its fame. Contrary, therefore, to the claims of bad translators, such translations do not so much serve the work as owe their existence to it. The life of the original attains in them to its ever-renewed latest and most abundant flowering. (page 72)

At this point translation as a mode has passed from the realm of an individual expressive text to the nature of language itself. Benjamin continues:

> Translation thus ultimately serves the purpose of expressing the central reciprocal relationship between languages. It cannot possibly reveal or establish this hidden relationship itself; but it can represent it by realizing it in embryonic or intensive form. This representation of hidden significance through an embryonic attempt at making it visible is of so singular a nature that it is rarely met with in the sphere of non-linguistic life. This, in its analogies and symbols, can draw on other ways of suggesting meaning than intensive—that is, anticipative, intimating—realization. As for the posited central kinship of languages, it is marked by a distinctive convergence. Languages are not strangers to one another, but are, a priori and apart from all historical relationships, interrelated in what they want to express. (page 72)

What Benjamin means by the "kinship of languages" ("Verwandschaft der Sprachen") and the role of translation in demonstrating this kinship is something quite at odds with notions of "similarity" in relation to works of art. Given that a translation comes into existence in the afterlife of an original work, a translation which strives to continue the original will not strive for "likeness" to the original, but will instead take into account the maturing process undergone by the original in the interim between its coming into existence and this point in its afterlife. Thus, according to Benjamin:

> Translation is so far removed from being the sterile equation of two dead languages that of all literary forms it is the one charged with the special mission of watching over the maturing process of the original language and the birth pangs of its own. (page 73)

Benjamin is here moving towards the formulation of his Idealist philosophy of language:

> Wherein resides the relatedness of two languages, apart from historical considerations? Certainly not in the similarity between works of literature or words. Rather, all suprahistorical kinship of languages rests in the intention underlying each language as a whole—an intention, however, which no single language can attain by itself but which is realized only by the totality of their intentions supplementing each other: pure language. (page 74)

All poetic and literary creations are couched in linguistic terms, yet in all language there remains an ineffable residue, resistant to communication. This other dimension of language is Benjamin's pure language, a language of truth, a sort of Platonic language to which all thought aspires that in the various tongues is tied contingently to linguistic elements. In these linguistic creations, specifically in literary works, this other dimension is obscured by alien meaning deriving from other associations connoted according to the context by the choice of words. The really significant task of the translator is the liberation of the pure language from its original context and the release of that pure language into his or her own language. That is the ultimate justification of genuine translation: its purpose is the transmission of pure language from one medium to another, for the sake of language, not for the sake of a reader. Benjamin expands on how the translator should set about this task:

> Fragments of a vessel which are to be glued together must match one another in the smallest details, although they need not be like one another. In the same way a translation, instead of resembling the meaning of the original, must lovingly and in detail incorporate the original's mode of signification, thus making both the original and the translation recognizable as fragments of a greater language, just as fragments are part of a vessel. For this very reason translation must in large measure refrain from wanting to communicate something, from rendering the sense, and in this the original is important to it only insofar as it has already relieved the translator and his translation of assembling and expressing what is to be conveyed. (page 78)

The practicality of this mode of transmission involves an appraisal and expansion of one's own language.[27] What Benjamin is proposing here is strict literalism as a strategy for translation, doing violence to the norms of the target language while transmitting the source language, and in so doing perhaps laying bare something of the language of truth.

Benjamin's argument is simple and profound. The theory may sound somewhat familiar to readers of Montale because it is the explicit formulation of the idea implicit in his cryptic "Intervista immaginaria" (1946), written during his most intense period of translation:

> E anche nel nuovo libro ho continuato la mia lotta per scavare un'altra dimensione nel nostro pesante linguaggio polisillabico, che mi pareva rifiutarsi a un'esperienza come la mia. Ripeto che la lotta non fu programmatica. Forse mi ha assistito la mia forzata e sgradita attività di traduttore. Ho maledetto spesso la nostra lingua.[28]

Montale's artistic interest in doing violence to the norms of Italian poetic language and his short but intense activity as a translator seem to link his practice with Benjamin's theory. Benjamin's model of translation applies to Montale in that it draws attention to the translator's opportunity for innovation of usage. Analysis of Montale's translations reveals his capacity for innovation, but that innovation is not generally achieved within the parameters of strict literalism. Nonetheless, the Benjamin model is a useful one as a theoretical approach to the examination of Montale's work as a translator of poetry.

The Jakobson Model

Montale's contention, reported above, that "chi legge, chi guarda, chi ascolta, modifica, traduce, adatta secondo la propria particolare sensibilità" would also find resonances of recognition in the work of Roman Jakobson. Jakobson's account of the linguistic aspects of translation is considerably more rigorous and scientific than Benjamin's and may, for that reason, form the basis of a more useful investigative tool for the analysis of Montale's activity as a translator.

Jakobson, in his seminal essay "On Linguistic Aspects of Translation", takes issue with the Logical Positivists' theory of meaning and posits a semiotic theory, according to which the meaning of any linguistic sign is its translation into some further sign, especially (in C. S. Peirce's phrase) a sign "in which it is more fully developed". Jakobson offers as an example the term "bachelor", which may be converted into the more explicit term "unmarried man" should a higher level of explicitness be required. He goes on to distinguish between three ways of interpreting a verbal sign:

1 intralingual: interpretation of signs by means of other signs of the same language;
2 interlingual: translation proper, from one language into another;
3 intersemiotic: transmutation through signs of non-verbal sign systems.

Intralingual translation is rewording, synonymy, near-synonymy or circumlocution, but even in this case there is inevitably *some* loss of meaning. The loss is likely to be greater in interlingual translation, where culture-specific terms will, as a rule, require componential analysis in passing from one language to another. Jakobson even argues that "translation from one language into another substitutes messages in one language not for separate code-units but for entire messages in some other language."

Against Benjamin's claim for a kinship of languages ("Verwandschaft der Sprachen"), Jakobson contends that:

> Languages differ essentially in what they *must* convey and not in what they *can* convey. Each verb of a given language imperatively raises a set of specific yes-or-no questions, for instance: is the narrated event conceived with or without reference to its completion? Is the narrated event presented as prior to the speech event or not? Naturally the attention of native speakers and listeners will be constantly focused on such items as are compulsory in their verbal code.[29]

It is not a difficult task to illustrate some of these yes-or-no questions which arise in translating between English and Italian. The following is a non-exhaustive list:

1 Morphology. English, being a hybrid descendant of the Teutonic group with a considerable Old French influence, is largely a language of monosyllables. Its historical development has taken in its stride the almost complete extinction of verb conjugation and noun declension. It has lost the thou–you distinction of familiar and polite address, which was already a strained convention in

Shakespeare's time. As a legacy of its hybrid nature English has two separate word-stocks from which to choose. In consequence, many polysyllabic verbs (which tend to have Greek or Latin roots) have synonyms which consist of two monosyllables (phrasal verbs), a verb and a preposition (e.g. "to telephone" = "to ring up"). In Italian, on the other hand, apart from basic conjunctions and a relatively small stock of other monosyllables, the vocabulary is at least bisyllabic. Montale's ways of dealing with the word-stock problem, as we shall see, are particularly interesting.

2 Gender. Differences of gender between languages cause problems for the translator because of what we may call grammatical personification. Jakobson cites as an example of such a difficulty a book of poems by Pasternak called *My Sister Life*, which would sound more natural in Italian than in English, but which caused his Czech translator to despair as the Czech noun meaning "life" is masculine. Italian poetry, from St Francis's "sora acqua" onwards, treats grammatical personification as a normal element of its poetic discourse, but literal translation into English is apt to sound too abstract and remote because English has virtually no gender left in its grammar.

3 Rhyme. Rhyme is the oldest form of metrical device and is present in both Italian and English poetry both as a means of structuring verse and as a feature which organizes the musical pattern of a poem. The potential for producing rhymes is far greater in Italian than in English because of some basic facts concerning the two languages. Most Italian words end in vowels, which makes rhyme a natural feature of the language. In fact Montale, as we shall see, took great care to minimize rhyme in some of his translations from English in order to preserve some of the effect of the original text. Rhyme involves the repetition of sounds; Montale tended towards avoiding repetition, and this is a feature which distinguishes some of his work from that of other translators. Montale also chose to use half-rhyme and assonance in his poems as methods of organization.

4 Abstraction. Dudley Fitts, commenting on an English translation of González Martínez's "Tuércele el cuello al cisne", has made the following point: "A Latin language can be more persuasive with such quasi-particularities as *the soul of things* and *the voice of the landscape*."[30] These expressions ring false in English, which as a language requires more empirical concrete detail to gain a

comparable power of incantation. The tendency in English is towards the sharp delineation of an object in order to universalize it. Fitts's suggested solution to the problem of translating "la voz del paisaje" is to combine a determinate part of the landscape with an oxymoron (for example, "the mute cry of the fields"). That sounds quite impressive in English but if we now translate it literally into Italian ("il grido muto dei campi"), the effect is more contrived or hermetic than "la voce del paesaggio".

5 Material and motion. Matthews makes a point about translating English into French which would also hold for translating English into Italian.[31] The following is a line from Eliot's "The Hollow Men": "Or rats' feet over broken glass". It will not translate literally into either French or Italian. Matthews took Saint-John Perse's translation as a model of how it should be done: "la course des rats sur le débris". The point of the exercise is to show that motion can be implied in English whereas it cannot in the Romance languages. The rats' paws loom too large in a literal version. They must give way to an abstraction ("la course") in order to make sense.

6 Syntax and velocity. Both Montale and Ungaretti observed the relative velocity of English and Italian syntax. Montale, as we have seen above, described Italian as "[il] nostro pesante linguaggio polisillabico". Likewise Ungaretti, coming from his translations of Góngora to work on Shakespeare, found difficulties of speed: "La difficoltà si risolveva dunque da sé tenendo conto che in un medesimo gruppo di vocaboli, la quantità di sillabe italiane è superiore a quella delle inglesi nel rapporto di circa sedici su undici."[32] One typical example of the problem is the two languages' different procedures in dealing with the genitive. The Saxon genitive can achieve a more concise phrase than the more cumbersome Italian one—compare "Montale's poems" with "le poesie di Montale", four syllables as against eight. Consequently, it is always a temptation to translate English blank verse into hypermetric Italian lines rather than traditional ones.

There are other grammatical features of English which cannot be translated into Italian without what Catford calls a "shift".[33] There are instances of singular English nouns shifting into plural Italian nouns because Italian cannot accommodate such singulars, e.g. "information" → "informazioni", "furniture" → "mobili". In other cases, an English adjective + noun structure must shift into an

Italian noun + adjective structure, e.g. "the Italian language" → "la lingua italiana", "the White House" → "la Casa Bianca", "the Appian Way" → "la via Appia". In these situations there are no choices—the languages themselves leave the translator with no alternatives—unless one is prepared to use inversion or hyperbaton or some other form of syntactic manipulation which might be acceptable in poetry but is not usually so in prose.

Language in its cognitive function, Jakobson argues, depends minimally on its grammatical structure, because "the cognitive level of language not only admits but directly requires recoding interpretation, i.e. translation". Thus to claim that cognitive data are untranslatable would be absurd. Poetry, however, is a special case. According to Jakobson:

> In poetry, verbal equations become a constructive principle of the text. Syntactic and morphological categories, roots, and affixes, phonemes and their components (distinctive features)—in short, any constituents of the verbal code—are confronted, juxtaposed, brought into contiguous relation according to the principle of similarity and contrast and carry their own autonomous signification. Phonemic similarity is sensed as semantic relationship. The pun [...] reigns over poetic art, and whether its rule is absolute or limited, poetry by definition is untranslatable. Only creative transposition is possible: either intralingual transposition—from one poetic shape into another, or interlingual transposition—from one language into another, or finally intersemiotic transposition—from one system of signs into another, e.g. from verbal art into music, dance, cinema or painting.[34]

Re-reading and Re-creation

The concept of *creative transposition* implies that absolute translation of poetic texts is an illusion: the transfer from one language to another cannot be total. But, as Walter Benjamin put it, "its goal is a final, conclusive, decisive stage of all linguistic creation. In translation, the original rises into a higher and purer air [...] but what reaches this region is that element in a translation which goes beyond transmission of subject-matter."[35] By this latter he meant the element in an original which seems to defy translation. Capturing the nuance, according to Benjamin, is the task of the genuine translator.

In practical terms that model of translation rejects a literal prose version of a poem (such as George Kay's procedure in the *Penguin Book of Italian Verse*).[36] Rejecting this option one is left with the prospect of making a poem in one language out of a poem in another. That raises two further difficulties. Given that the translator needs to find or invent formal effects in his own language to reproduce those of the foreign language, he or she is apt to swing to one of two extremes: the translator either copies the form slavishly to match the original or pays too little attention to the form and produces a flabby travesty of the original. Both extremes are parodies of tenable models of the creative transposition process: "concentrate on the content at the expense of the form" and "concentrate on the form at the expense of the content."

Translation as creative transposition has, as a necessary corollary, an aspect of interpretation. Given that a translator cannot translate everything that a text has to offer, he or she has to select, to keep what seems essential, and often in doing so to leave behind elements which cannot be accommodated within the constraints of the translation.[37]

This process of interpretation sometimes gives rise to what is called the equivalent effect principle, according to which the translator's task is to produce the same effect on the reader as was felt by readers of the original text. Thus the translator gives primacy to the reader, the addressee. Montale's translations do not always conform to that theory because he tended to approach translation as an extension of his own creative writing. What is fascinating in his translations is the interplay between the equivalent effect principle and creative transposition or appropriation.

On the linguistic question there is no doubt that Jakobson is correct: languages do differ essentially in what they *must* convey and not in what they *can* convey, and the Jakobsonian model is a useful one for the linguistic analysis of individual translations. But Montale's achievement as a translator is more in sympathy with Benjamin's synthetic model of translation. Through the process of translation Montale succeeded in making very Italian poems out of very English poems, but without appearing to lose the poetic nuance. Assessment of that achievement requires a pragmatic appropriation of both the vision of the Benjamin model and the practicality of the Jakobson model.

Translation, Intertextuality and Context

Intertextuality

Intertextuality is a term borrowed from text linguistics, and the concept of intertextuality will be used extensively in the following chapters. According to de Beaugrande and Dressler, intertextuality as a concept:

> subsume[s] the ways in which the production and reception of a given text depends upon the participants' knowledge of other texts. This knowledge can be applied by a process describable in terms of *mediation* (the extent to which one feeds one's current beliefs and goals into the model of the communicative situation [...]): the greater the expanse of time and of processing activities between the use of the current text and the use of previously encountered texts, the greater the mediation. Extensive mediation is illustrated by the development and use of *text types*, being classes of texts expected to have certain traits for certain purposes. Mediation is much smaller when people quote from or refer to specific well-known texts, e.g. famous speeches or works of literature.[38]

De Beaugrande and Dressler, after presenting the concept of intertextuality, go on to outline a typology of text types. In their view, literary texts and their sub-group, poetic texts, distinguish themselves from other text types by the characteristic of not intending "to increase and distribute knowledge about the currently accepted *real world*". This is a controversial judgement but it does have some intuitive plausibility.

A fundamental issue of intertextuality is the notion of *text allusion*, that is, where the producer of a text refers to an existing text. It may be significant that in order to explore this notion de Beaugrande and Dressler turn to poetic texts rather than *informative* texts (to use Newmark's terminology again). The significance of their choice would appear to be that poetic texts tend to refer to other texts or to language generally as much as they may refer to extralinguistic reality. The authors illustrate different degrees of intertextual mediation by presenting Christopher Marlowe's "Come live with me and be my love", written in 1600, and various other poems written after that date. Marlowe's poem begins:

> Come live with me and be my love,
> And we will all the pleasures prove
> That valleys, groves, hills, and fields,
> Woods, or steepy mountain yields.

In the same year Sir Walter Ralegh "replied" with gentle irony to Marlowe's poem, borrowing Marlowe's rhyme scheme and using the same metrical structure:

> If all the world and love were young,
> And truth in every shepherd's tongue,
> These pretty pleasures might me move
> To live with thee and be thy love.

Ralegh's poem clearly presupposes the existence of Marlowe's, and the reader will miss a great deal if unacquainted with the first poem. The intertextual connection here is vital. That link is less vital, though still important, in the case of John Donne's unlikely proposal of an improbable fisherman:

> Come live with me and be my love,
> And we will some new pleasures prove,
> Of golden sands and crystal brooks:
> With silken lines, and silver hooks.

The interlocutor is perhaps even more imaginary and less real here than in Marlowe's poem. What we have here is an intertextual joke which will be lost on those unaware of Marlowe's poem. (It may be noted that Donne's poem dates from 1612, and it could be safely assumed that his original readers were aware of the earlier poem.)

Intertextuality, to borrow Benjamin's phrase, continues the afterlife of a poem. In 1935 Cecil Day-Lewis extended the process of mediation with the following lines, put into the mouth of an unskilled labourer:

> Come live with me and be my love,
> And we will all the pleasures prove
> Of peace and plenty, bed and board,
> That chance employment may afford.

> I'll handle dainties on the docks
> And thou shalt read of summer frocks:
> At evening by the sour canals
> We'll hope to hear some madrigals.

This is devastating irony, quite unlike Ralegh's gentle wit. Day-Lewis is calling into question the *modus operandi* of a text type or genre. Poetry, he seems to be saying, must take some account of the *real world*. But the weapon he uses is intertextuality.

Montale and Intertextuality

Montale also had aesthetic difficulties with outmoded poetic conventions, and he explicitly encouraged an intertextual approach to reading poetry and indeed to reading his own work: "Sarebbe un errore leggere una sola poesia e cercare di anatomizzarla, perché c'è sempre un richiamo da un suono all'altro, ma anche da una poesia all'altra."[39] Montale's advice is interesting, but how useful is it in relation to his own work? The advice could send readers on an over-zealous investigation of texts motivated by a desire to trace *sources* for Montale's imagery, vocabulary, symbols and themes. That is one approach, but it is probably more genealogical than intertextual, and it is better suited to detecting plagiarism than to understanding the dynamics of intertextuality. Intertextual readings of poems are readings in which parts of a poem are clarified, or modified, by circumstances provided by other texts. These contextual texts may be *originals* by the same writer or they may be other writers' texts. Intertextuality is not so much a search for *influence* as an attempt to interpret texts in relation to each other. In Montale's case, the translations which were not commissioned are the key to his relationship with foreign literature. It is necessary to read these translations in the context of Montale's original work and of his authorial strategies in order to appreciate their significance.[40]

Intertextuality and Context

Montale's translations in the *Quaderno di traduzioni* may be broadly divided into two groups. The first group consists of poems for which Montale felt a significant empathy because of thematic, symbolic or linguistic content. This group includes texts such as Dickinson's "The Storm", Hopkins's "Pied Beauty" and Melville's "Billy in the Darbies". The second group consists of texts in which there is little affinity with Montale's own poetry. Here the most striking examples are Joyce's two poems "Watching the Needle-boats, at San Sabba" and "For a Flower Given to My Daughter", and Léonie Adams's "Lullaby". It is an easier task to assess the extent of innovation in Montale's translation procedure when his translations of the latter group are subjected to analysis.

Montale arranged the texts of the *Quaderno di traduzioni* in what is more or less chronological order according to the poets' dates of birth.[41] The collection represents a personal literary tradition which Montale created out of texts originally written by other poets. It is thus an act of appropriation, a reading, or, more precisely, a rewriting of the past. Borges, in an essay entitled "Kafka and his Precursors", has described an analogous process:

> If I am not mistaken, the heterogeneous pieces I have enumerated resemble Kafka; if I am not mistaken, not all of them resemble each other. This second fact is the more significant. In each of these texts we find Kafka's idiosyncrasy to a greater or lesser degree, but if Kafka had never written a line, we would not perceive this quality; in other words, it would not exist. The poem "Fears and Scruples" by Browning foretells Kafka's work, but our reading of Kafka perceptibly sharpens and deflects our reading of the poem. Browning did not read it as we do now. In the critics' vocabulary, the word *precursor* is indispensable, but it should be cleansed of all connotation of polemic and rivalry. The fact is that every writer *creates* his own precursors. His work modifies our conception of the past, as it will modify the future. In this correlation the identity or plurality of the men involved is unimportant. The early Kafka of *Betrachtung* is less a precursor of the Kafka of sombre myths and atrocious institutions than is Browning or Lord Dunsany.[42]

Borges's final point, that a writer's early work may be more remote from his later work than a text written by another writer, is probably one with which Montale would have agreed, given his theory of reading.[43] It would, however, be a more accurate description of Montale's interaction with his created tradition to claim that rather than translating individual texts Montale was trying to translate a tradition into Italian, and that in that ambitious process of translation he used his own particular idiolect as a standard. Consequently, his interaction with his precursors was as close as it could possibly be: they literally spoke his own language and he could feel perfectly justified in using his readings of these other texts to develop themes, images or symbols already latent in his own earlier work.

In analysing Montale translations and criticism I have departed from the order in which the texts are presented in the *Quaderno di traduzioni*. The reason for this is mainly chronological, although it could also be regarded as thematic. By chronological I here mean not the order of composition of the original English poems but the period in which Montale made his translation or wrote his essay. An interesting thematic pattern emerges from this Montalian chronology. In 1925, when he wrote his essay "Stile e tradizione", Montale seems to have had little interest in foreign literature, and evidence of his reading habits (presented in Chapter 1 of this book) suggests that his command of English was not very sure. In that year he discovered James Joyce's work (in French) and a few years later he was translating T. S. Eliot's poetry into Italian. He began translating some of Shakepeare's sonnets in the 1930s, more or less at the same time—ironically—as his rival Ungaretti was working on a similar project of translating Shakespeare. The differences between the translations made by the two poets illustrate their different poetics very clearly. Montale's translations from Emily Dickinson, Gerard Manley Hopkins, Herman Melville and W. H. Hudson correspond chronologically to a deepening interest in metaphysics in his own original work. The numbering of the chapters in this book reflects the development outlined above. The final chapters, however, do not fit strictly into the chronological pattern: they are arranged thematically and deal with the other poets included in the 1948 *Quaderno di traduzioni*. It may appear odd that Chapter 1 deals, in part, with Montale's reading of Joyce's short stories, while a discussion of his translations of Joyce's poems is included in a later chapter. The reason is that Montale's reading of Joyce in 1925 was something of a formative experience, whereas his translations, made nearly twenty years later, were essentially occasional pieces.

In discussing the various English poems and Montale's translations of them, I have not presented a review of criticism relating to the original English poems except where it is clear, or very likely, that Montale was aware of the criticism. An assessment of the

English poems is not the issue. In the case of variants of the poems, I present the text with which Montale was familiar, even if it is a corrupt one. What is at stake is what Montale made of the poems given the material at his disposal.

The translation industry in Italy in the 1930s and 1940s represented, as we have seen, a form of protest on various levels. Montale was a part of that translation industry. The concepts of intertextuality and creative transposition combine to complicate the job of discussing Montale as an interpreter of English. They are, nevertheless, important concepts which must be dealt with in Montale's case because there is no obvious division between Montale *anglista* and Montale *scrittore*—indeed there is a symbiotic relationship between the two aspects of his work. The following chapters attempt to clarify Montale's approach to the problems of translation and originality.

NOTES

1 C. Pavese, "L'influsso degli eventi", in his *La letteratura americana e altri saggi*, edited by I. Calvino (Turin, Einaudi, 1962), p. 247.

2 The list of contributors reads as follows: Giansiro Ferrata, Enrico Fulchignoni, Piero Gadda Conti, Carlo Linati, Eugenio Montale, Alberto Moravia, Umberto Morra, Cesare Pavese, Guido Piovene, Elio Vittorini.

3 Vittorini's commentaries were not cited specifically as the reasons for the book's unsuitability. There is no reasonable doubt, however, that they were in fact the stumbling-block. The following is an extract from Pavolini's letter to Bompiani (7 Jan. 1941): "L'uscita in questo momento dell'antologia americana non è opportuna. Gli Stati Uniti sono potenzialmente i nostri nemici. Il loro Presidente ha tenuto contro il popolo italiano il noto atteggiamento. Non è il momento per usare delle cortesie all'America nemmeno letterarie." The letter was printed in *La fiera letteraria* (19 Dec. 1968), and is cited by R. Powell, "Vittorini and America", *Journal of the Association of Teachers of Italian*, 22 (Summer 1977), 22–31 (p. 27).

4 The Ministero della Cultura Popolare (soon abbreviated to Minculpop) was founded in 1937 and originally directed by Dino Alfieri. It was modelled on Goebbels's Ministry for the Enlightenment of the People and Propaganda, and its aim was the politicization of all aspects of Italian culture by means of control over publishing, theatre, cinema and broadcasting.

5 See a 1929 article by Vittorini cited by N. Carducci, *Gli intellettuali e l'ideologia americana nell'Italia letteraria degli anni Trenta* (Manduria, Lacaita, 1973), p. 42.

6 C. Pavese, "Ieri e oggi" [1947], in *Letteratura e cultura del periodo fascista*, edited by G. Manacorda (Milan, Principato, 1974), pp. 228–30. For a detailed and critical account of the America myth see N. Carducci, *Gli intellettuali e l'ideologia americana*. For a brief account in English see L. Pertile, "Fascism and

Literature", in *Rethinking Italian Fascism*, edited by D. Forgacs (London, Lawrence and Wishart, 1986), pp. 162–84.

7 C. Pavese, "Ieri e oggi", p. 229.

8 G. Pintor, *Il sangue d'Europa*, quoted by N. Carducci, *Gli intellettuali e l'ideologia americana*, p. 30.

9 For information on the role of ghost translators in this period see M. A. Grignani, *Prologhi ed epiloghi: sulla poesia di Eugenio Montale* (Ravenna, Longo, 1987), pp. 198–99.

10. For an account of Montale's "American dream" see L. Rebay, "Montale, Clizia e l'America", in *La poesia di Eugenio Montale*, by various authors (Milan, Librex, 1983), pp. 281–308.

11 For a list of prose translations by Montale published in the 1940s, see the Bibliography.

12 E. Montale, "Intenzioni (intervista immaginaria)" [1946], in his *Sulla poesia*, edited by G. Zampa (Milan, Mondadori, 1976), pp. 561–69 (p. 567).

13 The question of plagiary has been raised several times in relation to Montale. One aspect of his work which has become an object of controversy is a series of five critical essays which were published under his name in *Il corriere della sera* in the 1950s. In October 1989 *Il giornale* published eight letters written by Montale to the American writer Henry Furst. The letters were written between April and November 1950 and had not previously been published. They are now the property of Marcello Staglieno. Staglieno decided to publish them with his own introductory note after discovering that the correspondence was alluded to in Mario Soldati's book *Rami secchi*, which was then due to be published by Rizzoli. In these letters Montale explained his predicament: "Vorrebbero da me articoli (e molti) su recenti libri italiani, francesi e inglesi. Per farlo bisognerebbe chiudersi in casa e non avere alcun obbligo di redazione; inoltre occorrerebbe avere una casa che io non ho. È una vita impossibile; tuttavia non oso lasciare il giornale perché non saprei come potrei vivere. [...] Nessuno può immaginare la vita che conduco; se qui lo sapessero—al giornale—invece di compiangermi mi metterebbero alla porta." See *Il giornale*, 24 Oct. 1989, p. 3; *Il corriere della sera*, 25 Oct. 1989, p. 3. Montale was living in a hotel in Milan at the time and was still working on poems for *La bufera e altro*. He could not find time to produce the articles and was terrified of losing his job at the *Corriere*; he appears to have seriously contemplated suicide. Evidently it was not the actual writing of reviews that posed Montale problems; the five essays commissioned all involved assessing work in English. (The authors included Hemingway, Oscar Wilde, Joyce Cary and Ivy Compton Burnett.) Montale, it is claimed, had a good knowledge of literature in English, but he seems to have found reading English irksome: "Provo gran fatica a leggere un libro italiano, figurarsi poi uno inglese," he wrote in one of the letters to Furst. In order to save time and to save his job, Montale asked of Furst an "immenso favore". Furst was to write the five essays (for which he would be paid the fee of 9,000 lire due to Montale) and to send them to Montale for minor revisions before they were presented to the *Corriere* as Montale's own work. Montale's biographer, Nascimbeni, quotes Montale's description of his terms of employment at the *Corriere*: "Secondo il contratto che avevo firmato col giornale due traduzioni valevano, agli effetti del compenso, come un racconto o una recensione" (G. Nascimbeni, *Eugenio Montale*, fourth edition [Milan, Longanesi, 1986], p. 100). Of course it

was not entirely Furst's work: Montale did retouch the essays before submitting them. Furst was merely an uncredited ghost writer, and it does not appear that he was unduly concerned by that arrangement. Montale had worked with other ghost writers during the war. Lucia Rodocanachi had provided ghost translations of texts in English for Montale as well as for other famous writers. Rodocanachi was paid but received no credit in the published translations. Working with uncredited translators did, however, put Montale in the way of temptation. Publishing work without giving due credit when there is an arrangement so to do may be acceptable, on pragmatic rather than ethical grounds; but publishing such work without such an arrangement is both unethical and illegal. Montale was guilty of the latter on one occasion. In 1942 he was consulted as an expert by Edizioni Teatro dell'Università di Roma to read an Italian translation of Eugene O'Neill's *Strange Interlude*. The translation was the work of Bice Chiappelli, a young scholar from Reggio Emilia. Montale rejected the translation maintaining that it failed to reach professional standards. Several months later Edizioni Teatro dell'Università published Montale's translation of *Strange Interlude*. Linguistic analyses of the two translations have suggested that Montale's version was produced by retouching Chiappelli's translation. Montale was successfully sued over this in the 1950s.

14 "Canto di Simeone" was published in *Solaria* [Florence], 4, xii (Dec. 1929), 11–12. It was reprinted in *Circoli* [Genoa], 3, vi (Nov–Dec. 1933), 50–57, along with a note on T. S. Eliot, Montale's translation of "La figlia che piange" and his translation of "Lullaby" by Léonie Adams ("Ninna nanna"). "Canto di Simeone" was later published in *Poeti antichi e moderni tradotti dai lirici nuovi*, edited by L. Anceschi and D. Porzio (Milan, Hoepli, 1945), pp. 69–71. The three poems have appeared in all editions of Montale's *Quaderno di traduzioni*.

15 Two of the sonnets (nos 22 and 33) appeared in *Città* [Rome] (7 Dec. 1944), under the title "Motivi". The following year Sonnet 22 was published, as "Motivo", in *Uomo* [Milan] (June 1945), 37, and included in *Poeti antichi e moderni*, p. 55. Montale's translation of Sonnet 48 was published, together with "Una voce è giunta con le folaghe", the facsimile of "Il sole d'agosto trapela appena" and his translations of Shakespeare sonnets 22 and 33, in *L'immagine* [Rome], 1, ii (June 1947), 109–15. The three "Motivi" have appeared in each edition of *Quaderno di traduzioni*.

16 The poems, "I giardini" ("Los jardines"), "Ramo d'autunno" ("Rama del otono"), "Albero autunnale" ("Arbol del otono"), "Avvenimento" ("Advenimiento"), "Presagio" ("Presagio") and "Il cigno" ("El cisne"), first published in *Circoli*, 1, i (Jan–Feb. 1931), 55–59, were subsequently published in *Poeti antichi e moderni*, pp. 75–80, in Montale's *Quaderno di traduzioni* (1948 and 1975), and as *Jorge Guillén tradotto da Eugenio Montale* (Milan, All'Insegna del Pesce d'Oro, 1958). They are reprinted in E. Montale, *L'opera in versi*, edited by G. Contini and R. Bettarini (Turin, Einaudi, 1980), pp. 745–50.

17 "Billy in catene" was also published in *Poeti antichi e moderni*, p. 65, and in *Quaderno di traduzioni*.

18 In *La ruota* [Rome], third series, 4, iv (April 1943), 105–06. It was also reprinted in *Poeti antichi e moderni*, pp. 83–84. Milosz was a Lithuanian diplomat who wrote poetry in French.

19 In *Il mondo* [Florence], 1, i (7 Apr. 1945), 9. "Tempesta" was also published in *Poeti antichi e moderni*, p. 61, and in *Quaderno di traduzioni*.

20 The poems appeared in *Il mondo*, 19 (5 Jan. 1946), 7, under the title "Due poesie di James Joyce". They were reprinted in *Quaderno di traduzioni*.

21 "Quinta poesia" (Dylan Thomas's "The force that through the green fuse drives the flower") was published in *Il mondo*, 23 (2 May 1946), 6, and included in *Quaderno di traduzioni*.

22 In *Il mondo europeo* [Rome–Florence], 39 (15 Mar. 1947), 15, with a note on Maragall. The translation was included in *Quaderno di traduzioni*.

23 In *La fiera letteraria*, year III, 28–29 (10 Oct. 1948), 1, and in *Quaderno di traduzioni*, also published in 1948.

24 See P. Newmark, *A Textbook of Translation* (Hemel Hempstead, Prentice Hall, 1988), pp. 39ff.

25 E. Montale, "Variazioni, V" [26 Feb. 1953], in E. Montale, *Auto da fé: cronache in due tempi*, edited by G. Zampa, second edition (Milan, Saggiatore, 1972), pp. 172–75 (pp. 173–74); Montale's italics.

26 See W. Benjamin, "Die Aufgabe des Übersetzers", in his *Schriften*, vol. IV, i (Frankfurt-am-Main, Suhrkamp, 1955), pp. 9–21; reissued in his *Illuminationen* (Frankfurt-am-Main, Suhrkamp, 1977), pp. 50–62. The standard English translation is Harry Zohn's "The Task of the Translator", in W. Benjamin, *Illuminations*, edited by H. Arendt (London, Fontana, 1973), pp. 61–82.

27 Benjamin (p. 81 of the English translation) cites Pannwitz: "He [the translator] must expand and deepen his language by means of the foreign language. It is not generally realized to what extent this is possible, to what extent any language can be transformed, how language differs from language almost the way dialect from dialect; however, this last is only true if one takes language seriously enough, not if one takes it lightly."

28 E. Montale, "Intenzioni", p. 567.

29 R. Jakobson, "On Linguistic Aspects of Translation", in *On Translation*, edited by R. A. Brower (Cambridge, Mass., Harvard University Press, 1959), pp. 232–39 (p. 236).

30 See D. Fitts, "The Poetic Nuance", in *On Translation*, pp. 32–47 (p. 37).

31 See J. Matthews, "Third Thoughts on Translating Poetry", in *On Translation*, pp. 67–77 (p. 72).

32 G. Ungaretti, *Saggi e interventi* (Milan, Mondadori, 1974), p. 552.

33 J. C. Catford, *A Linguistic Theory of Translation* (London, Oxford University Press, 1965), pp. 73–82. The following examples are based on Peter Newmark's observations on the problems of translating between English, French and German, in P. Newmark, *A Textbook of Translation*, pp. 85–88.

34 R. Jakobson, "On Linguistic Aspects of Translation", p. 230.

35 W. Benjamin, "The Task of the Translator", pp. 69–82.

36 See *The Penguin Book of Italian Verse*, edited and translated by G. Kay (Harmondsworth, Penguin, 1958).

37 Rachel Meoli Toulmin has made the same point: "Le versioni di Montale meritano di essere esaminate, perché l'impossibilità in cui egli si trova, come tutti i traduttori, di rappresentarci l'opera originale in tutti i suoi aspetti, e la necessità di operare una scelta, fa di ogni versione una critica non meno di una interpretazione dei versi tradotti"; see R. Meoli Toulmin, "Shakespeare ed Eliot nelle versioni di Eugenio Montale", *Belfagor*, 26 (1971), 453–71 (p. 453).

38 See R-A. de Beaugrande and W. U. Dressler, *Introduction to Text Linguistics* (London–New York, Longman, 1981), p. 182.

39 Montale in a radio programme with Maria Corti. The text of the interview appears in M. Corti, "*Satura* di Eugenio Montale", *L'approdo letterario*, year XVII, 53 (1971), 107–16 (p. 115).

40 In Montale's case, philological criticism has been facilitated by some very important publications. Firstly, the *Autografi di Montale: fondo dell'Università di Pavia*, edited by M. Corti and M. A. Grignani (Turin, Einaudi, 1976); this was the first really significant publication of Montale's manuscripts. It was followed in 1980 by *L'opera in versi*, which contains all Montale's public poems together with all the available variants and full publication details of each poem; this volume contains some very early work. Another publication with a bearing on the early Montale is the *Quaderno genovese*, edited by L. Barile (Milan, Mondadori, 1983). This *Quaderno genovese* is a diary which Montale kept between February and August 1917, before his conscription into the Italian army. His 1940s translation of W. H. Hudson's *Green Mansions* (*La vita della foresta*) finally came into print in 1987 (Turin, Einaudi). The *Concordanza di tutte le poesie di Eugenio Montale*, 2 vols (Florence, Olschki), compiled by Giuseppe Savoca, was also published in 1987.

41 There are anomalies: for example, Joyce (1882–1941) precedes Yeats (1865–1939), Hopkins (1844–89) precedes Hardy (1840–1928) and Dickinson (1830–86) precedes Melville (1819–91).

42 J. L. Borges, "Kafka and his Precursors", translated by J. E. Irby, in Borges's *Labyrinths* (Harmondsworth, Penguin, 1970), pp. 234–36.

43 See above, p. 18. Montale is, incidentally, reported as having said, "Ogni poeta crea i suoi predecessori"; see G. Nascimbeni, *Eugenio Montale*, p. 60.

Chapter 1

THE ENCOUNTER WITH MODERNISM

Montale's "Stile e tradizione"

Creating a literary tradition, according to T. S. Eliot, is an essential part of an artist's activity.[1] Montale's essay "Stile e tradizione" was published in 1925, six years after Eliot's "Tradition and the Individual Talent". Montale's essay is essentially a negative document. It includes the following: "Il problema della tradizione è il problema di tutti noi, e porlo con chiarezza è già impresa difficile; ché tanto varrebbe averlo risolto, per metà. Ma siamo lontani da questo."[2]

Montale described his position as a Crocean one:

> Evitare il generico, costruirsi dei limiti e dei piani concreti, e siano pure modesti, è questa la difficoltà maggiore a cui va incontro, oggi piú che ieri, una rassegna di letteratura; ed una rivista come la presente, che non ha temuto di rifarsi esplicitamente all'insegnamento di quel maestro di chiarezza che è il Croce. Pensando al quale, e ai frutti tuttora incerti e controversi della sua scuola, che accettiamo in piú parti come nostra, non è facile davvero resistere alla tentazione di crearsi storici del tempo presente e suoi giudici, se non proprio suoi giustizieri. ("Stile e tradizione", p. 15)

His tone was reserved and pessimistic, not to say despondent. As a literary manifesto it was, in effect, a manifesto against manifestos. Marinetti's Futurist Manifesto, and the appeal to the irrational explicit in Futurism and implicit in Fascism, were the probable targets of the following remarks:

> Il concetto di tradizione che ci guida, i propositi di chiarezza e di concretezza che ci vengono dall'insegnamento crociano, sono,

> per esempio, assai chiari, e per nostro conto decisivi, per quanto si riferisce a problemi di cultura e di critica, e ai programmi di lavoro pel futuro, che a questi si riferiscono. C'è qui materia per l'opera di piú di una generazione; e intanto già si parla, d'attorno, di buttar via il certo per l'incerto. Se i poeti hanno perduto la fiducia nelle parole, i critici che non vogliono essere da meno si raccomandano quando alla provvidenza, quando a Freud e alla contingenza; è in tutti un gran disprezzo dell'arte e un palese desiderio di pescare nel torbido. ("Stile e tradizione", p. 16)

He lamented the lack of a "letteratura civile" and attributed that lack to "un diffuso benessere e comfort intellettuale senza cime ma senza vaste bassure". The absence of a reading public, in Montale's view, had a significant implication for writers. A writer's relationship with Italian society was bound to be a lonely one: "Si dovrà dunque lavorare in solitudine, e per pochi: di fronte non è che grossezza, e non solo quella borghese, ma quell' altra verniciata di cultura e di sufficienza" ("Stile e tradizione", p. 16).

Next Montale took on D'Annunzio, attacking the Dannunzian mixture of politics and poetry, and rejecting D'Annunzio's contribution and influence as aberrations in Italian literary history: "Il problema dello stile, inteso come qualcosa di organico, di assoluto, momento supremo della creazione letteraria, è tuttora aperto al punto in cui lo lasciarono il Manzoni e il Leopardi; e parve non vi fosse dopo che abbassamento, compromessi, dialetto e falsetto" ("Stile e tradizione", pp. 17–18). He explicitly rejected not just D'Annunzio but also Carducci, Pascoli and all the lesser poets after Leopardi:

> Lo stile, il famoso stile totale che non ci hanno dato i poeti dell'ultima illustre triade, malati di furori giacobini, superomismo, messianismo ed altre bacature, ci potrà forse venire da disincantati savi e avveduti, coscienti dei limiti e amanti in umiltà dell'arte loro piú che del rifar la gente. In tempi che sembrano contrassegnati dall'immediata utilizzazione della cultura, del polemismo e delle diatribe, la salute è forse nel lavoro inutile e inosservato: lo stile ci verrà dal buon costume. ("Stile e tradizione", p. 19)

In this essay Montale identified his targets and turned his invective against them. There was, however, very little about "Stile e tradizione" which could be described as constructive. The statement which came closest to being positive is well known: "Non continua chi vuole la tradizione, ma chi può, talora chi meno lo sa. A questo intento poco giovano i programmi e le buone intenzioni" (p. 17). But this statement, which sounds very like the determinism present in Montale's poetry of that period, is too vague to be useful as a contribution to the idea of a tradition. The conclusion to be drawn from the essay is that in 1925 Montale knew which writers he did *not* want to claim as literary ancestors, but was not so sure about which writers he did want to claim. In the essay he was resistant to the temptation to look outside Italy for models.[3] "Stile e tradizione", however, was published in early January 1925, and 1925 was to be an important year for Montale as a critic, not least because of his discovery (via Svevo) of James Joyce.

Twenty years later, again on the subject of tradition, Montale wrote:

> Volgiamoci indietro, risaliamo a ritroso la corrente, anche se su questo filo piú di una grande tradizione poetica scomparirà per un momento dal nostro sguardo. Eliot, Valéry, poco piú addietro nel tempo due altri: Yeats (piú anziano ma ringiovanito al contatto dei giovani) e Apollinaire, che non si possono esaurire nel dono della loro apparente spontaneità; e piú addietro ancora i simbolisti della prima generazione, i "maledetti", e il loro quasi contemporaneo Hopkins, e in fondo—non già iniziatrice della serie—Emily Dickinson, sospesa tra la sublimità e i *nonsenses*... In meno di cent' anni, quali voci può lasciare *una certa idea* (un'idea sbagliata, secondo alcuni) della poesia, al mondo di domani, se il mondo d'oggi potrà avere ancora una storia![4]

This passage from "Eliot e noi" (1947) offers a very different perspective on Montale's idea of a tradition, based on writers from outside Italy writing in French and in English—but mainly in English. In another essay from the mid-1940s Montale reflected on his transition from the Mediterranean world to the wider world: "Negli *Ossi di seppia* tutto era attratto e assorbito dal mare fermentante, piú tardi vidi che il mare era dovunque, per me, e che persino le classiche architetture dei colli toscani erano anch' esse movimento e fuga."[5] Montale's discovery of and interaction with English poetry and prose was an important part of the process which took his poetry away from the Mediterranean and into wider cultural traditions.

Montale, Joyce and Modernism

Joyce and Montale are linked together by a literary coincidence. In Trieste, Joyce had established a friendship with Italo Svevo, who had written two novels in the last years of the nineteenth century and seen them pass into critical oblivion. Svevo wrote his third novel, *La coscienza di Zeno*, while Joyce was writing *Ulysses*, and Joyce helped to bolster Svevo's literary reputation in Paris when *La coscienza di Zeno* was in print. Montale read Svevo's novels in the early 1920s after being introduced to them by Bobi Bazlen, who also came from Trieste. Montale then wrote three essays on Svevo, and the two men began a correspondence which lasted until Svevo's death. Montale's essays brought Svevo out of obscurity and helped to establish him as an important and widely read novelist.

Montale was proud of the success which his critical judgement had achieved and disputed claims that the French critic Benjamin Crémieux had *discovered* Svevo first.[6] Montale's essays on Svevo not only revived Svevo's literary career, they also gave Montale himself the status of a credible man of letters. It was on the basis of his essays on Svevo that he was invited to contribute a review of *Dubliners* to *La fiera letteraria* in 1926. The first edition of *Ossi di seppia* appeared in 1925; within the next four years T. S. Eliot had published Praz's translation of "Arsenio" in *The Criterion* and Samuel Beckett had translated "Delta" into English.

Montale's Review of *Dubliners*: A Poet not a Critic

Montale's review of *Dubliners*, written in 1926, gave expression to his appreciation of Joyce's writing. He had read *Dubliners* in a French translation. He did not have an English copy to hand until Svevo sent him one which he bought at Montale's request during a visit to Paris in 1926, after the publication of Montale's essay.[7] In this essay Montale described Joyce as a "poeta irlandese", and *Ulysses* as "un poema", an epic poem, rather than as a novel. (It is very unlikely that Montale had read *Ulysses* in English by that stage.) It seems that Joyce's model of composition may well have held an attraction for Montale.

The review itself contains passages which evoke aspects of Montale's own poetry and offer a bridge between Montale's critical interest in Joyce and his own artistic concerns. The following is taken from Montale's analysis of "Two Gallants": "Le parole piú usuali sono prossime a rompersi in un grido che dica tutta la stanchezza di una vita [...] si sente condannato alla coscienza di se stesso, e troppo lontano dalla tranquilla indifferenza degli alberi e degli astri."[8]

Montale eulogized Joyce here for his ability to transform representational language ("le parole piú usuali") into a cognitive instrument, an instrument which could take the reader to the limits of physical appearance and metaphysical reality. Montale found this quality in Joyce's writing and could more readily appreciate it because the transformation of representational language into a cognitive tool was one of his own articles of faith. He had already given expression to this aspiration five years earlier in one of *Ossi di seppia*'s programme poems, "I limoni". After describing familiar Ligurian scenes in the first two stanzas using colloquial language quite ostentatiously (for instance, "Ascoltami, i poeti laureati/si muovono soltanto fra le piante/dai nomi poco usati"), he had declared his metaphysical credentials:

> Vedi, in questi silenzi in cui le cose
> s'abbandonano e sembrano vicine
> a tradire il loro ultimo segreto,
> talora ci si aspetta
> di scoprire uno sbaglio di Natura,
> il punto morto del mondo, l'anello che non tiene,
> il filo da disbrogliare che finalmente ci metta
> nel mezzo di una verità.
>
> (*L'opera in versi*, p. 9)

The language of the *Dubliners* review, in particular "prossime a rompersi" and the subjunctive "un grido che dica tutta [...]", seems to be so close to the language of the poem (especially—in relation to the two expressions cited—"vicine/a tradire il loro ultimo segreto" and the subjunctive "che finalmente ci metta/nel mezzo di una verità") as to be almost self-pastiche. Of course it is not pastiche: it is an indication of just how closely Montale identified his own artistic aspirations with what he found in Joyce's stories.

The other aspect of Montale's analysis of "Two Gallants" quoted above, the tiredness of life, the coming to conscience and the calm indifference of the natural world, was also part of the Montalian metaphysics. The opposition between harmony in the external world and discord in the observer is a long-standing Montalian conviction, and his early poetry was largely an attempt to clothe that conviction in successful poetic form. His critical appraisal of Joyce's stories, then, appears to be based on his own experience of writing poems. How much, for example, of what he wrote about Joyce's work would apply to his own early poems?

Montale would have his readers believe that "Meriggiare pallido e assorto" was composed in 1916, with some later modifications in the final stanza.[9] It would thus precede the *Quaderno genovese* and the "Accordi".[10] Ramat has argued that "Meriggiare" in its present form (and he refers to more than the alleged modification of the last stanza) is almost certainly subsequent to the "Accordi" suite.[11] His argument, in brief, is that the idea behind "Meriggiare" may have begun in 1916 but that at that stage the poem did not take the form which is familiar to readers of the published collections. To illustrate his point Ramat examines the probable metamorphosis of "Elegia" into "Flauti-fagotti" (which is one component of the "Accordi").[12] He then poses the question of why, after schooling himself in the subtleties of "Meriggiare", Montale should have spent so much time on such meagre and artificial poems. Ramat's argument is in the tradition of Montale criticism initiated by Pancrazi, in that it stresses the superiority of those of Montale's poems which treat of objects in Nature or specific memories over those of his poems which do not.[13] The judgement runs parallel to Montale's eulogy of Joyce's writing.

Pancrazi, in 1934, argued that Montale is "piú sicuro [...] quando può concentrare una scena di natura, una figura definita, un singolo ricordo". This sense of images, symbols or talismans drawn from reality is almost entirely absent from the "Accordi", but it informs "Meriggiare". "Meriggiare" does have a musical element in its structure, but it is not an ingenuous attempt to imitate the sounds of musical instruments. Rather it is an exploration of the music inherent in the Italian language. The onomatopoeia of the "schiocchi di merli, frusci di serpi" is part of the internal logic of the poem, which is constituted by a network of assonance and rhyme.

The tautness of structure in "Meriggiare" is matched by a thematic subtlety quite alien to the "Accordi". The theme is not new: the situation of waiting and immobility is already familiar from "Elegia" and some poems of the "Accordi". What distinguishes "Meriggiare" from those other poems is the scope and coherence of its imagery and its compact organization. Four of the poem's six infinitives ("ascoltare", "spiare", "osservare" and "sentire") are verbs of perception. That reflects a decision in favour of observing the external world in detail and in an adult fashion rather than registering directly the sensations of an adolescent or announcing a metaphysical theory. The latter two elements are still residually present but they are held in check by the precision of the images taken from the external world. Montale in "Meriggiare" presents his old problem of immobility through those elemental images.

Three of the four elements are represented in the poem. The earth provides a stage for the snakes and the red ants. The wind causes the sea to shimmer in the distance beyond the branches. There is noonday heat but no fire. Noonday heat frames the psychological immobility and makes a crucible of the "orto", and that heat is essentially destructive: "Meriggiare pallido e assorto/ presso un *rovente* muro d'orto" (lines 1–2). The scorching wall, Man's invention, is counterpointed by the dynamism and harmony in Nature, whether that be the manoeuvres of the ants:

> Nelle crepe del suolo o su la veccia
> spiar le file di rosse formiche
> ch'ora si rompono ed ora s'intrecciano
> a sommo di minuscole biche
> (lines 5–8)[14]

or the movement of the sea: "il palpitare/lontano di scaglie di mare" (lines 9–10). The symbolic wall returns in the final stanza to seal Man's fate:

> E andando nel sole che abbaglia
> sentire con triste meraviglia
> com' è tutta la vita e il suo travaglio
> in questo seguitare una muraglia
> che ha in cima cocci aguzzi di bottiglia.
> (lines 13–17)

The importance of "Meriggiare" lies not in its theme, which is Montale's old conviction, but rather in the precision of its imagery. Abstractions are eschewed and objects of the external world are brought into focus. Nature does not have an allegorical role; it has a vital position in the breath of the poem. "Meriggiare" breathes the specificity of Liguria. The Ligurian sea, the *canicola*, the parched earth and the crumbling walls as well as the regional flavour of words such as "orto" contribute to the specificity of the landscape, and that particularity or objective rendering of Liguria which is developed in the "Ossi brevi" section of *Ossi di seppia* becomes the basis of Montale's symbolic landscape.

This type of specificity, the universal in the particular, is a feature of Joyce's work to which Montale draws particular attention:

> Il procedimento di Joyce in queste novelle consiste tutto, piú o meno consapevolmente, nel trarre partito dalla regolarità stessa del taglio di coteste sue *tranches* e della lacerazione che ne consegue. Il senso di tali composizioni è in quella frangia di parole non dette, di reazioni non constatate e di vita inosservata che accompagna i tronconi mutilati di questi pezzi di vita dublinese; è nel paradosso con cui lo scrittore riesce, individuando la sua città nativa nei suoi tratti piú realistici, le sue figure nei loro segni minuti, a fare di questa Dublino concreta e provinciale una città rigorosamente astratta e fuori del tempo. ("*Dubliners*")

Joyce's Dublin and Montale's Liguria are counterparts. They are different stages on which to play the same contemporary drama. The drama, in both cases, is understated. Montale's understatement is idiomatic to his poetry, probably a reaction against D'Annunzio initially, but cultivated as an artistic ideal. Montale recognizes the same quality of understatement in Joyce's stories:

> Ma ecco, con tali qualità che avrebbero potuto fare di lui uno dei piú efficaci "specialisti" del brivido contemporaneo, lo scrittore rifiutarsi ad ogni insistenza su questi temi a condannarsi ad una forma di constatazione sempre meno commossa dell'eterna avventura umana. Ed ecco il dato stesso, il "fatto" ridursi sempre piú a una materia *of no importance*, al puntiglioso relievo di ogni sussulto delle esistenze piú povere, a una testimonianza, infine, che cerca la sua maggiore gravità nel fatto stesso di escludere da sé, in qualsiasi aspetto, l'eccezionale. ("*Dubliners*")

This artistic strategy of concentrating on what appear to be arbitrary particulars in order to express the universal represents a fundamental affinity between Montale and Joyce, as indeed between Montale and Hopkins. Montale draws attention to Joyce's Catholic education and to his "senso di corpo", his corporeal or bodily sense. Montale's appreciation of Joyce's "senso di corpo" had important implications for Montale's own metaphysics and poetry. Montale distinguishes Joyce's "senso di corpo" from that of other writers and schools:

> Il "senso di corpo" di Joyce è altro da quello dei romanzieri francesi; ed è rimasto in lui fondamentalmente cattolico. Un realismo, in questo senso, assoluto, qualora sia, com' è qui, spogliato dalla cristiana speranza della redenzione; un senso preciso della fatalità di condurre seco, per le vie del mondo, uno scheletro pesante e insopprimibile, una carne vorace e peritura che è da sola una condanna della nostra miserabile condizione di esseri viventi. Non è l'atteggimento spirituale dei russi [...] nei quali è sempre possibile, come ha dimostrato da par suo Scestof [Chestov], veder trapelare dalla foresta spessa delle affermazioni nichilistiche, una speranza *à rebours*: come dire una luce assurda e lontana ch'è rifranta sull'opera loro, ne è riassorbita e la sostenta. ("*Dubliners*")

Montale had read and been influenced by the Russian Existentialists. Chestov's existentialism forms the philosophical basis of Montale's early poems. Chestov's is a system of hope which posits necessary conditions as tyrannies to be overthrown by privileged contingencies. It is a philosophy which exalts the One over the Many, the miracle over the treadmill. Montale contrasts Chestov with Joyce in 1926, and this is very significant in relation to his own poetry of that time. The Chestov influence (which was at its strongest in "Movimenti") is very much diminished in the poems added to the second edition of *Ossi di seppia*.[15] Of these poems "I morti" is the most striking in terms of its title. Montale's Italian title is a precise translation of Joyce's "The Dead". In fact, in all four of the poems the dead have more presence than the living observer. The "return of the dead in memory" theme is one which entered Montale's poetry around 1926, the year in which he wrote the review of *Dubliners*.

Montale's dead mingle with the living on the coast, a symbolic dividing line.[16] The dead sink into the sea, which is their habitat, while the living linger on the tired earth:

> Cosí
> forse anche ai morti è tolto ogni riposo
> nelle zolle: una forza indi li tragge
> spietata piú del vivere, ed attorno,

larve rimorse dai ricordi umani,
li volge fino a queste spiagge, fiati
senza materia o voce
traditi dalla tenebra; ed i mozzi
loro voli ci sfiorano pur ora
da noi divisi appena e nel crivello
del mare si sommergono...
(from "I morti": *L'opera in versi*, pp. 93–94)

The dead are as real as the living and they communicate at the moments when the two worlds intersect. Esterina had been tempered and matured by the sea;[17] in the later poems, however, "sommersa" is a synonym for "dead". The interlocutor of "Incontro" (referred to as Arletta in an earlier draft) returns to the observer's memory at the coastline. Montale worked on this poem and on the *Dubliners* review at the same time, and Arletta's return, prompted by the wind and the sea, does suggest some kinship with Michael Furey's return, which is prompted by the song "The Lass of Aughrim".

Michael Furey returns on the memory of a song he used to sing, an involuntary memory, an unannounced guest to haunt Gretta Conroy's frustrated marriage. The notion of memories being triggered by external stimuli was to become an important part of Montale's later poetics. The following is the narrator's reaction to a visit from the dead as described in "La piuma di struzzo":

> Rimasi a lungo agitato [...]. Che partissero a cavallo di una scopa non mi pare probabile. Dormii pochissimo ripetendomi sempre "Del mondo i disinganni..." e cercando di dipanare il senso recondito di quella visita notturna. Avevo assistito all'appuntamento di un morto con un vivo o all'escursione serale di due defunti? E se i due non sapevano nulla di me, come mai avevano trovato la mia casa? E se, infine, dovevo considerarli come un frutto del mio subconscio, un'allucinazione, perché non avevo partorito qualche personaggio di maggior peso nella mia vita?[18]

In the earlier meeting ("Incontro"), Arletta is a talismanic figure whose presence acts as a form of respite from the swarms of the living:

Prega per me
allora ch'io discenda altro cammino

che una via di città,
nell'aria persa, innanzi al brulichio
dei vivi; ch'io ti senta accanto; ch'io
scenda senza viltà.
(*L'opera in versi*, pp. 96–97)

"Arsenio" was a new development in Montale's poetry, though there was, of course, continuity with the earlier poems. The continuity took various forms, such as the immobility/impotence theme which had a history in Montale's works stretching back beyond the "Accordi". The contrast between Arsenio's miserable state and the zest in nature was also familiar. One of the principal aspects of the poem's novelty was the image of Arsenio dragging his roots, in the final stanza. The image seems to be a cognate of Man's burden as Montale described it in his review of *Dubliners*.[19]

The previous year Montale had written:

Penso che per i piú non sia salvezza,
ma taluno sovverta ogni disegno,
passi il varco, qual volle si ritrovi.
("Casa sul mare": *L'opera in versi*, p. 91)

That is a modified version of Chestov's existentialism. The existentialist hope is tempered with a resigned realism. In "Arsenio" Chestov has practically disappeared and has been replaced by a philosophy which seems to have been suggested to Montale by his reading of Joyce. Arsenio's immobility does not consist merely in stasis, waiting for a miracle. It is not a physical condition. He drags his roots around as he descends to the sea. His immobility is metaphysical. Chestov's miracles are replaced by Joycean epiphanies, moments of metaphysical progress or inspiration.[20]

So Montale first read Joyce's *Dubliners* and *Ulysses* in the mid-1920s. In the course of writing the *Dubliners* review he complained in a letter to Svevo that he was not a critic by nature.[21] Reading Joyce, Montale recognized important affinities with his own writing. The affinities were threefold. Firstly there was Joyce's obsessive realistic detail, the care with which he reproduced Dublin in words. Montale was trying to make of Liguria what Joyce had made of Dublin, a specific model to express the universal human condition. Secondly, Joyce's language, or rather the way in which Joyce could use ordinary language and invest it with deep metaphysical insight, held a fascination for Montale. Montale, in his poetry, also cultivated attempts to give representational language cognitive power, to write in language which would express the complexity of relations between the observer and the observed objects. Thirdly, Montale found in "The Dead" a philosophy of memory. According to this, memory had the ability to interrupt the flow of time and present the dead as more real entities than the living, in the manner of Chestov's existentialism and Boutroux's philosophy of momentary liberation. The place of memory, and particularly of memories involuntarily triggered by external stimuli, becomes more significant in Montale's later work, but the roots are there in 1926, nourished by his reading of Joyce.

Montale and Eliot

It is really only in the wake of *Ossi di seppia* that one should begin to consider Montale's translations of poetry, because his first published translations date from the late 1920s. His career as a translator began with T. S. Eliot's two poems "A Song for Simeon" and "La Figlia Che Piange" (lent to him by Mario Praz), which he translated in 1928–29.

Montale's decision to translate Eliot's poetry suggests some level of affinity between the work of the two poets. Eliot had published Mario Praz's translation of "Arsenio" in *The Criterion* in 1927 and had noted what Praz described as a "kindred inspiration" shared by Montale and himself. Praz was the human connection between the two poets, and it may be instructive to summarize some points from his essay "T. S. Eliot and Eugenio Montale", which was published in 1948.[22]

Praz was the first critic to note affinities between Eliot and Montale. In the 1948 essay he stated his view of these affinities. Firstly, there is in "The Waste Land" and *Ossi di seppia* "the same vision of a barren, disconsolate world, of a desperate aridity searching every cranny of the rocks for a drop of water", which is "symbolical of a state of the soul". Secondly, Praz argued that Montale developed a formula similar to Eliot's objective correlative through his reading of Eliot's poetry in the 1930s. Montale, according to Praz, learned some or all of the following from Eliot:

> Covert allusions to personal experiences, which, puzzling to the reader as they are, diffuse an intimate atmosphere in a poem, so that one seems to share them in a dream-like fashion, as if with a little effort one might remember them as parts of one's own past, and still that effort will not be undertaken, since the lyrical import of the experience is already transfused into the verse; quotations often in a foreign language embedded in the texture of a poem, which receives illumination from them; notes throwing light on the text, though often in a non-committal way: these are traits of Eliot's technique which Montale seems to have mastered in his second volume of verse *Le occasioni* (1939).[23]

Praz's three points—that Montale's poems often stimulate vicarious experiences in the reader, that Montale uses a device which we might call intertextuality and that Montale's "clarifications" about his poems are often no more clear that the poems themselves—may all be sustainable, but the nature of Eliot's influence on Montale is a little more dubious. Indeed Praz's contentions have not passed without dissenting critical comment. Rachel Meoli Toulmin has taken issue with his claims that Montale and Eliot make similar use of quotations from authors of different epochs and cultures and that both poets mix conversational and literary levels of language in their poetry.[24] On the first point Meoli Toulmin paraphrases Bonfiglioli in claiming that "è stato notato che nell'opera del poeta italiano le citazioni sono piú rare e piú difficili da isolare."

On the second point Meoli Toulmin has observed that

> Eliot spesso inserisce nelle sue poesie richiami al linguaggio quotidiano piú prosaico; e certe frasi dell'inglese popolare, in particolare nelle opere del periodo della "Terra desolata", servono ad evocare la malinconia banale e niente affatto lirica di molti aspetti della vita umana.
>
> Non troviamo nel lessico, personale e scelto, di Montale nessun elemento paragonabile a questi frammenti di "conversazione" comune e immediata, "quasi del giornale stracciato", come li caratterizza Bigongiari, ma in realtà ben al di là della prosa giornalistica. Un passo del genere si trova nella seconda parte di "The Waste Land", nella quale, in una strofa che poi termina con una citazione dell'*Amleto*, viene rievocato con spietato realismo un tipico dialogo da *Public Bar* londinese.[25]

She concludes that "l'affinità tra i due scrittori ci pare sia di carattere generale, di atmosfera, ed è difficile reperire dei luoghi in cui Eliot, anche attraverso le versioni, abbia esercitato un'influenza precisa sul poeta italiano".[26]

Meoli Toulmin does not argue that Montale did not make innovations in Italian poetic diction, whether in terms of linguistic register or of metre. Contini had noted Montale's innovative mixture of linguistic register in his poetry as early as 1933:

> Il discorso di Montale è un discorso di tono e timbro "familiare" [...] il quale si presuppone per lo piú, ben vicino, un interlocutore [...]. E il linguaggio preferito ricorre a parole determinatissime, "dialettali" addirittura, diremmo [...]. In una simile funzione stanno i termini piú letterarî [...] con un valore, pertanto, press' a poco opposto a quello che l'estetismo o il purismo potevano rispettivamente assegnare.[27]

Likewise Pinchera has provided detailed arguments for the case that Montale had made considerable metrical innovation in his early poetry.[28] Meoli Toulmin's point is that there is little or no discernible influence between Eliot and Montale.

Influence may not be a very useful concept. Italian and English are such different languages that for an Italian poet to learn from English poetry requires not an ability to imitate but a strong disposition towards originality. Meoli Toulmin's assertion that "tutto sommato, sentiamo che la presa di contatto di Montale con Eliot non è dipesa tanto dalle versioni delle *Ariel Poems*, quanto da un contesto culturale piú generale: dall'eredità poetica europea comune ai due poeti e dalla conoscenza di Praz, di Pound, e piú tardi dello stesso Eliot" may provide the basis for another relationship between Montale and Eliot, one which Montale himself alluded to in an essay on Eliot.

Montale wrote four essays dealing specifically with Eliot's poetry. The first of these introduced his translations of "A Song for Simeon" and "La Figlia Che Piange" in *Circoli* (1933). The second, "Eliot e noi", was published in 1947 on the occasion of Eliot's visit to Rome. In typically self-deprecating style Montale states that his essay should not be taken as the work of a specialist.[29] He goes on to distance himself further from Eliot, calling Eliot's poetry,

> da "The Waste Land" (che conobbi dopo le poesie di *Ariel*) ad "Ash Wednesday" fino agli ultimi "Quartetti", con i grandi

> intervalli della produzione drammatica, la piú difficile da giudicarsi da parte di un lettore italiano. Ma in definitiva varii testi di Eliot—non solo poeta ma critico e saggista acutissimo—restarono per me semplici schede di biblioteca, e temo ormai che un vero e proprio *expert* in materia di studi eliotiani io non potrò piú diventare. ("Eliot e noi", p. 442)

The last few words are revealing. Montale wrote, "io non potrò *piú* diventare". The implication is that Montale's interest in Eliot's work belongs principally to an earlier period.

Rather than merely providing thematic or stylistic models for imitators Montale argues that Eliot's contribution to the state of poetry lies in his ability to indicate a direction. Eliot's most influential achievement, according to Montale, was "la riscoperta [...] dell'Europa da parte di un americano di vecchio ceppo" ("Eliot e noi", p. 442).

Eliot's rediscovery of European literary traditions, whether French Symbolism, the *dolce stil novo* or the poetry of the English Metaphysical poets, gave a foundation on which international Modernism could build. The specifically modern techniques, such as sprung rhythm—which, according to Montale, Eliot learned from the Imagists—, required the presence of a tradition behind them in order to constitute an innovation.

Montale tied Eliot's innovation to a tradition. For Montale, Eliot was another link in a chain which stretched from Coleridge and Poe to the post-Surrealist French poets.[30] Eliot's poetry was a development beyond *poesia pura*:

> Eliot non è un poeta puro come lo era Mallarmé (e assai meno il Valéry) e come lo sono i recenti post-surrealisti ai quali s'è accennato (p. es. René Char): non è un poeta puro nel senso ch'egli elimini dall'atto poetico ogni elemento razionale. Come Gerard Manley Hopkins, come parecchi altri dei migliori poeti moderni passati attraverso Baudelaire, Eliot tenta di investire musicalmente l'atto dell'ispirazione, senza ridurlo a semplice, "aurorale" ineffabilità, senza ridursi allo stato di un automa che diffidi del proprio pensiero e scriva solo in stato di sonnambulismo. ("Invito a T. S. Eliot", p. 461)

That was a positive judgement on Montale's part. Eliot's poetry aspired to the conditions imposed by Montale's recurrent definition of poetry—"un sogno fatto alla presenza della ragione".[31] That combination of music and reason or sound and sense as criteria of poetic acceptability is a more fundamental affinity between Montale and Eliot than the three noted by Praz. In Montale's view, the contributions of reason (irony, sarcasm and invective) were the principal aspects of Eliot's originality:

> Ma qui sta appunto l'originalità di Eliot: nell'aver scritto solo dopo una profonda accumulazione interiore. Non per questo, però, egli si è attenuto al pregiudizio di quei poeti puri che riducono la lirica al momento della semplice contemplazione, dell'elegia. In Eliot troviamo anche l'ironia, il sarcasmo, l'invettiva. Certe sue parodie ("Sweeney Agonistes") fanno pensare al *Mikado,* ai libretti musicati da Sullivan. ("Invito a T. S. Eliot", p. 463)

How does Eliot achieve this balance of music and reason in his poetry? According to Montale:

> In lui [Eliot] la parola prosastica convive accanto a quella aulica, il tono diventa lirico per accensione interiore, non già perché obbedisca alle leggi di un metronomo. Eliot giunge spesso al canto dal recitativo, al tono alto dal tono piú parlato che possa darsi. È soprattutto (diciamo la parola) un poeta-musicista; e non è mai o quasi mai (come lo era Valéry e lo fu spesso Rilke) un neoclassico. È questa la sua maggiore modernità; e sia detto senza voler porre confronti, che sarebbero inaccettabili. Non per nulla Eliot è giunto dopo; e s'è visto quanto per lui conti "arrivare a tempo". ("Invito a T. S. Eliot", p. 463)

But Eliot's technical innovations in English were not always easily appreciated by a foreign audience, according to Montale. The diction of Eliot's poetry, Montale claims, had generally not been well served by his French and Italian translators. Comparing Eliot's European reception with that of Edgar Allan Poe, Montale wrote:

> Ma a parte le infinite differenze, e a parte il fatto che crediamo ingiusta e antistorica, in arte, una rigida distinzione fra reprobi ed eletti, resta da osservare che il Poe fu servito in Europa da un traduttore di genio—Baudelaire—che gli dette una forma definitiva e lo inserí in un ambiente e in una cultura; mentre Eliot fu sinora (tranne rare e parziali eccezioni) disservito da interpreti volenterosi ma in perpetua lotta con mezzi espressivi inadeguati, con lingue che appiattiscono inevitabilmente la leggerezza del suo recitativo. I francesi—si veda l'esempio migliore, il "Little

> Gidding" di Gide—conservano molto bene lo sfumato, il *fading* dei testi originali, ma sono costretti a non pochi annacquamenti voluti dal carattere razionale del loro linguaggio; e gli italiani quando non si appagano di una modesta letteralità, sono forzati a una ricerca di monosillabi, di elisioni e di cesure che certo stravolgono il genio originariamente plastico e disteso del nostro discorso. Un Eliot tedesco, poi, è da credere che riuscirebbe troppo inchiostrato alla romantica, come dicono sia avvenuto al Valéry rilkiano. ("Eliot e noi", p. 444)

In view of this verdict on the French and Italian translations of Eliot's poems, it may be interesting to examine the relative success or failure of Montale's translations in relation to his own criteria.

The Eliot Poems

"A Song for Simeon"

The following is the text of Eliot's "Song for Simeon" (1928):

> Lord, the Roman hyacinths are blooming in the bowls and
> The winter sun creeps by the snow hills;
> The stubborn season had made stand.
> My life is light, waiting for the death wind,
> Like a feather on the back of my hand.
> Dust in sunlight and memory in corners
> Wait for the wind that chills towards the dead land.
>
> Grant us thy peace.
> I have walked many years in this city,
> Kept faith and fast, provided for the poor,
> Have given and taken honour and ease.
> There went never any rejected from my door.
> Who shall remember my house, where shall live my children's children
> When the time of sorrow is come?
> They will take to the goat's path, and the fox's home,
> Fleeing from the foreign faces and the foreign swords.
>
> Before the time of cords and scourges and lamentation
> Grant us thy peace.

Before the stations of the mountain of desolation,
Before the certain hour of maternal sorrow,
Now at this birth season of decease,
Let the Infant, the still unspeaking and unspoken Word,
Grant Israel's consolation
To one who has eighty years and no to-morrow.

According to thy word.
They shall praise Thee and suffer in every generation
With glory and derision,
Light upon light, mounting the saints' stair.
Not for me the martyrdom, the ecstasy of thought and prayer,
Not for me the ultimate vision.
Grant me thy peace.
(And a sword shall pierce thy heart,
Thine also).
I am tired with my own life and the lives of those after me,
I am dying in my own death and the deaths of those after me.
Let thy servant depart,
Having seen thy salvation.

Eliot's poem is an elaboration on the Biblical text known as the Song of Simeon or by its Latin name *Nunc dimittis*.[32] It occurs in Luke 2. 29–32. Eliot uses the King James Bible and the *Book of Common Prayer* as a linguistic background against which to achieve allusive resonance. The opening vocative of the poem is a deliberate echo of the *Nunc dimittis*. Likewise the final and penultimate lines of the poem echo the opening of the canticle. The last stanza of the poem begins with a direct quotation from the canticle ("According to thy word"). There is a saturation of liturgical language in the poem, the clearest example of which is the refrain "Grant us thy peace."

The poem has an austere and majestic tone which Eliot produces through an imitation of the metre of his Biblical and liturgical background. The *Nunc dimittis* has an irregular metre, its lines ranging from very short (e.g. "Depart in peace") to quite long (e.g. "And to be the glory of thy people Israel"); it has no rhyme scheme and its cadence follows the rhythm of speech. In Eliot's poem there are occasional rhymes (e.g. "and":"stand":"hand":"land", lines 1, 3, 5, 7) but there is no specific rhyme scheme and there is great metrical variety. Eliot does make use of *enjambement*, and there is in the first stanza an underlying iambic pentameter movement which is disguised in places. The underlying metre of the other stanzas is not as clear (though the first part of the second stanza is also substantially iambic pentameter).

A comparison between the poem and the *Nunc dimittis* reveals the differences on which Eliot's poem is predicated. The *Nunc dimittis* is a prayer of hope, in which Simeon expresses no doubts about the fate of mankind enlightened by the Incarnation. Eliot's poem evinces less hope and has its elements of despair concerning mankind's fate:

> Who shall remember my house, where shall live my
> children's children
> When the time of sorrow is come?
> They will take to the goat's path, and the fox's home,
> Fleeing from the foreign faces and the foreign swords.

Simeon, having seen the Infant, looks forward to glory and salvation. Eliot's *persona* looks to the Last Judgement and the Stations of the Cross:

> Before the time of cords and scourges and lamentation
> Grant us thy peace.
> Before the stations of the mountain of desolation,
> Before the certain hour of maternal sorrow,
> Now at this birth season of decease [...].

The final stanza makes the cleanest break with the Biblical Simeon, who clearly says, "For mine eyes have seen thy salvation." Eliot's *persona* says instead:

> Not for me the martyrdom, the ecstasy of thought and
> prayer,
> Not for me the ultimate vision.

The Biblical Simeon attained salvation, the Modernist Simeon renounces all hope of it.

Eliot's poem was published in 1928. The following year Montale published his translation, which carried the (mistranslated) title "Canto di Simeone":

Signore, i giacinti romani fioriscono nei vasi
e il sole d'inverno rade i colli nevicati:
l'ostinata stagione si diffonde...
La mia vita leggera attende il vento della morte
come piuma sul dorso della mano.
La polvere nel sole e il ricordo negli angoli
attendono il vento che corre freddo alla terra deserta.

Accordaci la pace.
Molti anni camminai tra queste mura,
serbai fede e digiuno, provvedetti
ai poveri, ebbi e resi onori ed agi.
Nessuno fu respinto alla mia porta.
Chi penserà al mio tetto, dove vivranno i figli dei miei figli
quando arriverà il giorno del dolore?
Prenderanno il sentiero delle capre, la tana delle volpi
fuggendo i volti ignoti e le spade straniere.

Prima che tempo sia di corde verghe e lamenti
dacci la pace tua.
Prima che sia la sosta nei monti desolati,
prima che giunga l'ora di un materno dolore,
in quest' età di nascita e di morte
possa il Figliuolo, il Verbo non pronunciante ancora e impronunciato
dar la consolazione d'Israele
a un uomo che ha ottant' anni e che non ha domani.

Secondo la promessa
soffrirà chi Ti loda a ogni generazione,
tra gloria e scherno, luce sopra luce,
e la scala dei santi ascenderà.
Non martirio per me—estasi di pensiero e di preghiera—
né la visione estrema.
Concedimi la pace.
(Ed una spada passerà il tuo cuore,
anche il tuo cuore.)
Sono stanco della mia vita e di quella di chi verrà.
Muoio della mia morte e di quella di chi poi morrà.
Fa' che il tuo servo partendo
veda la tua salvezza.

(*L'opera in versi*, pp. 740–41)

This translation is of particular interest because it was Montale's first published work as a translator and also the first Italian translation of Eliot's poem.[33] Montale's choice of words and of metre should reveal some of his earliest solutions to the problems of translating an English poem into Italian.

Montale had no religious background comparable with Eliot's High Church Anglo-Catholic tendencies on which to draw. The attraction which this poem held for Montale almost certainly lay in its tone of renunciation, consonant with the tone of his own poems, such as "Casa sul mare", written in 1925:

> Penso che per i piú non sia salvezza,
> ma taluno sovverta ogni disegno,
> passi il varco, qual volle si ritrovi.
> Vorrei prima di cedere segnarti
> codesta via di fuga
> labile come nei sommossi campi
> del mare spuma o ruga.
> Ti dono anche l'avara mia speranza.
> (*L'opera in versi*, p. 91)

There is very little thematic distance between these lines and Eliot's "Not for me the martyrdom, the ecstasy of thought and prayer,/ Not for me the ultimate vision."

In the absence of Eliot's background of religious language, Montale had to structure his translation along different lines from those of Eliot. Firstly, Eliot's monosyllabic rhymes and half-rhymes (e.g. "and":"stand":"hand":"land" or "swords":"Word") were removed. Montale was under no illusions concerning the difficulties of using monosyllables in Italian. On the other hand, his metrical procedure is comparable to Eliot's. The translation begins with the vocative "Signore", which opens a hypermetric line. There is, however, in the first stanza an underlying structure composed of hendecasyllables and *settenari*. Two of the lines (3 and 5) are quite clearly hendecasyllables. *Settenari* appear embedded within hypermetric lines, e.g. "[...] il vento della morte" (line 4), "La polvere nel sole [...]" (line 6) and "alla terra deserta" preceded by a hendecasyllable in line 7. The *settenario* metre acts as a type of refrain. The first line could be read as apostrophe + *settenario* + *settenario*:

Signore,
i giacinti romani
fioriscono nei vasi;

and this metrical pattern is also discernible in the final line: "veda la tua salvezza". The repetitions in the original ("Grant us thy peace") are treated as a pretext for variation ("Accordaci la pace", "dacci la pace tua", "Concedimi la pace"), but all Montale's three alternatives for "Grant us thy peace" are *settenari*. The words on the surface may be different but the rhythm establishes a deeper structure at which Montale seems to have been aiming. His translation is built on a contrast between two rhythms, the *settenario* and the hendecasyllable.[34]

The other area of interest is Montale's choice of linguistic register in the translation. This is connected with the notion of fidelity to Eliot's text but it is in fact a more ample question. Fidelity, however, is a useful starting-point. It has been contended that Montale's translation aspires to being a faithful and complete interpretation of Eliot's poem.[35] To what extent may that contention be sustained?

Montale's first major translation problem presents itself in the second line: it consists of a verb + preposition ("creeps by") and a vague collocation ("snow hills"). The latter gave Montale no great difficulty ("colli nevicati"), but the former proved to be a more interesting case. To translate "to creep" Montale used the verb *radere* (the primary meaning of which is "to shave") instead of the more obvious *strisciare*. Two factors probably influenced his choice, one internal and one external. Firstly, there is a link through assonance connecting "rade" with "romani" and "vasi" in the first line. Secondly, *radere* is a verb which occurs in three of the later *Ossi di seppia* poems (two of which were added in the second edition). It occurs in "Arsenio" as a transitive verb: "un frúscio immenso rade/la terra."[36] It appears in line 50 of "Crisalide":

Spicca una d'esse un volo senza rombo,
l'acque di piombo come alcione profugo
rade.

(*L'opera in versi*, p. 86)

It appears again in an adjectival form in the penultimate stanza of "Incontro":

> nella luce
> radente un moto mi conduce accanto
> a una misera fronda che in un vaso
> s'alleva s'una porta di osteria.
> (*L'opera in versi*, pp. 96–97)

Of the three occurrences in Montale's own poetry this is the only one where the sense of *radere* corresponds to its use in the translation. It is worth noting that "vaso" is one line away from "radente" in "Incontro", almost as a calque for "Canto di Simeone"; in other words, there is a definite intertextual echo between "Incontro" and "Canto di Simeone". So in his first translation Montale translated Eliot's poem not just into Italian but into his own idiolect of Italian. It is likely that the internal assonance factor and the external or intertextual factor were both at work motivating Montale's linguistic choice in this case.

In the third line a further problem was posed for Montale by the form of Eliot's elliptical verb "to make stand". Montale eventually chose "diffondersi", a verb with a nuance of "insinuation", and while it is an infidelity it might well be an improvement on the original.[37] The real infidelity of the stanza occurs in the place of greatest emphasis, the very last word. Montale translated Eliot's "dead land" not as the literal "terra morta" but as "terra deserta". Why? Again there are two factors. The last line of the first stanza is a hypermetric line composed of a hendecasyllable and a *settenario*. "Morta" is bisyllabic and therefore not rhythmically possible, as a trisyllabic word is required. This seems a likely explanation though perhaps not quite convincing. The external factor concerns the opening of "Arsenio", which acts as another linguistic seed-bed for lines 6 and 7 of "Canto di Simeone":

> I turbini sollevano la *polvere*
> sui tetti, a mulinelli, e sugli spiazzi
> *deserti*, ove i cavalli incappucciati
> annusano la *terra*.
> (*L'opera in versi*, p. 82)

"Dust" and "earth" ("polvere" and "terra") were present in the English text almost as an invitation for Montale to mistranslate "dead" as "deserta", not in order to render homage to the first man to publish "Arsenio" in English, but to cohere with a trace in his own poetic memory. That element of coherence, between translation and his own work, was to become a characteristic of Montale's translation procedure.

The second stanza of the translation is metrically very tight, containing one *settenario*, five hendecasyllables and three hypermetric lines, two consisting of hendecasyllable + *settenario* and one being a *settenario doppio*. It is a close though not entirely literal translation. Montale avoided a masculine ending in the second line by avoiding a literal translation ("città" for "city"). Instead he opted for synecdoche, translating "in this city" by "fra queste mura". Eliot's stanza is quite regular but Montale chose to interrupt this regularity in his translation by introducing an *enjambement* between the third and fourth lines, causing a caesura after "poveri" in the fourth line. The effect, to use Montale's own musical terminology, is *recitativo* rather than *canto*.

The third stanza is also a close translation but in a looser metre. There are some interesting infidelities. Eliot's "the stations of the mountain of desolation" has the specific nuance of Calvary and the Via Crucis, but Montale's "sosta nei monti desolati" is relatively context-free. The next line is an analogous case. Eliot wrote, "Before the certain hour of maternal sorrow", which Montale mistranslated as "prima che giunga l'ora di *un* materno dolore". Both examples testify as much to Montale's lack of Eliot's religious concerns as to his reluctance to produce a faithful crib for the foreign poem. There is a further example in the last stanza. Eliot's ending, "Let thy servant depart,/Having seen thy salvation", was translated by Montale as "Fa' che il tuo servo partendo/veda la tua salvezza." The translation shifts the focus of the original poem, in which the gerund is in the past tense (and thus a completed action). In other words, Eliot's Simeon almost repeats the words of the Biblical Simeon; he is content to die because he has seen God's salvation. Montale's Simeone wants something quite different: what he wants to see as he leaves is the sudden flash of revelation, the *barbaglio* which is characteristic of Montale's poetry.

To return to the question posed at the start of this analysis, it is clear from the foregoing that Meoli Toulmin's claim about completeness and fidelity in relation to Montale's interpretation of Eliot's poem is illusory. Completeness and fidelity are not approximate or relative terms, and Montale's translation does not satisfy either of them. Neither is there much evidence of Montale's having aspired to either concept as a criterion of successful translation. He translated into his own idiom, both linguistic and thematic, and it may be instructive at this point to refer back to his remarks on Eliot's other translators:

> Eliot fu sinora (tranne rare e parziali eccezioni) disservito da interpreti volenterosi ma in perpetua lotta con mezzi espressivi inadeguati, con lingue che appiattiscono inevitabilmente la leggerezza del suo recitativo. [...] Gli italiani quando non si appagano di una modesta letteralità, sono forzati a una ricerca di monosillabi, di elisioni e di cesure che certo stravolgono il genio originariamente plastico e disteso del nostro discorso. ("Eliot e noi", p. 444)

In the light of this statement, how well was Eliot served by Montale's "Canto di Simeone"? Montale was more aware than many others of Eliot's metrical innovations, and his translation reflects that awareness. He was also aware of the difficulties of maintaining a *recitativo* tone in Italian poetry, and made a significant effort to achieve that tone through the absence of rhyme and the use of elision, *enjambement* and caesura. Eliot does not appear to have been quite so well served by the nuances which the translator introduced into the text. Montale effectively appropriated the poem, bringing into it linguistic and thematic echoes of his own poems. Once appropriated, the translation became part of his poetic memory, ready to be used later on in other poems. Simeon's concern for his descendants is alluded to in "Voce giunta con le folaghe", the poem in which the shade of Montale's father speaks with Clizia. The textual memory involves the "sentiero delle capre" in the second stanza of "Canto di Simeone", which reappears as a "sentiero da capre".[38]

"La figlia che piange"

The following is the text of T. S. Eliot's "La Figlia Che Piange" (1911):

O quam te memorem virgo...

Stand on the highest pavement of the stair—
Lean on a garden urn—
Weave, weave the sunlight in your hair—
Clasp your flowers to you with a pained surprise—

Fling them to the ground and turn
With a fugitive resentment in your eyes:
But weave, weave the sunlight in your hair.

So I would have had him leave,
So I would have had her stand and grieve,
So he would have left
As the soul leaves the body torn and bruised,
As the mind deserts the body it has used.
I should find
Some way incomparably light and deft,
Some way we both should understand,
Simple and faithless as a smile and shake of the hand.

She turned away, but with the autumn weather
Compelled my imagination many days,
Many days and many hours:
Her hair over her arms and her arms full of flowers.
And I wonder how they should have been together!
I should have lost a gesture and a pose.
Sometimes these cogitations still amaze
The troubled midnight and the noon's repose.[39]

This is one of Eliot's earliest poems, and Mario Praz has traced in it several textual echoes of Dante Gabriel Rossetti's "Blessed Damozel".[40] "La Figlia" is thus a remote descendant of the lady of the *stilnovisti*. But Eliot's free rhythm has more life than Rossetti's ponderous metre in "The Blessed Damozel", of which the following is a sample:

The blessed damozel leaned out
From the gold bar of Heaven;
Her eyes were deeper than the depth
Of waters stilled at even;
She had three lilies in her hand,
And the stars in her hair were seven.

The "figlia" in Eliot's poem is addressed in the first stanza as an interlocutor, and there is dramatic urgency in the monosyllabic imperatives "stand", "lean", "weave", "clasp" and "fling". Eliot's free verse was not confined within a strict rhyme scheme. There are rhymes, such as "stair":"hair":"hair" (lines 1,3,7), but they give the impression of being casual. The stanzas are of uneven length: seven lines in the first, nine in the second and eight in the third. Eliot allied sense to syntax, making clean semantic and syntactic breaks at the end of each line, unlike Rossetti, who had used occasional *enjambement*, for example:

He shall fear, haply, and be dumb:
  Then will I lay my cheek
To his, and tell about our love [...].
(stanza 20)

Eliot's text derives an incantatory power from the frequent repetitions, such as "Weave, weave the sunlight in your hair/[...]/But weave, weave the sunlight in your hair" (lines 3, 7), "So I would have had him leave,/So I would have had her stand and grieve,/ So he would have left" (lines 8–10), and "As the soul leaves the body torn and bruised,/As the mind deserts the body it has used" (lines 11–12). The text contains none of the metaphysical complexities of the *Ariel Poems*, but exactly what that entails for the translator is a matter for discussion.

Montale's translation reads as follows:

La figlia che piange

O quam te memorem virgo...

  Sosta sul piú alto piano della scala—
appoggiati ad un'urna di giardino—
tessi, tessi la luce del sole nei tuoi capelli—
stringi i tuoi fiori a te con sorpresa attristata—
gettali a terra e volgiti
con un rapido cruccio negli sguardi:
ma tessi, tessi la luce del sole nei tuoi capelli.

  Cosí avrei voluto vederlo andare,
cosí avrei voluto ch'ella restasse e soffrisse,
cosí egli sarebbe partito
come l'anima lascia il corpo contuso e lacero,
come lo spirito lascia il corpo che ha logorato.
E troverei
un modo incomparabilmente lieve e abile,
un modo che capiremmo tutt' e due,
semplice e infido come un sorriso e una stretta di mano.

Ella si volse, ma col tempo di autunno
sforzò per molti giorni la mia mente,
molti giorni e molte ore:
la sua chioma sulle sue braccia, le sue braccia piene di
fiori,
e mi chiedo com' essi sarebbero stati insieme!
Avrei perduto un gesto ed una posa.
Questi pensieri a volte meravigliano ancora
la mezzanotte turbata e la pace del mezzodí.
(*L'opera in versi*, p. 742)[41]

In his 1933 note published in *Circoli* Montale described "La Figlia Che Piange" as "meno notevole" than the *Ariel Poems*.[42] Unlike "Canto di Simeone", his translation of this poem has no significant variants. The implication of this is either that the translation caused Montale less effort or that he was not prepared to give it more effort than he did.

Montale's translation of "La Figlia Che Piange" is a very faithful version both syntactically and semantically. Apart from the inevitable rhyme of "capelli" with "capelli" (lines 3 and 7), he avoided end-rhymes. He also avoided, as Eliot had done, the use of *enjambement* and caesura. That is more serious in the case of Italian than of English. English, because of its stock of monosyllables, uses fewer syllables to express meaning than Italian does. So, starting from the modest aspiration to literal translation, we may expect longer and hypermetric Italian lines as translations of Eliot's free but concise stanzas. Montale's lines conform to this expectation.

The interlocutory *tu* of the first stanza fits easily into Montale's idiom, as do the five imperatives. Monosyllabic imperatives such as the ones used by Eliot, however, are impossible in Italian and thus constituted Montale's first problem. He found bisyllabic equivalents for three of the imperatives ("sosta" for "stand", "tessi" for "weave" and "stringi" for "clasp"), but had to resort to longer, *sdruccioli* imperatives for the remaining two: "appoggiati" for "lean" and "gettali" for "fling".

Meoli Toulmin has taken issue with some of Montale's linguistic choices in this translation.[43] She has argued that Montale's "urna" (line 2) is not an appropriate rendering of Eliot's "urn". The Italian word has more immediate funereal and indeed electoral contexts that does the English word, so Meoli Toulmin has suggested *vaso* instead. Montale was faced with several English collocations for which he had to resort to relative periphrasis, such as "urna di giardino" for "garden urn", "luce del sole" for "sunlight" and "pace di mezzodí" for "noon's repose". In each case the (accurate) Italian translation is more cumbersome that the original English expression. In other words, the Italian language is at odds with the type of expression to which Montale aspired. Elsewhere Montale avoids the most obvious Italian equivalent of an English word, as in his translation of "fugitive" as "rapido" instead of "fugace" and of "deft" as "abile" instead of "destro". What is most clearly absent from Montale's "La figlia che piange" is the tendency towards variation which characterizes many of his translations, including "Canto di Simeone". He followed Eliot's lead in all the repetitions noted above, that is, "tessi, tessi la luce del sole nei tuoi capelli/[...]/ma tessi, tessi la luce del sole nei tuoi capelli" (lines 3, 7), "Cosí avrei voluto [...]/cosí avrei voluto [...]/cosí egli sarebbe partito" (lines 8–10) and "come l'anima lascia il corpo [...]/come lo spirito lascia il corpo [...]" (lines 11–12).[44] Montale's linguistic choices in his translation are consistent in that he knew Italian to be a heavier, more polysyllabic language than English but wanted to achieve greater concision in Italian, which led him to use the shortest words available.

Such a level of repetition is uncharacteristic of Montale's translation procedure, and it should be remembered that "La figlia che piange" is one of his early translations and one in which he probably had relatively little interest.

"Animula" is a different case. The poem was translated in the 1940s and first published as an appendix to the 1947 essay "Eliot e noi".

"Animula"

The following is the text of Eliot's "Animula" (1929):

> "Issues from the hand of God, the simple soul"
> To a flat world of changing lights and noise,
> To light, dark, dry or damp, chilly or warm;
> Moving between the legs of tables and of chairs,
> Rising or falling, grasping at kisses and toys,
> Advancing boldly, sudden to take alarm,
> Retreating to the corner of arm and knee,
> Eager to be reassured, taking pleasure
> In the fragrant brilliance of the Christmas tree,

Pleasure in the wind, the sunlight and the sea;
Studies the sunlit pattern on the floor
And running stags around a silver tray;
Confounds the actual and the fanciful,
Content with playing-cards and kings and queens,
What the fairies do and what the servants say.
The heavy burden of the growing soul
Perplexes and offends more, day by day;
Week by week, offends and perplexes more
With the imperatives of "is and seems"
And may and may not, desire and control.
The pain of living and the drug of dreams
Curl up the small soul in the window seat
Behind the *Encyclopaedia Britannica*.
Issues from the hand of time the simple soul
Irresolute and selfish, misshapen, lame,
Unable to fare forward or retreat,
Fearing the warm reality, the offered good,
Denying the importunity of the blood,
Shadow of its own shadows, spectre in its own gloom,
Leaving disordered papers in a dusty room;
Living first in the silence after the viaticum.

Pray for Guiterriez, avid of speed and power,
For Boudin, blown to pieces,
For this one who made a great fortune,
And that one who went his own way.
Pray for Floret, by the boarhound slain between the
yew trees,
Pray for us now and at the hour of our birth.

"Animula" is an elaboration upon part of Marco Lombardo's speech in *Purgatorio*, XVI. 85–93.[45] The theme of the speech is free will and the nature of the Good. The title "Animula" is both Latin and Italian. In both languages it is a diminutive of *anima*, thus it means literally "little soul". The Zingarelli dictionary offers a figurative meaning: "persona dall'interiorità debole, incerta".[46]

Eliot's poem consists in two stanzas, the first (which is much longer than the second) containing five sentences, the second containing two. The poem is cast in free verse composed mainly of pentameter, hendecasyllables and alexandrines. The first line, a hendecasyllable, is inside quotation marks as it is a loose translation of *Purgatorio*, XVI. 85. Eliot takes Marco's speech as a reference-point for a meditation on the growing up and eventual dying of the simple soul in the modern world. Referring to Dante's image of the infant distracted by competing appearances of pleasure, Eliot describes a child in a Christmas scene, and, in the second stanza, various fictitious characters who followed one particular course of action. Eliot's conclusion is bleak: conscious life begins only after the last rites ("Living first in the silence after the viaticum", line 31).[47]

The following is Montale's translation of "Animula":

"Lascia la mano di Dio la semplice anima" e volge
a un piatto mondo di luci mutevoli e di rumore,
al chiaro, al buio, all'asciutto o all'umido, al fresco o al caldo;
s'indugia tra le gambe delle sedie o dei tavoli,
alzandosi o cadendo, baci afferrando o gingilli,
s'avanza franca, poi s'allarma subito,
si rifugia nell'angolo di un braccio e d'un ginocchio,
pronto a rassicurarsi, a rallegrarsi
del fragrante lucore che dà l'albero
di Natale, del vento e del sole e del mare;
sul pavimento scruta il trapunto dei raggi,
intorno a una sottocoppa d'argento una fuga di cervi,
verità e fantasia scambia e confonde,
carte da gioco e re e regine l'appagano,
ciò che fanno le fate, ciò che dicono i servi.
Il pesante fardello dell'anima che cresce
è sempre maggiore imbarazzo e offesa di giorno in giorno,
di settimana in settimana, è offesa
d'imperativi—l'essere e il parere,
il si può, il non si può, il desiderio e il possesso.
Pena di vita e narcotico di sogni torcono l'anima
piccoletta che accanto alla finestra
siede al riparo dell'*Enciclopedia Britannica*.
Lascia la mano del tempo la semplice anima, incerta
ed egoista, storta e zoppicante,
incapace di starsi avanti o indietro,
teme la realtà calda, l'offerta bene,
rifiuta il sangue come un importuno,
ombra delle sue ombre e spettro del suo buio,
disperde le sue carte tra buio e polvere
e comincia la vita nel silenzio che segue il viatico.

> Prega per Guiterriez, avido di successo e di potere,
> e per Boudin ch'è crollato,
> per chi s'è fatto ricco e chi ha tirato
> per la sua strada; prega per Floret che i segugi
> sbranarono fra gli alberi di tasso; per noi prega
> ora e nell'ora della nostra nascita.
> (*L'opera in versi*, pp. 743–44)

Since "Animula" is an elaboration on Marco Lombardo's speech in *Purgatorio*, it offers a literary game to Italian translators. Should they reproduce Dante's lines where Eliot has translated directly from them or should they translate the translation without reference to Dante's text?

Montale's translation avoids not only Dante's words but also the hendecasyllable which is characteristic of the *Commedia* and which Eliot had used in his quotation from Dante.[48] Montale's translation is written in free verse composed mainly of hypermetric lines. The intention is to achieve an accurate transmission of the poem's content at the expense of form. That is an unusual decision on Montale's part, considering his procedure in the other translations. His version of "Animula" is almost a paradigm of literal translation. It does compress more than the English poem in places, but without any serious change of nuance. For instance, Eliot's

> taking pleasure
> In the fragrant brilliance of the Christmas tree,
> Pleasure in the wind, the sunlight and the sea;

becomes

> a rallegrarsi
> del fragrante lucore che dà l'albero
> di Natale, del vento e del sole e del mare;

Montale excises the redundant repetition of the noun "pleasure". There are some echoes of the language of Marco Lombardo's speech, but these ("Pena di vita e narcotico di sogni *torcono* l'anima/ *piccoletta*" for "The pain of living and the drug of dreams/Curl up the small soul") are also accurate and literal translations of Eliot's poem.[49] One of Eliot's lines seems to have caused Montale some difficulty. The penultimate line of the first stanza contains a passive nuance: "Leaving disordered papers in a dusty room". Montale's final solution reads "disperde le sue carte tra buio e polvere", while a variant reads "nella stanza scompiglia i fogli tra la polvere".[50] The variant is more literal except for the active nuance in the verb *scompigliare*. Both *scompigliare* and *disperdere* have Montalian echoes, and neither is entirely faithful to Eliot's meaning.[51]

Montale's three translations from T. S. Eliot are not unified by a common approach. "Animula" is essentially an accurate semantic translation in hypermetric lines; it is the least innovative of the three. It was translated about twenty years after the other two poems as an act of homage to Eliot on Eliot's visit to Rome. "La figlia che piange", a much earlier piece of work, is also a relatively close translation, guided by the criterion of literalness. Of the three translations only "Canto di Simeone" exhibits evidence of an appropriation by Montale of Eliot's text. It is a partial interpretation (or even a partial re-interpretation) of Eliot's poem, and the interpretation is more consistent with Montale's own poetics. The reworking in this translation is reflected in the structure, which is more deliberate and calculated than that of the other two translations.

The Return of the Mayflower

Eliot's principal contribution to Montale's poetics was that he offered a direction.[52] Montale described the direction, quoting the title of an article by Georges Cattaui, as "il ritorno del Mayflower" (see above, pages 50–55). Eliot's interest in Dante and the *dolce stil novo* stimulated Montale's deeper awareness of his Italian poetic patrimony, and set an example which could provide a bridge from *Ossi di seppia* to his later poems. *Ossi di seppia* and "Stile e tradizione" belong to the same period. In that period Montale was still writing in the shadow of D'Annunzio, and, while there are allusions to the older Italian tradition in *Ossi di seppia*, the real poetic context of the volume, as Sanguineti, Bonfiglioli and Mengaldo have demonstrated, is formed by D'Annunzio, Gozzano, Pascoli and the *crepuscolari*.[53]

In the mid-1920s Montale came into contact with international Modernism, particularly with Joyce and Eliot, albeit at one remove (through French translations) at least in Joyce's case. These encounters as a critic and a translator were suggestive to Montale as a poet in different ways. The example which Joyce gave him was of a foreign writer with whom he could feel a creative affinity which could be exploited in his own poetry, firstly because Joyce was a foreigner and secondly because he wrote prose rather than poetry. Eliot is a different case. Critics have made much of Montale's apparent affinities with Eliot and the influence of Eliot's poetry which, it has been claimed, appeared in Montale's poetry throughout the 1930s and 1940s. By and large the affinities are incidental and the influences illusory. What Montale did derive from Eliot was a new way of looking at Dante and the *stilnovisti*. Not that Montale was at all convinced by the American Modernists' interpretations of the *dolce stil novo*. He was, for example, sceptical about Pound's erudition: "Erudito, ma di una erudizione che sapeva di digesto, di corso accelerato, fluido ma non corretto parlatore della nostra lingua, aveva allestito una discussa edizione delle poesie di Cavalcanti e collaborava a riviste italiane con note spesso illuminanti."[54] Pound and Eliot provided a means by which Montale could escape the shadows of D'Annunzio and the *crepuscolari* and enter the older Italian tradition not as an archivist but as a modern poet.

It is no coincidence that Montale's early translations of Eliot corresponded to this new realization in his poetics. But the paradoxical claim that Montale became more consciously an Italian poet through the act of translation requires some disentangling in the following chapters.

NOTES

1 See T. S. Eliot's "Tradition and the Individual Talent" [1919], in his *Selected Prose*, edited by J. Hayward (Harmondsworth, Penguin, 1953), pp. 21–30, and specifically the following (pp. 23–24): "No poet, no artist of any art, has his complete meaning alone. His significance, his appreciation is the appreciation of his relation to the dead poets and artists. You cannot value him alone; you must set him, for contrast and comparison, among the dead. I mean this as a principle of aesthetic, not merely historical criticism. The necessity that he shall conform, that he shall cohere, is not one-sided; what happens when a new work of art is created is something that happens simultaneously to all the works of art which preceded it. The existing monuments form an ideal

order among themselves, which is modified by the introduction of the new (the really new) work of art among them. The existing order is complete before the new work arrives; for the order to persist after the supervention of novelty, the *whole* existing order must be, if ever so slightly, altered; and so the relations, proportions, values of each work of art toward the whole are readjusted; and this is conformity between the old and the new."

2 "Stile e tradizione" was published in *Il Baretti*, 2, i (15 Jan. 1925), 15. It is reprinted in E. Montale, *Auto da fé: cronache in due tempi*, edited by G. Zampa (Milan, Saggiatore, 1966), pp. 15–19. References are to the latter edition. The passage quoted here is on pp. 15–16.

3 See E. Montale, "Stile e tradizione", p. 17: "Al desiderio di frontiere troppo vaste, di cieli troppo distanti, porremmo innanzi il confine del nostro paese, la lingua della nostra gente. Troppo lavoro rimane da compiere oggi, perché ci tentino questi salti nel buio."

4 E. Montale, "Eliot e noi", *L'immagine* [Rome], 1, v (Nov–Dec. 1947), 261–64, now included in his *Sulla poesia*, edited by G. Zampa (Milan, Mondadori, 1976), pp. 441–46. The passage quoted is on pp. 445–46; Montale's italics.

5 E. Montale, "Intenzioni (intervista immaginaria)" [1946], in his *Sulla poesia*, edited by G. Zampa (Milan, Mondadori, 1976), pp. 561–69 (p. 567).

6 See, for example, the essay "Un panorama letterario" [1928], in E. Montale, *Sulla poesia*, pp. 163–67. For a very different account of Svevo's "discovery" by Italian critics, see A. Gramsci, "La 'scoperta' di Italo Svevo", in his *Letteratura e vita nazionale* (Turin, Editori Riuniti, 1975), pp. 116–17.

7 See *Carteggio Svevo–Montale*, edited by G. Zampa (Milan, Mondadori, 1976), p. 23. The letter is dated 3 July 1926 (i.e. probably after the *Dubliners* article had been written). The following is added to it as a postscript: "Crede Lei che a Londra o Parigi potrà trovarsi una edizione in *inglese* di *Dubliners*? (parlo di edizioni di *poco prezzo*). In caso, la compri per me. Ma badi che desidero *assolutamente* ch'Ella mi sappia dire il costo, per pagare il debito."

8 E. Montale, "*Dubliners*", *La fiera letteraria*, year II, 38 (19 Sept. 1926).

9 See E. Montale, "Intenzioni", p. 563: "Ma nel '16 avevo già composto il primo frammento *tout entier à sa proie attaché*: *Meriggiare pallido e assorto* (che modificai piú tardi nella strofa finale). La preda era, s'intende, il *mio* paesaggio." "Meriggiare pallido e assorto" may be read in Montale's *L'opera in versi*, edited by G. Contini and R. Bettarini (Turin, Einaudi, 1980), p. 14.

10 See E. Montale, *L'opera in versi*, pp. 765–72.

11 See S. Ramat, "Un pre-Accordo", in his *L'acacia ferita e altri saggi su Montale* (Venice, Marsilio, 1986), pp. 19–36.

12 For "Elegia" see E. Montale, *L'opera in versi*, p. 759. The poem is dated 1918.

13 See P. Pancrazi, "Eugenio Montale: poeta fisico e metafisico" [1934], in his *Scrittori d'oggi* (Bari, Laterza, 1944), pp. 248–58.

14 The rhyme "formiche":"biche" is an early example of Montale's Dantean echoes. The rhyme occurs in *Inferno*, XXIX. 64–66: "Non credo ch'a veder maggior tristizia/fosse in Egina il popol tutto infermo,/quando fu l'aere sí pien di malizia,/che li animali, infino al picciol vermo,/cascaron tutti, e poi le genti antiche,/secondo che i poeti hanno per fermo,/si ristorar di seme di formiche;/ch'era a veder per quella oscura valle/languir li spirti per diverse biche" (ll. 58–66).

15 The poems added to the second edition were "Arsenio", "I morti", "Delta" (the poem which Beckett liked well enough to translate in the late 1920s) and "Incontro" (originally entitled "Arletta").
16 The symbolic significance of the coastline is examined by both R. J. West, *Eugenio Montale: Poet on the Edge* (Cambridge, Mass., Harvard University Press, 1981), Ch. 1, and F. J. Jones, *The Modern Italian Lyric* (Cardiff, University of Wales Press, 1986), especially p. 441.
17 See "Falsetto": "L'acqua è la forza che ti tempra,/nell'acqua ti ritrovi e ti rinnovi" (E. Montale, *L'opera in versi*, pp. 12–13).
18 E. Montale, "La piuma di struzzo", in his *Farfalla di Dinard* (Milan, Mondadori, 1960), pp. 70–75 (pp. 74–75).
19 See, for example, in Montale's review of *Dubliners*: "Cosí in 'Una nuvola' un impiegato [...] ha l'improvvisa sensazione, ricascando, della miseria e della monotonia della propria esistenza strangolata."
20 Montale stated in a letter to Gadda Conti: "I miei motivi sono semplici e sono: il paesaggio (qualche volta allucinato, ma spesso naturalistico: il nostro paesaggio ligure, che è universalissimo); l'amore, sotto forma di fantasmi che *frequentano* le varie poesie e provocano le solite 'intermittenze del cuore' (gergo proustiano che io non uso) e l'evasione, la fuga dalla catena ferrea della necessità, il miracolo, diciamo cosí, laico" (quoted by A. Valentini, *Lettura di Montale: Ossi di seppia* [Rome, Bulzoni, 1971], p. 11).
21 Montale found his own interest in Joyce quite unnerving. In a letter to Svevo (6 Dec. 1926) he wrote: "Joyce [...] mi dà preoccupazioni infinite di tutte le specie [...]. Rimpiango d'essermi impegnato per Joyce. Io non sono un critico. E non voglio neppure presentarmi come tale" (*Carteggio Svevo–Montale*, p. 41).
22 M. Praz, "T. S. Eliot and Eugenio Montale", in *T. S. Eliot: A Symposium*, edited by R. March and M. J. Tambimuttu (London, Poetry Editions, 1948), pp. 244–48.
23 M. Praz, "T. S. Eliot and Eugenio Montale", pp. 246–47.
24 See R. Meoli Toulmin, "Shakespeare ed Eliot nelle versioni di Eugenio Montale", *Belfagor*, 26 (1971), 453–71.
25 R. Meoli Toulmin, "Shakespeare ed Eliot", p. 462.
26 R. Meoli Toulmin, "Shakespeare ed Eliot", p. 466.
27 G. Contini, "Introduzione a *Ossi di seppia*", *Rivista rosminiana* (1933), now in his *Una lunga fedeltà: sulla poesia di Montale* (Turin, Einaudi, 1974), pp. 5–16. The passage quoted is on pp. 6–7.
28 See A. Pinchera, "La versificazione tonico-sillabico nella poesia di Montale", *Quaderni urbinati*, 7 (1969), 155–84.
29 "Ancor meno d'oggi, quando tradussi 'A Song for Simeon' (*Solaria*, 1929) e 'La Figlia Che Piange' per il numero americano di *Circoli* (1933) e le feci precedere da una notizia che resta una delle prime apparse in Italia sull'autore di 'The Waste Land', io potevo credermi uno specialista in questo argomento" (E. Montale, "Eliot e noi", p. 441).
30 See E. Montale, "Invito a T. S. Eliot", first published in *Lo smeraldo* [Milan], 4, iii (30 May 1950), 19–23, and reprinted in his *Sulla poesia*, pp. 457–65, from which the quotations are taken.

31 The definition is not Montale's but that of Tommaso Ceva. Montale quotes it in "Variazioni", *Il mondo*, 2 (21 Apr. 1945), 6. The essay is reprinted in his *Sulla poesia*, pp. 104–06, where the quoted phrase appears on p. 105.

32 Eliot would have known the *Nunc dimittis* as an evening canticle in the Anglican liturgy. It appears as follows in the 1662 *Book of Common Prayer*: "Lord, now lettest thou thy servant/Depart in peace/According to thy Word./For mine eyes have seen thy salvation,/Which Thou hast prepared/Before the face of all people;/To be a light to lighten the Gentiles/And to be the glory of thy people Israel."

33 Montale's "Canto di Simeone" was first published in *Solaria* [Florence], 4, xii (Dec. 1929), 11–12.

34 Further examples of *settenari* include "Chi penserà al mio tetto" (l. 13), "la tana delle volpi" (l. 15), "Secondo la promessa" (l. 25), "Non martirio per me" (l. 29) and "né la visione estrema" (l. 30). The final line of the second stanza is a *settenario doppio*. Hendecasyllables abound in each stanza.

35 See R. Meoli Toulmin, "Shakespeare ed Eliot", p. 466: "Nelle sue attente versioni delle poesie di Eliot sembra che egli [Montale] cerchi soprattutto di dare una interpretazione completa e fedele al testo."

36 "Arsenio", l. 42 (E. Montale, *L'opera in versi*, p. 82).

37 Variants include "l'ostinata stagione è sopraggiunta" and "l'ostinata stagione rincrudisce"; see E. Montale, *L'opera in versi*, p. 1159.

38 See E. Montale, *L'opera in versi*, p. 250.

39 There is a story behind Eliot's title and epigraph. The following is Grover Smith's account: "While Eliot was travelling in Europe in 1911, he visited a museum in Northern Italy possessing a *stele* designated, according to a friend who suggested that he take a look at it, 'La figlia che piange' ('young girl weeping'). For some reason, when he searched for this tablet he was unable to find it. The subject of his resulting lines being nameless, he understandably in reprinting the poem used as an epigraph the phrase from Aeneas's address to Venus: 'Maiden, by what name shall I know you?' (*Aeneid*, I. 327)." See G. Smith, *T. S. Eliot's Poetry and Plays*, second edition (Chicago, University of Chicago Press, 1974), p. 27.

40 See M. Praz, "Eliot and Dante", in his *The Flaming Heart* (Gloucester, Mass., Smith, 1966), pp. 365–66.

41 Montale's translation of "La Figlia Che Piange" was first published in *Circoli* [Genoa], 3, vi (Nov–Dec. 1933), together with a translation of Léonie Adams's "Lullaby" ["Ninna nanna"] and a reprint of "Canto di Simeone".

42 See an extract from the note printed in E. Montale, *L'opera in versi*, pp. 1160–61.

43 See R. Meoli Toulmin, "Shakespeare ed Eliot", p. 465.

44 There is in fact a slight variation here. Eliot repeated the verb "to leave" (ll. 8, 10), whereas Montale alternated *andare* and *partire*.

45 *Purgatorio*, XVI. 85–93: "Esce di mano a lui che la vagheggia/prima che sia, a guisa di fanciulla/che piangendo e ridendo pargoleggia,/l'anima semplicetta che sa nulla,/salvo che, mossa da lieto fattore,/volontier torna a ciò che la trastulla./Di picciol bene in pria sente sapore;/quivi s'inganna, e dietro ad esso corre,/se guida o fren non torce suo amore."

46 *Vocabolario della lingua italiana di Nicola Zingarelli*, edited by M. Dogliotti and L. Rosiello, eleventh edition (Bologna, Zanichelli, 1989).

47 The invocations of the second stanza have an interesting Montalian parallel in a similar invocation at the end of "Incontro" (1926): "Prega per me/allora ch'io discenda altro cammino/che una via di città,/nell'aria persa, innanzi al brulichio/dei vivi; ch'io ti senta accanto; ch'io/scenda senza viltà" (E. Montale, *L'opera in versi*, p. 97).

48 The first line: "'Issues from the hand of God, the simple soul.'"

49 R. Meoli Toulmin in "Shakespeare ed Eliot" has traced the following echoes: "torcono":"torce" (*Purgatorio*, XVI. 93) and "piccoletta":"semplicetta" (*Purg.*, XVI. 88). "Piccoletta" is in fact a subtler solution than Meoli Toulmin has suggested because it echoes both the diminutive "semplicetta" and the "picciol bene" of *Purg.*, XVI. 91.

50 See E. Montale, *L'opera in versi*, p. 1162.

51 For *scompigliare* see "Vento e bandiere", l. 3, "S'è rifatta la calma", l. 6 and "Marezzo", l. 88 (E. Montale, *L'opera in versi*, pp. 23, 70, 88). For *disperdere* see "A Liuba che parte", l. 4, "Elegia di Pico Farnese", l. 49 and "Due nel crepuscolo", l. 26 (*L'opera in versi*, pp. 123, 175, 213).

52 See E. Montale, "Eliot e noi", p. 442: "Creava in me il senso di un arco gettato tra due pilastri, indicava una direzione."

53 See E. Sanguineti, "Da Gozzano a Montale" [1954], in his *Tra liberty e crepuscolarismo*, second edition (Milan, Mursia, 1977), pp. 17–39; P. Bonfiglioli, "Pascoli e Montale", in his *Studi per il centenario della nascita di G. Pascoli* (Bologna, Commissione per i Testi di Lingua, 1962), pp. 219–43; P. V. Mengaldo, "Da D'Annunzio a Montale", in his *La tradizione del Novecento* (Milan, Feltrinelli, 1975), pp. 13–106.

54 E. Montale, "Se i biglietti da mille fossero quelli di Ezra Pound", first published in *Corriere d'informazione*, 18–19 Nov. 1955, and now included in his *Sulla poesia*, pp. 490–94 (p. 492).

Chapter 2

SHAKESPEARE: TRADITION AND INNOVATION

Divergent Traditions

Two Perceptions of Shakespeare

As we have seen, the first tangible evidence of Montale's interaction with English poetry was his translation of two poems by T. S. Eliot. They were soon followed by translations from Shakespeare. Montale made a number of these. The *Quaderno di traduzioni* contains fragments from *A Midsummer Night's Dream* and three sonnets. Montale also translated *The Comedy of Errors, Timon of Athens* and *The Winter's Tale* for Mario Praz's *William Shakespeare: Teatro* (1949), as well as translating *Hamlet* independently.[1] His critical writings on Shakespeare include "Sotto il nome di Shakespeare" and "Letture: Shakespeare; Donne".[2]

It is probably true to say that the translations of each generation will differ—must differ—from those of the preceding generation because a generation can only distinguish itself by its difference from the generation which has come immediately before. Yet such a theory of literary history contains an assumption which is debatable and rather too glib. Two writers of the same generation, although working as contemporaries, may belong to quite different traditions. When two contemporaries who belong to different literary traditions concentrate their energies on translating the same text, we may expect to find conflicting theories and practices of translation. The differences between Montale's and Ungaretti's translations of Shakespeare's "Full many a glorious morning have I seen" provide an object-lesson in different approaches to translation practice.

Ungaretti's Shakespeare

Ungaretti, unlike Montale, suffered no ill effects of censorship during the Fascist period. This was due partly to his six-year sojourn in Brazil (1936–42) as professor of Italian at São Paolo University, and partly to the fact that his writing was admired by Mussolini.[3] Generally speaking, each of his translations was the result of a personal interest in the foreign text, whether it were Brazilian folk-poetry, Góngora or Shakespeare, rather than being the result of a commission by an Italian publisher.[4] His choice of poetry for translation was usually guided by his aesthetic concerns, and unlike Montale he left to posterity essays specifically relating to the topics of translation and aesthetics. By coincidence both Ungaretti and Montale worked on translating Shakespeare's sonnets during the 1930s and 1940s. While Montale translated only three sonnets, Ungaretti published twelve in a limited edition (1942) and incorporated them into his *40 sonetti di Shakespeare* in 1946. The latter contains an important introductory essay. The other relevant essays, "Significato dei sonetti di Shakespeare" and "Della metrica e del tradurre" date originally from the same period.[5]

The Translations

The Case of Sonnet 33

Sonnet 33 is the only sonnet translated by both Montale and Ungaretti. Shakespeare's poem reads as follows:

> Full many a glorious morning have I seen
> Flatter the mountain-tops with sovereign eye,
> Kissing with golden face the meadows green,
> Gilding pale streams with heavenly alchemy;
> Anon permit the basest clouds to ride
> With ugly rack on his celestial face,
> And from the forlorn world his visage hide,
> Stealing unseen to west with this disgrace.
> Even so my sun one early morn did shine
> With all triumphant splendour on my brow;
> But out, alack! he was but one hour mine,
> The region cloud hath mask'd him from me now.

Yet him for this my love no whit disdaineth;
Suns of the world may stain when heaven's sun staineth.

This poem conforms to the familiar formal structure of a Shakespearean sonnet. The rhyme scheme is ABAB CDCD EFEF GG. There is an implied *enjambement* between the first and second lines, which is relatively unusual, in that semantic and syntactic periods tend to coincide in the sonnets. A combination of hyperbaton and periphrasis distances the poem from the conventions of spoken English. The sun, the first grammatical subject of the poem, is referred to by a variety of epithets (such as "a glorious morning", line 1, "golden face", line 3 and "his celestial face", line 6), but is not explicitly mentioned until the third quatrain. The sonnet has an underlying dialectical structure: the first quatrain is positive, the second negative; the first half of the third quatrain is positive, the second negative; and the closing couplet turns on an ambiguity. This ambiguity concerns the internal rhymes "dis*dain*eth": "*stain*":"*stain*eth". "Stain" is a verb with negative connotations, but the implication of the final line seems to be positive.

Ungaretti's version reads as follows:

Ho veduto piú d'un mattino in gloria
con lo sguardo sovrano le vette lusingare,
baciare d'aureo viso i verdi prati,
con alchimia di paradiso tingere i rivi pallidi,
e poi a vili nuvole permettere
di fluttargli sul celestiale volto
con osceni fumi sottraendolo all'universo orbato
mentre verso ponente non visto scompariva, con la sua disgrazia.
Uguale l'astro mio brillò di primo giorno
trionfando splendido sulla mia fronte;
ma, ah! non fu mio che per un'ora sola,
e dell'umano clima nubi già l'hanno a me mascherato.
Non l'ha in disdegno tuttavia il mio cuore.
Astri terreni possono macchiarsi se il sole nel cielo si macchia.

Ungaretti dispenses with Shakespeare's rhyme scheme and does not develop another one in its place. He opts for long lines consonant with his own form of free verse rather than trying to match Shakespeare's metre. This free metre allows him to retain a relatively prosaic syntax and thus enables him to convey (in theory at least) more of the sense of Shakespeare's words to the reader, without elements of the hyperbaton and periphrasis which characterize the original. Ungaretti does retain the dialectical structure of Shakespeare's sonnet. There is hyperbaton in his first quatrain, but it works independently of Shakespeare's syntactic structure. Ungaretti begins with "Ho veduto", which makes his translation appear more personal in tone than the original poem. His first two quatrains form a single sentence, and his opening makes the poet's *io* the subject of the whole sentence. In Shakespeare's sonnet the focus was on the object, the sun; in Ungaretti's translation the focus is on the observer. Ungaretti's solution to the problem of translating the Teutonic adjective "heavenly" is more prosaic than the original, if only because of the number of syllables required to accommodate "alchimia di paradiso". Ungaretti's strategy there is essentially literal. The literal strategy also works with "permettere" for "permit", but Ungaretti's "disgrazia" for Shakespeare's "disgrace" is a dubious translation: the nuances of the words are quite different. Ungaretti may have been well aware of the difference in nuance, because he does not always stick to his literal strategy. But he makes very little of Shakespeare's connection between "disgrace" and the verb "stain". Ungaretti's "macchiarsi" is an accurate and literal translation of "stain", but it fails to connect with the earlier part of the poem. In fact the whole thrust of Ungaretti's poem bears his personal stamp, and this is essentially a free version based on Shakespeare's sonnet and exploiting its hermetic aspect.

The following is Montale's translation of Sonnet 33:

> Spesso, a lusingar vette, vidi splendere
> sovranamente l'occhio del mattino,
> e baciar d'oro verdi prati, accendere
> pallidi rivi d'alchimie divine.
> Poi vili fumi alzarsi, intorbidata
> d'un tratto quella celestiale fronte,
> e fuggendo a occidente il desolato
> mondo, l'astro celare il viso e l'onta.
> Anch' io sul far del giorno ebbi il mio sole
> e il suo trionfo mi brillò sul ciglio:
> ma, ahimè, poté restarvi un'ora sola,
> rapito dalle nubi in cui s'impiglia.
> Pur non ne ho sdegno: bene può un terrestre
> sole abbuiarsi, se è cosí il celeste.[6]

Montale retains Shakespeare's rhyme scheme, though he makes extensive use of half-rhyme, for instance "mattino":"divine" (lines 2,4), rather than perfect rhyme. He translates into hendecasyllables. That makes his translation appear more compact than Ungaretti's.

How does Montale achieve greater concision than Ungaretti? A contrast between the opening quatrains of the two translations is a good starting-point. Ungaretti avoids Shakespeare's syntax in order to put a different focus on the poem. Montale also makes changes in the syntax but his motivation differs from Ungaretti's. Montale reduces Shakespeare's long phrase to a one-word synonym ("Spesso" for "Full many a glorious morning": compare Ungaretti's "piú d'un mattino"). Strictly speaking Ungaretti's translation of the phrase is more literal, but is it not really, in Benjamin's words, "the inaccurate transmission of inessential content"? Against Montale it could be argued that "spesso", while it does translate "full many", ignores "glorious" and "morning". Montale does sacrifice "glorious" through lack of space, but he retains "morning", putting it later in the sentence. His hyperbaton is different from Shakespeare's, but unlike Ungaretti's it does not substantially alter the sense of Shakespeare's quatrain. Both Montale and Ungaretti chose *lusingare* and *vette* for "flatter" and "mountain-tops". Montale brings the phrase forward in the sentence and reduces it by removing the definite article (*le*) and by apocopation (*lusingar* for *lusingare*). Montale performs further reductions in his first two lines by avoiding Ungaretti's auxiliary verb + tensed verb structure ("vidi" instead of "ho veduto"), and by turning Shakespeare's adjectival structure into an adverbial structure ("vidi splendere/ *sovranamente* l'occhio del mattino" for "Flatter the mountain-tops with sovereign eye"). Montale's "occhio del mattino" is thus a *creative transposition* which grows out of his reading of Shakespeare's first quatrain, but it is not a *forzatura* of the text. Ungaretti's "tingere" for Shakespeare's "gilding" is more literal than Montale's "accendere", but taken in the context of "alchemy", "accendere", with its nuance of lighting a fire, seems more fitting to the alchemical process than "tingere". Montale, like Ungaretti, opts for a Romance alternative to Shakespeare's Teutonic adjective "heavenly", but Montale's choice of "divine" gains two syllables on Ungaretti's more cumbersome "di paradiso". So Montale's translation appears more compact than Ungaretti's. Does that make it a better translation?

In itself, compactness cannot be an infallible criterion for choosing between translations. There are, however, other features of the translations on which a rational argument for preference could be built. For example, the translations of "the forlorn world"—Ungaretti's "universo orbato" and Montale's "desolato / mondo"—could be contrasted on the basis of hyperbole, those in favour of hyperbole lauding Ungaretti and disapproving of Montale, and vice versa. There is also a more objective test of good reading. Ungaretti's "disgrazia" for Shakespeare's "disgrace" appears to be a weak point in his translation. Montale shows himself more wary of the *faux amis* by using "l'onta" (an end-rhyme with "fronte"). Montale's "onta" does make a connection with his translation of "stain" in the final line. "Abbuiarsi" is not as literal a translation of the English verb "to stain" as Ungaretti's "macchiarsi", but in the context of the sun hidden behind the clouds it is decidedly *ben trovato*: "abbuiarsi", as well as its primary meaning, "to become overcast", has figurative meanings which include "to lapse into melancholy" and (of sight) "to grow dim".

So of the two approaches outlined in the earlier, theoretical discussion, Ungaretti tends towards concentrating on the content rather than the form while Montale tends the other way. But in fact Ungaretti's method, far from catching more of the nuance in the poem, actually catches less of it than Montale's. Montale's reading of the sonnet is selective, as every interpretation must be, but his selection produces a more coherent Italian poem than Ungaretti's.

Shakespeare's sonnet has several features which were likely to be congenial to Montale's poetics. The images in the first quatrain—of sunlight on the mountain-tops, on the meadows and in the streams—are suggestive of the descriptions of light and iridescent colours which are characteristic of Montale's mature poetry.[7] The dialectical structure of the sonnet also has something in common with Montale's idea of an *occasione*. Shakespeare's conclusion (the couplet) was open to interpretation. And the image of alchemy (turning base metals into gold), read as a meditation on the impermanence of events, would be likely to appeal to a writer schooled in the Crocean / Hegelian tradition. The implication of the alchemical image when referred to a person (as it is in the final couplet) seems to be that the presence (or even the memory of the presence) of one person could change another's perception of the world. Shakespeare's "I" in the sonnet contemplates the natural world (mornings, sun, clouds and so forth) in terms of a human relationship which was alive only in his memory. That is similar to the position of Montale's *io* in the *mottetto* "La speranza di pure rivederti" (1937). In that poem, written around the time of the Shakespeare translation, Montale's *io* is reminded of Clizia (who has gone away) by his meeting a uniformed man with two jackals on a leash.[8] The dialectical relationship between the observer and the natural world is essentially the same in both the Shakespeare sonnet and Montale's *mottetto*: in both poems ordinary perceptions of the natural world are reinterpreted by the observer in the light of the observer's memory.

In fact Montale's reading of the sonnet amounts to an appropriation. The following is an example of the process of appropriation at work. Shakespeare's line "Stealing unseen to west with this disgrace" was translated by Ungaretti as "mentre verso ponente non visto scompariva, con la sua disgrazia". Apart from the slight inversion and the dubious "disgrazia", that is a literal translation. Montale instead combines the line with the previous one and translates as "e fuggendo a occidente il desolato/mondo, l'astro celare il viso e l'onta". Montale excises "unseen", and his verb "celare", as well as being an accurate translation, has a place in the internal pattern of his poem, connecting "celestiale" (line 6) with "celeste" (line 14). That internal patterning is a characteristic of Montale's poetry from the 1930s onwards, and its presence in the translation demonstrates the degree to which Montale conceived of translation as an extension of creative writing.

Montale, Shakespeare, Dante and Tradition

Consolidation: One Approach

When Montale translated the Shakespeare sonnets he was aware of T. S. Eliot's poetry and criticism. He had probably read Eliot's book on Dante, from which the following is a quotation:

> For the science of writing verse, one has learned from the *Inferno* that the greatest poetry can be written with the greatest economy of words, and with the greatest austerity in the use of metaphor, simile, verbal beauty and elegance. When I affirm that more can be learned about how to write poetry from Dante than from any English poet, I do not mean that Dante is thereby greater than

> Shakespeare or, indeed, any other English poet. I put my meaning into other words by saying that Dante can do less *harm* to anyone trying to learn to write verse, than can Shakespeare. Most great English poets are *inimitable* in a way that Dante was not. If you try to imitate Shakespeare you will certainly produce a series of stilted, forced, and violent distortions of language. The language of each great English poet is his own language; the language of Dante is the perfection of a common language. In a sense, it is more pedestrian than that of Dryden or Pope. If you follow Dante without talent, you will at worst be pedestrian and flat; if you follow Shakespeare or Pope without talent, you will make an utter fool of yourself.[9]

Mario Praz, commenting on the above passage, has made the point that an argument parallel to Eliot's could be easily constructed in relation to Italian poets:

> Whenever Italians have tried to imitate Dante, they have produced sometimes flat and pedestrian verse, but more frequently they have written precisely in that stilted and forced style which Eliot thinks proper to the worst imitators of Shakespeare. [...] Italians who read Shakespeare, on the other hand, frequently find his language direct and possessing the very accent of life. In either case it could be easily shown that the illusion is caused by the ignorance in which one naturally is of the conventions of a foreign language.[10]

Several critics have scrutinized Montale's relationship with Dante.[11] Such critical scrutiny has produced some quite extravagant claims, such as this one by Arshi Pipa:

> Does the use of allegory in some of the latest works of Montale warrant a search for an allegorical interpretation of his whole work? The present essay attempts that search within the broader design of interpreting Montale with Dante as a guide. The method is simple. Once a Dantean expression is identified in Montale, the situation in which it occurs is tested to see whether it corresponds to a similar situation in Dante. If the correspondence in situation is matched by a correspondence in expression, we have a correspondence in poetic thought. This method, an application of logical analysis to linguistic data, yields tangible results. Their sum total justifies the conclusion that some of Dante's texts supply a commentary on Montale's poetry.[12]

Generally speaking, the application of logical analysis to linguistic data does produce tangible results of all sorts, but their relevance to the aesthetic act of reading poetry is sometimes dubious. The postulates underlying the logical analysis should be examined critically in order to evaluate the relevance of the logical results. The concept of "poetic thought" is neither clear nor distinct. There are Dantean echoes in Montale's poetry just as there are echoes of Foscolo, Leopardi, D'Annunzio, Pascoli, Sbarbaro and the Ligurian poets. That is beyond question, and Montale was probably as aware of them as anyone else; but the notion that Montale was somehow writing poetry in the margins of Dante's *Commedia* represents a misunderstanding of Montale's use of his poetic sources. Montale does borrow from other poets but what he borrows becomes his own. His borrowings cohere internally in his own work: they do not, as Pipa seems to suggest, justify a claim that the source texts may be used as a commentary on Montale's poetry.[13]

Pipa's other dubious axiom is contained in the following:

> It is small wonder that Dante's lens applied to Montale's poetry discovers meanings that would otherwise have remained latent. The allusiveness thus described goes hand in hand with allegory. Some of the linguistic clues in Montale point to a different use of Dante: he is evoked by devious allegorical devices to voice Montale's political accusations and to sanction his apocalyptic visions. Finally, not a few cases of contact between the two poets seem to be mere coincidence, explainable by identical points of view on the same subject.[14]

There are several points here. Firstly, not only is it "small wonder that Dante's lens applied to Montale's poetry discovers meanings that would otherwise have remained latent", it is no wonder at all. Reading any major modern poet through a medieval lens is as anachronistic an enterprise as the image of the lens suggests, and it is as likely to produce much *forzatura* and distortion as it is to be a useful interpretive tool. The theory that Montale used Dante "to voice political accusations and to sanction his apocalyptic visions", and further that this might be "explainable by identical points of view", is interesting. Most of the interest lies in the equation of similarity with identity. The similarity theory holds: both Dante in his day, and Montale in his, were disillusioned with politics in the Italian peninsula and particularly in Florence, and both poets had a strong metaphysical disposition. The substitution of identity for similarity, however, does not hold: Dante's so-called imperial politics nourished by his Christian vision and conception of the world had little in common with Montale's political and religious beliefs. There is some justification for checking Montale's Dantean sources in order to contrast the one with the other in the hope of interpreting Montale's meaning by his difference from Dante, but when it goes beyond similarity the search is an inconclusive exercise.

Consolidation: Another Approach

For Montale Dante represented a reference-point in his native Italian tradition. Montale's translations of the three Shakespeare sonnets (22, 33 and 48) reflect a linguistic background that is formed by the language of Dante and the other poets of the *dolce stil novo*. In looking for a linguistic register suitable for the transplanting of Shakespeare into Italian, Montale chose Dante, Petrarch and the *stilnovisti* as his model. According to Maria Pia Musatti:

> Memorie dantesche soprattutto, stilnovistiche e petrarchesche, che non si limitano al singolo prestito lessicale, applicato di preferenza all'area della rima, ma incidono sull'andamento sintattico, offrono il modello formale che permette la difficile mediazione culturale, nello sforzo di riprodurre entro le coordinate del nuovo sistema, sia pure con un inevitabile slittamento, il significato e l'effetto originario dell'esperienza shakespeariana.[15]

Analysis of the variants of Montale's translation of Sonnet 22 is illuminating because it demonstrates how the translation became more Dantean in the course of rewriting. Shakespeare's sonnet reads as follows:

> My glass shall not persuade me I am old
> So long as youth and thou are of one date;
> But when in thee time's furrows I behold,
> Then look I death my days should expiate.
> For all that beauty that doth cover thee
> Is but the seemly raiment of my heart,
> Which in thy breast doth live, as thine in me;
> How can I then be elder than thou art?

O, therefore, love, be of thyself so wary,
As I not for myself but for thee will;
Bearing thy heart, which I will keep so chary
As tender nurse her babe from faring ill.
Presume not on thy heart when mine is slain;
Thou gav'st me thine, not to give back again.[16]

Montale's first published version begins:

Allo specchio, guardandomi mi credo
giovane perché tu sei Giovinezza.
Ma se una ruga sul tuo volto io veda
saprò che i miei dí la morte spezza.

Montale evidently had second thoughts about "guardandomi", perhaps because it seems to intrude from the spoken register. His "tu sei Giovinezza" is uncharacteristic in that it is very direct and not a particularly good translation. Musatti has suggested that in his brooding over the first attempt Montale remembered Dante's *Vita nuova* sonnet "Amore e 'l cor gentil sono una cosa", which begins:

Amore e 'l cor gentil sono una cosa,
sí come il saggio in suo dittare pone,
e cosí esser l'un sanza l'altro osa
com' alma razional sanza ragione.[17]

Dante's identification of "Amore" with the "cor gentil" is analogous to Shakespeare's identification of "youth" with a person; or rather, Montale probably read the two identifications as analogous. His definitive version reads:

Allo specchio, ancor giovane mi credo
ché Giovinezza e te siete una cosa.
Ma se una ruga sul tuo volto io veda
saprò che anche per me morte non posa.
Quella beltà che ti ravvolge è ancora
parvenza del mio cuore che nel tuo
alberga—e il tuo nel mio—; e come allora
decidere chi è il vecchio di noi due?
Poni in serbo il tuo cuore, ed io lo stesso
farò di me: del tuo cosí zelante

come fida nutrice in veglia presso
la cuna, che ogni morbo sia distante.
 Spento il mio cuore, invano il tuo riprendere
 vorresti: chi l'ha avuto non lo rende.
(*L'opera in versi*, p. 711)

The Dantean solution ("ché Giovinezza e te siete una cosa") removes the "Giovinezza":"spezza" rhyme, which has no *stil novo* precedent, and replaces it with "cosa":"posa", which is characteristic of Dante, the *stilnovisti* and (to a lesser extent) Petrarch; in fact the rhyme appears in "Amore e 'l cor gentil sono una cosa".[18] Montale's first version had "culla" instead of "cuna" in line 12. Musatti has an explanation for the change: "cuna" is a linguistic echo of *Inferno*, XIV. 100 ("Rea la scelse già per *cuna fida*"). In the sonnet's final quatrain Montale echoes Dante's two-word expression, dividing it between two lines:

 Poni in serbo il tuo cuore, ed io lo stesso
farò di me: del tuo cosí zelante
come *fida* nutrice in veglia presso
la *cuna*, che ogni morbo sia distante.

There are many Dantean echoes in the three sonnets, but their significance, rather than being just Dantean echoes, is that they are part of the linguistic register into which Montale (eventually) chose to translate Shakespeare.[19]

Unlike Ungaretti, then, Montale in his translations deliberately retains the basic form of the Shakespearean sonnet as a cultural equivalent in Italian. Given the relative velocities of the two languages, that required departures from the original syntactic structures. One of Montale's basic techniques is the reduction of the number of adjectives or the substitution of an adjective + noun phrase in English with a single (but semantically equivalent) Italian noun. Compare, for example, "For all that beauty that doth cover thee/Is but the seemly raiment of my heart" with "Quella beltà che ti ravvolge è ancora/parvenza del mio cuore che nel tuo/alberga": the Dantean "parvenza" translates the "seemly raiment" to confine the line to a hendecasyllable.

Montale consistently adopts the hendecasyllable as a cultural equivalent of Shakespeare's iambic pentameter, and defended his choice in an invective against Ungaretti in 1958:

> Ci si è accorti che la lirica ha pochissimo bisogno di libertà, e che non si rinunzia a determinati schemi senza che sorga il bisogno di crearne altri, ben piú ardui di quelli offerti dalla tradizione, e soggetti a piú rapida usura, in ragione della loro troppo evidente singolarità.[20]

Apart from the polemic against Ungaretti, Montale here makes an important point about traditional metre. Its chief claim on our interest is the fact that in his early poems Montale implicitly rejected traditional Italian metre and form. Before his reworkings of the Shakespeare poems he had never published a sonnet. Indeed the pseudo-sonnets of "Finisterre" represent a tangent linking his poetry to that of the Petrarchan tradition. The hendecasyllable—the basic unit of currency in the Italian tradition—fared little better in the *Ossi di seppia* poems. It is the unifying principle of some of them ("Meriggiare pallido e assorto", for instance), but it is not the only, or even the most important, metrical principle at work in the collection. Some poems, notably "In limine", are written in *ottonari*, but the dominant metrical concept is an individual type of free verse which relies on assonance, harsh rhymes and *enjambements* for the setting of its tone.

The Shakespeare *rifacimenti* are significant for that very reason. They represent Montale's coming to terms with traditional verse forms. The more controversial point is that this apparently belated acceptance of tradition takes place *through the mediation of a foreign language*. Furthermore, Montale comes to the sonnet—a form characteristic of Dante, Petrarch and every other memorable Italian poet until Leopardi—through Shakespeare, a reference-point of English poetry. But while Montale did decide to retain the Shakespearean form, his choice of language is very firmly rooted in the Italian *registro aulico*. It would thus appear that his experience of translating Shakespeare into Italian helped him overcome his rancour towards the "eloquenza della nostra vecchia lingua aulica", which, he claimed, contributed to the character of his first book.[21]

Innovation

It is a view widely held by critics, and acknowledged by Montale himself, that the poems of *Le occasioni* are metrically tighter than those of *Ossi di seppia*.[22] Therefore the importance of Montale's translations from and reading of English in the period of transition should not be underestimated. His choice of Shakespeare as a poet to translate reflected a profound interest in the English language, its literature and its sensibilities. But this interest is not isolated from his work as a whole: the case of Shakespeare and his role in Montale's reconciliation with his own tradition indicates the importance of English in his poetic development.

Montale successfully appropriated Shakespeare as a reference-point for his own work. He achieved this in several ways including direct quotation, as in the epigraph to Part IV of *Le occasioni* ("Sap check'd with frost, and lusty leaves quite gone, / Beauty o'ersnow'd and bareness every where"), and indirect quotation, as in in the *mottetti*:

Luce di lampo

invano può *mutarvi in alcunché*
di ricco e strano. Altro era il tuo stampo.[23]

But these direct and indirect quotations were not gratuitous. Montale was using intertextuality to create his own elective tradition out of literature of the past. At the same time as he was writing allusions to Shakespeare into his poems he was also writing allusions to Dante into them, for instance those to *Inferno* in the first *mottetto,* one of a minority of Italian poems which begin with two monosyllables:

Lo sai: devo riperderti e non posso.
Come un tiro aggiustato mi sommuove
ogni opera, ogni grido e anche lo spiro
salino che straripa
dai moli e fa l'*oscura* primavera
di Sottoripa.

Paese di ferrame e alberature
a *selva* nella polvere del vespro.
Un ronzío lungo viene dall'aperto,
strazia com' unghia ai vetri. Cerco il segno
smarrito, il pegno solo ch'ebbi in grazia
da te.
E l'*inferno* è certo.[24]

Of course Montale's Dantism began much earlier than the 1930s: even his very early poems contain Dantean echoes.[25] The point is that in looking for a cultural equivalent in Italian to Shakespeare's sonnets he chose Dante's language. The implication for his own original poetry was that, while he continued alluding to Dante's poetry as before, his own poetry was now written in a spare, tight idiom which translation from English in general, and Shakespeare in particular, had helped him develop.

Montale, then, translated Shakespeare's sonnets into the *registro aulico* derived from Dante, Petrarch and the *stilnovisti*. That in itself could scarcely be called innovation. At the same time, however, he introduced Clizia, his *donna angelicata* into his own poetry, occasionally using Shakespearean imagery to compound the Shakespeare–*dolce stil novo* connection, for example in the *mottetto* "Ecco il segno", dated 1938 and thus written after the Shakespeare translations:

> Il passo che proviene
> dalla serra sí lieve,
> non è felpato dalla neve, è ancora
> tua vita, sangue tuo nelle mie vene.[26]

The image expressing metaphysical identity of two physically different people ("sangue tuo nelle mie vene") is a cognate of Shakespeare's two hearts in "My glass shall not persuade me I am old": "Presume not on thy heart when mine is slain;/Thou gav'st me thine, not to give back again." As we have seen, before writing "Ecco il segno" Montale had translated Shakespeare's couplet as "Spento il mio cuore, invano il tuo riprendere/vorresti: chi l'ha avuto non lo rende".

That is not to argue for the couplet as "source" of the *mottetto*. Montale's innovation in relation to the tradition of the *dolce stil novo* consists in his ability to present it as a vehicle for modern poetry by reviving it from a reference-point outside the tradition. In one sense Montale held to the ideas about tradition he had expressed in the 1925 essay "Stile e tradizione", and in another sense he broke with them. In 1925 he had written: "Al desiderio di frontiere troppo vaste, di cieli troppo distanti, porremmo innanzi il confine del nostro paese, la lingua della nostra gente. Troppo lavoro rimane da compiere oggi, perché ci tentino questi salti nel buio".[27] Thirteen years later Montale had become reconciled with his own Italian tradition, not by "leaps into the dark" but by a deliberate and thorough cultivation of English literature, through the medium of translation.

NOTES

1 See *William Shakespeare: Teatro*, edited by M. Praz, 3 vols (Florence, Sansoni, 1949), I, 411–73, III, 635–712, 849–994; W. Shakespeare, *Amleto*, translated by E. Montale (Milan, Cederna, 1949).

2 Both articles were published in *Il corriere della sera*, on 2 Feb. 1951 and 14 Mar. 1953. The section on Shakespeare is now reprinted in E. Montale, *Sulla poesia*, edited by G. Zampa (Milan, Mondadori, 1976), pp. 480–81.

3 See Mussolini's preface to *Il porto sepolto* in G. Ungaretti, *Tutte le poesie* (Milan, Mondadori, 1969), pp. 552–53.

4 In 1936 Ungaretti had published a volume of translations which included poems by Saint-John Perse, Blake, Góngora, Essenin and Paulhan: *Traduzioni* (Rome, Novissima).

5 All these texts are included in G. Ungaretti, *Saggi e interventi* (1974), pp. 551–76.

6 E. Montale, *L'opera in versi*, edited by G. Contini and R. Bettarini (Turin, Einaudi, 1980), p. 712. Montale's translation was first published in *Città* [Rome] (7 Dec. 1944). In his note to the *Quaderno di traduzioni* Montale claimed that all three *rifacimenti* were done before 1938 (see *L'opera in versi*, p. 1154).

7 See, for example, "guizzo argenteo della trota" in "L'estate" (1935), "mischia d'acque e cielo schiude / finestre ai raggi della sera,—sempre / piú raro, astore celestiale, un cutter / bianco-alato li posa sulla rena" in "Proda di Versilia" (1946) or "Nubi color magenta s'addensavano / sulla grotta di Fingal d'oltrecosta" in "Nubi color magenta..." (1950): E. Montale, *L'opera in versi*, pp. 169, 245, 261.

8 See E. Montale, *L'opera in versi*, p. 138.

9 T. S. Eliot, *Dante* (London, Faber, 1929), p. 28.

10 M. Praz, "Eliot and Dante", in his *The Flaming Heart* (Gloucester, Mass., Smith, 1966), pp. 348–74 (p. 360).

11 For example, G. Cambon, "Montale dantesco e bruegheliano", *Aut-aut*, 35 (1956), 371–91; P. Bonfiglioli, "Dante Pascoli Montale", in *Nuovi studi pascoliani* (Bolzano–Cesena, Società di studi romagnoli, 1963), pp. 35–92; A. Pipa, *Montale and Dante* (Minnesota, University of Minnesota Press, 1968). I should acknowledge here an unpublished essay, "Tre versioni montaliane da Shakespeare: *La commedia degli errori*, *Timone d'Atene* e *Il racconto d'inverno*" by M. Antonello, and thank Paolo Acquaviva and Prof. J. C. Barnes, both of University College, Dublin, for bringing it to my attention.

12 See A. Pipa, *Montale and Dante*, p. 14.

13 The most forthright rejection in English of Pipa's thesis is Z. G. Barański's "Dante and Montale: The Threads of Influence", which was delivered as a lecture in the Dante Series at University College, Dublin in 1983 and pub-

lished in *Dante Comparisons*, edited by E. Haywood and B. Jones (Dublin, Irish Academic Press, 1985), pp. 11–48.

14 A. Pipa, *Montale and Dante*, p. 14.

15 M. P. Musatti, "Montale traduttore: la mediazione della poesia", *Strumenti critici*, 41 (Feb. 1980), 129–30. The present section expands on points made in Musatti's essay, which is very incisive but also, unfortunately, very short.

16 Montale's translation of this sonnet was first published together with his version of Sonnet 33 in *Città* on 7 December 1944.

17 *Vita nuova*, edited by D. De Robertis, in Dante Alighieri, *Opere minori*, 2 vols in 3 (Milan–Naples, Ricciardi, 1979–88), I, i, 1–247 (pp. 133–34).

18 It appears as a rhyme between quatrains: "Amore e 'l cor gentil sono una *cosa*,/sí come il saggio in suo dittare pone,/e cosí esser l'un sanza l'altro osa/com' alma razional sanza ragione./Falli natura quand' è amorosa,/Amor per sire e 'l cor per sua magione,/dentro la qual dormendo si ri*posa*/tal volta poca e tal lunga stagione" (ll. 1–8; *Vita nuova*, pp. 133–35). The "cosa"/"posa" rhyme also appears in *Purgatorio*, VI. 64/66 (Sordello), *Paradiso*, XIV. 128/132 (the Cross of Souls) and *Paradiso*, XVI. 83/85 (Florence and Fortuna), though not all these occurrences of *posa* are verbs. M. P. Musatti, "Montale traduttore", p. 145 n. 19, has also traced the rhyme to two of Petrarch's poems, the sonnet "Di dí in dí vo cangiando il viso e 'l pelo" (*Canzoniere*, 195; ll. 9/12) and the *canzone* "Ben mi credea passar mio tempo omai" (*Canzoniere*, 207; ll. 28/30).

19 One echo which Musatti did not pursue but is worth mentioning is Montale's "abbuiarsi" in line 14 of "Spesso, a lusingar vette". The verb appears twice in the *Commedia*, in *Purgatorio*, XVII. 62 and *Paradiso*, IX. 71. The latter makes an interesting aside in the context of the Shakespeare sonnet: "L'altra letizia, che m'era già nota/per cara cosa, mi si fece in vista/qual fin balasso in che lo sol percuota./Per letiziar là sú fulgor s'acquista,/sí come riso qui; ma giú s'abbuia/l'ombra di fuor, come la mente è trista."

20 E. Montale, "Ungaretti" [1958], in his *Sulla poesia*, pp. 306–07 (p. 306).

21 E. Montale, "Intenzioni (intervista immaginaria)" [1946], in his *Sulla poesia*, pp. 561–69 (p. 565).

22 This view was first expressed by G. Contini in "Dagli *Ossi* agli *Occasioni*" [1938], an essay now reprinted in his *Una lunga fedeltà: sulla poesia di Montale* (Turin, Einaudi, 1974), pp. 17–45. It has been reiterated by many critics, most notably in recent times G. Cambon, *Eugenio Montale's Poetry: A Dream in Reason's Presence* (Princeton, Princeton University Press, 1982), pp. 54–89 and C. de C. L. Huffman, *Montale and the Occasions of Poetry* (Princeton, Princeton University Press, 1983), pp. 74–113.

23 "Il ramarro, se scocca", in E. Montale, *L'opera in versi*, p. 141. The allusion is to Ariel's song in *The Tempest*, I. 2. 396–402: "Full fathom five thy father lies;/Of his bones are coral made;/Those are pearls that were his eyes;/Nothing of him that doth fade/But doth suffer a sea-change/Into *something rich and strange*./Sea-nymphs hourly ring his knell."

24 E. Montale, *L'opera in versi*, p. 133. The poem alludes primarily to *Inferno*, I. 1–3.

25 See Z. G. Barański, "Dante and Montale", pp. 37–38.

26 See E. Montale, *L'opera in versi*, pp. 140, 910.

27 E. Montale, "Stile e tradizione" [1925], in his *Auto da fé: cronache in due tempi*, edited by G. Zampa, second edition (Milan, Saggiatore, 1972), pp. 15–19 (p. 17).

Chapter 3

EMILY DICKINSON AND THE ANTINOMIES

DICKINSON, GOETHE AND MONTALE

There are two essays dedicated to Emily Dickinson's poetry which are attributed to Montale. The first of these was published in 1939, the second in 1957. Given the doubt cast on the true authorship of some of "Montale's" articles published during the 1950s while he was a full-time employee of *Il corriere della sera*, the 1957 article must be treated with some caution. Dickinson's poetry, however, was quite well known to Montale, as is clear from the 1939 essay.[1]

The article published in 1939 was a review of Emilio and Giuditta Cecchi's book on Emily Dickinson.[2] After giving a summary of critical works on Dickinson's life and poetry, Montale uses the review as an opportunity to make his own assessment of the poet and the poems. He describes her work in relation to its influence on Italian poetry:

> Crediamo che il suo [Dickinson's] influsso, con quello di vari poeti inglesi cattolici o cattolicheggianti, dal Thompson al Patmore fino al Hopkins, rimarrà mediato, marginale, operando su giovani aggiornati solo di terza mano e in perpetua ricerca di *contenuti*. Ma influsso non mancherà in qualche modo. ("La poesia di Emily Dickinson", p. 437)

The 1939 essay closes with the following quotation from Ludwig Lewisohn:

> La Dickinson talvolta giunge a una concisione verbale e a una ricchezza di significati quasi degne del Goethe epigrammatico. Ha accresciuta di una nota nuova ed eroica l'eterna litania dell'amore. Può toccare altezze che soltanto conobbero i piú

> intensi poeti mistici del secolo diciassettesimo. Nitida e visionaria, esatta ed esaltata, sa schernire come Heine, e mostrare il lato frusto e ridicolo dell'universo. ("La poesia di Emily Dickinson", p. 441).

The allusion to Goethe is an interesting one. Barile has made a case concerning the title *Le occasioni* (1939) which involves Goethe. According to Barile's argument, Montale had certainly read Sergio Baldi's translation of and commentary on Hopkins's poem "The Wreck of the Deutschland". In his commentary Baldi had written that the request to Hopkins from his rector to write a long poem came to him as an "occasione, ma in senso goethiano per sperimentare la sua musica". Baldi's commentary was published in March 1939, Montale's review came out the following July and *Le occasioni* appeared in October. It seems that Baldi's essay suggested to Montale a comparison between himself and Goethe which resulted in the title of his second collection. Further, having identified himself with Goethe and then having found Dickinson compared to Goethe too, Montale may have started to look to Dickinson's work for inspiration. In this regard it is significant that Montale refers specifically to only one poem in the 1939 essay; that poem is "The Storm", which was published in his own translation about six years later.

The Texts

Montale's translation of "The Storm" is based on a corrupt version of Dickinson's poem. It is therefore necessary, as a preliminary, to quote the corrupt version in full, as it is printed in the *Quaderno di traduzioni*:

> There came a wind like a bugle;
> it quivered through the grass,
> and a green chill upon the heat
> so ominous did pass
> we barred the windows and the doors
> as from an emerald ghost;
> the doom's electric moccasin
> that very instant passed.
> On a strange mob of panting trees
> and fences fled away

and rivers where the houses ran
the living looked the day.
The bell within the steeple wild
the flying tidings whirled.
How much can come
and much can go
and yet abide the world.[3]

This is the version of Dickinson's text which Montale had before him and which developed into "Tempesta". The seventeen lines of text alternate longer and shorter lines, except in the final three lines where the pattern changes slightly: the last line contains six syllables like the other short lines of the poem but lines 15 and 16 each contain four syllables, making them an eight-syllable line divided into two parts (the longer lines are all of eight syllables). The shorter lines rhyme in pairs, giving four sets of end-rhymes ("grass":"pass", "ghost":"passed", "away":"day" and "whirled": "world"). There are no caesuras, and the four sentences are made to fit the metrical pattern of the poem through a series of hyperbatons: "and a green chill upon the heat/so ominous did pass" (lines 3–4), "On a strange mob of panting trees/[...]/the living looked the day" (lines 9–12) and "The bell within the steeple wild/ the flying tidings whirled" (lines 13–14). These hyperbatons seem to be motivated partially by a concern with making rhymes.

"The Storm" is constructed on a dramatic vision of the Apocalypse. This, at least, is Montale's interpretation of it.[4] The scene is set with the bugle's blast. This simile introduces the trumpet which we are told will herald the Last Judgement. But a bugle is not quite a trumpet: it is smaller, it is higher in pitch and it has no connotations of triumph. The point is that Dickinson's "bugle" is an obvious variation on the Biblical "trumpet", and as such a type of intertextual understatement. As understatement it may well have appealed to Montale's sensibilities.

The bugle sounds an alarm, and is thus related by its function to the bell (line 13). The relationship is underscored by the bell's location: it is "within the steeple", and the *l* sounds in "b*ell*" and "steep*le*" refer back through "the *li*ving *loo*ked the day", "*ele*ctric moccasin" and "green ch*ill*" to the "bug*le*" of the first line. This music underpins the dread and awe which the poem probes.

The adjectives play their part in the process of revelation. Firstly, there is an oxymoron, "a green chill upon the heat": Heat and cold are thought of in common sense as colourless natural phenomena. Likewise a ghost is a colourless, unnatural phenomenon. Ghosts are rarely described as green, and still more rarely perhaps as "emerald". Emily Dickinson evidently has a wholesome respect for colours: fear and dread are green. "Doom's electric moccasin" is an interesting collocation. "Doom" is personified and "moccasin" is a metonymy for Doom's footfall. Again it is the adjective which is especially suggestive: "electric" hovers between nuances of dynamic, dangerous and spectacular like a thunderbolt or a flash of lightning. "Very" is an intensifier which is otherwise empty, but it does isolate the particular instant: it is *this* instant, a frozen still in the flux of time, and not any other. To sum up the first sentence, we have an instant isolated from all others, fraught with sudden dread which has been carried by the cold wind. It is an existential moment: Death appears and the poet gingerly senses her own mortality.

The second sentence is the outward sign of inner turmoil. Personifications abound: the trees are panting, the fences have fled away and houses are on the run. Synecdoche, the part for the whole, is also at work here. The trees, panting like horses, represent Nature *in extremis*. The fences are boundaries or fixed categories which are now blurred or obscured. The houses, standing perhaps for home and stability, are no longer stable. In short, this is a crisis-point. There is an element of obscurity in "the living looked the day", the allusion to the *Dies irae, dies illa* having been lost in this version of the text. Montale compensates for the obscurity with a clarification in his translation.

The adjective "wild" in the third sentence is ambiguous: it may qualify either the bell or the steeple. It is in effect a floating adjective which stresses the frenetic and dreadful quality of the instant but also forges a structural link with "wind", giving echo (perhaps unconsciously) to Shelley's apostrophe "O Wild West Wind". Leaving Shelley aside, the "wind" of the first line lurks in the thirteenth line as a type of anastomosis inside "*with*in *the*". The wind is wild and it does violence to boundaries and stability.

Dickinson's conclusion is also ambiguous, the ambiguity resting on the verb "abide", which reiterates the /ei/ diphthong of "wild". It is not clear whether the subject of the verb is the "much [that] can come/and much [that] can go" or "the world" itself, though it seems more likely that "world" is the subject. In this case

Dickinson is setting up a contrast between the world, which continues to exist, and transient mortals, who come and go.

Montale's "Tempesta" retains the seventeen-line structure of "The Storm". It also divides grammatically into four sentences:

> Con un suono di corno
> il vento arrivò, scosse l'erba;
> un verde brivido diaccio
> cosí sinistro passò nel caldo
> che sbarrammo le porte e le finestre
> quasi entrasse uno spettro di smeraldo:
> e fu certo l'elettrico
> segnale del Giudizio.
> Una bizzarra turba di ansimanti
> alberi, siepi alla deriva
> e case in fuga nei fiumi
> è ciò che videro i vivi.
> Tocchi del campanile desolato
> mulinavano le ultime nuove.
> Quanto può giungere,
> quanto può andarsene,
> in un mondo che non si muove![5]

Unlike "The Storm", "Tempesta" does not have four sets of end-rhymes. There are end-rhymes and half-rhymes in "Tempesta" but they do not follow a schematic pattern: "caldo":"smeraldo" (lines 4, 6), "deriva":"vivi" (lines 10, 12) and "nuove":"muove" (lines 14, 17). Montale's use of assonance is more extensive than Dickinson's. It starts in the first line with "C*o*n un s*u*o*n*o di c*o*rno" and continues with "scosse l'*er*ba:/un v*er*de br*i*vido diaccio/cosí sin*i*stro", "uno sp*et*tro di smeraldo:/e fu certo l'el*et*trico", culminating in the long broad vowels of the last four lines:

> mulinavano le *u*ltime n*uo*ve.
> Q*ua*nto p*uò* gi*u*ngere,
> q*ua*nto p*uò* andarsene,
> in *u*n mondo che non si m*uo*ve!

In "Tempesta" the wind is no longer like a bugle: it arrives, literally, with the sound of a horn. "Vento" is not in a position of stress in "Tempesta", unlike "wind" in "The Storm". Instead Montale emphasizes the wind's activity: "Con un s*uo*no di c*o*rno/

il vento arrivò." Dickinson's phrasal verb "to quiver through" would be hard to match in Italian. Montale reduces it to "scosse l'erba", so that the wind in "Tempesta" does not quiver through the grass, it shakes it. The two words which draw attention to themselves in the opening lines, *corno* and *scotere*, are, as we shall see, words of relatively high frequency in Montale's poetry.

Lines 3–4 must be treated together in both "The Storm" and "Tempesta". Montale drops the conjunction, but amplifies "chill" into "brivido diaccio". "Brivido" has several functions in the poem. Firstly, the stressed narrow vowel, contrasting with the previous broad vowels, introduces a note of tension, which is continued in the next line by "cosí" and "sinistro". Secondly, "brivido" accounts for the nuance of "quiver" which had been left untranslated in the second line. "Diaccio" is a dialect word corresponding to "gelido", and is probably a late addition to the poem, suggested—because of a rhyming relationship—by "Giudizio", which almost certainly came first. Again it is more than just a coincidence that both "brivido" and "diaccio" are favoured words in Montale's poetic language. There is a subtle semantic shift in Montale's preposition: in "Tempesta" the "verde brivido diaccio" passes *in* the heat ("passò nel caldo"), whereas Dickinson's "green chill" passes "upon the heat". Montale's "cosí" for Dickinson's "so" is perfectly accurate, but Montale expands the word's scope by turning it into a "cosí [...] che" construction, which links up further on with an imperfect subjunctive ("entrasse"). Dickinson's "the windows and the doors" becomes a stimulus for Montale's linguistic ingenuity. He plays on /rt/ and /tr/ sounds in the next three lines:

> che sbarrammo le po*rt*e e le fines*tr*e
> quasi en*tr*asse uno spe*ttr*o di smeraldo:
> e fu ce*rt*o l'ele*ttr*ico [...].

In doing this Montale sets up a structural link with "sinis*tro*" and "ve*rd*e" in the first four lines.

"Doom's electric moccasin", Dickinson's most complex figure, is modified substantially in "Tempesta". Firstly, the personification of doom is reduced to "Giudizio", the Biblical term. With personification eliminated, the moccasin becomes redundant. Bulgheroni has approached this figure from a more historical angle.[6] She has argued that the allusion to American Indians implicit in "moccasin" would have been out of place in Montale's poem because it would not have been relevant to the Italian historical ambience. The argument is a specific version of the argument for normalization of cultural terms in translation. Yet Montale was not a poet who made concessions to his readers. A "moccasino elettrico" would hardly have been more incongruous in Montale's work than the two jackals on a leash in Modena in the *mottetto* "La speranza di pure rivederti".

There is a slight inconsistency between the article published in 1957 and Montale's practice in the translation. The essay is nominally a review of Guido Errante's translations of some 400 lyrics by Emily Dickinson. The only serious criticism of Errante's procedure is the following:

> Spinto dalla convinzione che si debbano mantenere "chiuse" ad ogni costo le strofe della Dickinson, l'Errante parafrasa, annacqua e cosparge di facili rime poesie che nell'originale si accontentano di allitterazioni o di eleganti rime *faux-exprés* [*sic*].
>
> È un peccato perché se Errante si fosse rassegnato a tradurre letteralmente, migliaia di lettori italiani forniti di una mediocre conoscenza dell'inglese avrebbero potuto facilmente seguire le non facili anfrattuosità del testo. ("Emily", pp. 498–99)

In the case of "doom's electric moccasin" it seems more likely that Montale deletes the personification and its attendant metonymic footfall because he has a point of his own to make. "Certo" is not a direct translation of anything in Dickinson's poem. We have already noted its structural role but it also has a semantic function. The only part of Dickinson's complex figure that Montale translates directly is "elettrico": the "moccasin" becomes "segnale". *Segno* and *segnale* are both keywords in Montale's idiolect. The signal or sign in this poem is qualified by the adjective "electric". The electric sign of the Last Judgement which comes in a storm is quite unambiguous. Dickinson's footfall has become a flash of lightning, obeying the structure of a Montalian *occasione*. The intertextual function of "certo" is now clear. It is a cross-reference to at least one of those seminal poems from *Le occasioni*:

> Pareva facile giuoco
> mutare in nulla lo spazio
> che m'era aperto, in un tedio
> malcerto il certo tuo fuoco.
>
> (from "Il balcone": *L'opera in versi*, p. 106)

That is an example of the cross-reference process at work in "Tempesta", but while it is an interesting one it is far from being the most important, as we shall see.

Montale translates "strange" by "bizzarra" despite the facts that "strange" has a more transparent cognate in Italian (*strano*) and that *bizzarro* is a stronger term than *strano*. Lines 9–12 are quite obscure in the corrupt text from which Montale worked. He compensates for the obscurity by placing the only verb of the sentence in the twelfth line, thus interpreting the trees, fences and houses as things which the living saw. (This is, incidentally, the sense of Dickinson's "uncorrupt" text.) "Siepi alla deriva" for "fences fled away" is clearly a textual liberty but it has a structural function in Montale's poem in that "deriva" is related by a half-rhyme to "vivi".

Dickinson's floating adjective "wild" is modified to "desolato" and tied to the "campanile". Montale replaces object by function in his "Tocchi del campanile" for "The bell within the steeple", and his verb, *mulinare,* catches a nuance of Dickinson's "whirled". Montale makes a departure from Dickinson's poem in the final three lines. He imitates her refrain, "How much can come/and much can go", with his "Quanto può giungere,/quanto può andarsene". His closing line, however, ("in un mondo che non si muove!"), besides rhyming with the "ultime nuove" of the fourteenth line, contains an echo of a different writer and a different context: there seems to be an allusion to Galileo's famous statement, referring to the Earth, "Eppur si muove." But Montale's allusion is a negative one. Earth is "un mondo che *non* si muove". This unwarranted negation departs from Dickinson's poem and foregrounds Montale's own attraction towards negation. The final line of his translation follows the grammatical if not the metrical pattern of his conclusion to the opening poem of *Le occasioni,* "Il balcone":

> A lei ti sporgi da questa
> finestra che non s'illumina.
> (*L'opera in versi,* p. 107)

The concluding line of "Tempesta" raises more difficulties of interpretation than does the "elettrico/segnale del Giudizio", which represents the other substantial liberty taken in the text. The two major interpretive problems concern the allusion to Galileo (it is inconceivable that Montale was unaware of Galileo's phrase) and the negation of Galileo's belief.

Montale seems to bring science and religion into opposition and then make no definite choice between the two different conceptions of the world. Dickinson's poem, according to Bulgheroni, is imbued with a "religiosità eretica" in which an anthropomorphic god strides through the world of a dream.[7] The anthropomorphism is almost absent from Montale's poem, but the religiosity is there explicitly in the vision of the Last Judgement with the tolling bell. Yet the poem's religious content is undercut by the final allusion to Galileo's "Eppur si muove", which seems to represent the rational, scientific and perhaps materialist conception of the world, in which natural phenomena obey natural laws. Accordingly, a storm is a storm and no more: it is not a divine visitation. Lightning is an electrical charge: it has no meaning over and above itself. In other words, the scientific conception of the world, of which Galileo is a sponsor, is the arena of necessary laws, the "rete/che ci stringe" against which Montale had railed since *Ossi di seppia* and before.[8]

Given Montale's self-collocation between the chain of necessary events and his poetic need for the privileged instant, what were his reasons for introducing the scientific outlook into a translation when it is absent from the foreign text?

Montale made poetry out of indecision. The tension of indecision seems to have been necessary for many of his poems, and he seems to have felt the need to undercut the frenzied religiosity of Emily Dickinson's poem with a sobering draught of rationalism. The instant ("the doom's electric moccasin/ *that very instant* passed") which Montale implied but did not translate is privileged or precious only if it is threatened by something. The threat, in Montale's view of things, comes from science because science denies the possibility of the still in the flux of time. Without the backdrop of necessary connections there would not have been enough tension for Montale to fashion a poem.

Still, to recognize the scientific backdrop is not to accept it as binding: hence Montale's negation of Galileo's "Eppur si muove." It is an example of what Emerico Giachery, writing about Montale, has recently described as a "condizione ossimorica".[9] In "Tempesta" Montale undercuts religion with science and then rejects the claims of science. But "Tempesta" can only generate a broader interpretation when read in the context of other of Montale's poems to which it seems to be tied in bonds of intertextuality.

"Tempesta" in Contexts

There are several different contexts into which "Tempesta" may be inserted. They may be divided into three rough and overlapping categories: linguistic, thematic and figurative. Bulgheroni and Lonardi have both noted the linguistic correspondences between "Tempesta" and "Corno inglese".[10] "Corno inglese", the only component of the "Accordi" suite to be included in *Ossi di seppia*, was written about twenty years before Montale's translation of Dickinson's poem. Consequently there can be no argument for influence of the translation on the original text. The argument runs entirely in the other direction.

The linguistic correspondences between the two poems are based on their openings. "Corno inglese" begins:

> Il vento che stasera suona attento
> —ricorda un forte scotere di lame— [...].
> (*L'opera in versi*, p. 11)

"Tempesta" starts:

> Con un suono di corno
> il vento arrivò, scosse l'erba [...].

The opening of "Tempesta", although it is not a literal translation, does no particular violence to the sense of Emily Dickinson's poem, except for the replacement of "bugle" with "corno" rather than one of the other alternatives suggested by Bulgheroni (*buccina*, *tromba* and *fanfara*). That the opening lines of the two poems have four words in common is a coincidence, and it may be that the coincidence induced Montale to mistranslate "bugle" as "corno". Of the four words in common only "vento" can really be considered a keyword in Montale's poetry, and it is important for thematic rather than purely linguistic reasons.[11]

Both "Tempesta" and "Corno inglese" have the wind as an activating principle. In *Ossi di seppia* the wind is a source of motion and activity, and it is a recurrent symbol in Montale's poetry. The wind is one of the four elemental powers in the external world, and this objective fact produces more than one kind of poetic reaction. The liminal poem in *Ossi di seppia* introduces the wind as a fundamental element of Montale's symbolic world. The reader is exhorted to be glad if the wind steers him or her towards the surge of life:

> Godi se il vento ch'entra nel pomario
> vi rimena l'ondata della vita.
> (from "In limine": *L'opera in versi*, p. 5)

The wind, then, offers an escape from immobility, a state which is tantamount to death. The wind is thus an inspiration.

The wind also informs the development of "Corno inglese", though this is a very different type of poem from "Tempesta". "Corno inglese" is included in the "Movimenti" section of *Ossi di seppia*, just after "I limoni". The wind plays through the trees in a huge orchestra of Nature. The sea throws trumpets of seething foam onto the coast. The firmament resonates the sound, but only the fleeting clouds offer the human observer any comfort as they uncover patches of blue sky, reminding him of the doors ajar in "I limoni", through which he glimpses the sudden bright flash of inspiration. Here, however, there are no golden trumpets, no flash of sunlight to set the imagination adazzle: "Corno inglese" is essentially a poem about an absence of poetry. The wind animates harmony in Nature but discord in the observer; it inspires a realization that Nature and the individual belong to different orders of being. Nature will continue to exist, the individual observer will not. "L'agave su lo scoglio" (1922) takes this line of reasoning a step further. Its first section frames the Montalian activity/immobility dilemma in terms of the natural world and the individual.[12] Here again the wind is the activating principle. The sirocco burns the yellow-green earth and blows clouds in the sky:

> O rabido ventare di scirocco
> che l'arsiccio terreno gialloverde
> bruci;
> e su nel cielo pieno
> di smorte luci
> trapassa qualche biocco
> di nuvola, e si perde.
> (*L'opera in versi*, p. 68)

The activity of the wind, as set out in the first seven lines, is then, in the rest of the poem, contrasted with the plight of the individual consciousness, tormented by its own immobility. The underlying objective-versus-subjective structures of "L'agave su lo scoglio" and of Dickinson's poem are thus similar. The objective phenomena—in the first case a wind flaying the parched earth and scattering the clouds, in the second the sudden blast of a storm—are pretexts for subjective dread and shivers of mortality.

The "brivido diaccio" is an original figure in "Tempesta" which does not directly translate anything in Dickinson's text. "Brivido" is a word which Montale uses quite sparingly in his poetry and criticism.[13] The "brivido" here is a transposition which gives the Italian line ("un verde brivido diaccio") an adjective + noun + adjective structure in place of the English adjective + noun structure ("green chill"). Nonetheless, "brivido" is an addition, and (this may be more significant than the superficial correspondence with "Corno inglese") it is a word which Montale had previously used in "L'agave su lo scoglio":

> Ore perplesse, brividi
> d'una vita che fugge
> come acqua tra le dita;
> inafferrati eventi;
> luci—ombre, commovimenti
> delle cose malferme della terra;
> oh alide ali dell'aria
> ora son io
> l'agave che s'abbarbica al crepaccio
> dello scoglio
> e sfugge al mare da le braccia d'alghe
> che spalanca ampie gole e abbranca rocce;
> e nel fermento
> d'ogni essenza, coi miei racchiusi bocci
> che non sanno piú esplodere oggi sento
> la mia immobilità come un tormento.
> (*L'opera in versi*, p. 68)

"Brivido" may thus be seen as one of those keywords which import into a "translated" text a hint of Montalian preoccupations. In "L'agave su lo scoglio" the wind in the external world corresponds to a shiver in the inner world because wind is the extreme manifestation of activity, of life and of infinite possibility.

Montale's antithetical imagination treated life and death as the two sides of an equation. Mutually exclusive concepts, in his imagination they overlap.[14] Life and death (or activity and stasis) are respectively positive and negative. But in positing a positive object of desire (such as life or activity) Montale tends to cleave to its opposite, because he refuses to exercise his will in order to make a distinction. Distinction implies exclusion, eliminating a field of possibilities, and Montale will not be lured away from the richness of diversity. So the wind is a symbol representing life and activity, and also a symbol representing death and immobility.

By the 1940s, when Montale translated "The Storm", the wind had become a storm. Commenting on "La bufera" twenty-five years after writing the poem, Montale wrote: "La Bufera (la poesia iniziale) è la guerra, in ispecie *quella* guerra dopo *quella* dittatura (vedi epigrafe); ma è anche guerra cosmica, di sempre e di tutti."[15] What process of the imagination had turned inspiration into cosmic war?

Montale's identification with the damned and his stoic acceptance of life in Hell prompt some reference to Dante. The word "bufera" in the context of the *Commedia* suggests, of course, Paolo and Francesca in *Inferno* v, buffeted around without respite as *contrapasso* for their earthly transgression. The nature of that transgression was a frenzied passion which defeated their powers of reason. There is a political dimension to the storm symbolism in "La bufera" which was absent from Montale's earlier symbol of the wind. The storm represents the War because the War was the living reality of the time. War has eclipsed life, the irrational has defeated reason. Montale's Enlightenment values of rationalism and liberalism, reason and freedom, had been subjugated by irrational force, and his only remaining weapon against force is immobility. For Montale, to resist the force, if only as an individual, is already to act against it.

Yet this attitude caused difficulties for Montale, and "Tempesta" gave him the opportunity to tease out some of those difficulties. He had a distaste for creeds of certainty, and he could not resist the temptation to cast doubt even on Emily Dickinson's heretical certainties. He achieved this in his final line, "in un mondo che non si muove!", by juxtaposing science and religion. The philosophical basis of action is certainty; immobility is the product of doubt and indecision. Montale invoked Galileo (whose philosophy is entirely absent from Dickinson's poem) only to question Galileo's theory, and by implication the whole of scientific theory. That was Montale's response to a fundamental tension in his own work. The rationalism which is so evident in his journalism (whether political essay, book review or concert review) contains an irrational streak within itself. While he defended reason against the irrational political forces which Fascism presupposed, Montale defended himself, in his poems, against the natural laws propounded by reason. His defence was his myth of the secular epiphany, or, in Contini's terminology, the privileged instant.

The myth of the privileged instant is developed in *Ossi di seppia*, it is alluded to in the title *Le occasioni*, and it appears again in "La bufera", the opening poem of the third collection:

> il lampo che candisce
> alberi e muri e li sorprende in quella
> eternità d'istante—marmo manna
> e distruzione.[16]

It is heralded as usual by a flash of light. Dickinson had isolated an instant of inspiration in the flow of time ("the doom's electric moccasin/that very instant passed"), but Montale veers away from literal translation, producing instead "fu certo l'elettrico/segnale del Giudizio." Montale implants the lightning-flash into the poem, and its function is to act as a token of his familiar *occasione*.

Montale's "Tempesta" has a life of its own independent of Emily Dickinson's poem. He took few liberties in the translation, and even the most obvious deviation from the original, "l'elettrico/ segnale del Giudizio", could not really be described as blatant mistranslation. Yet "Tempesta" is a very Montalian poem. There are several factors which combine to explain that paradoxical state of affairs. The structure of Emily Dickinson's poem is one with which Montale could be familiar, having himself used the device of an external event as a pretext for metaphysical reflection in some of his own poems. Much of Montale's artistic success consists in placing limits on his own freedom of expression. His poetry is suspicious of freedom, as if freedom were to be equated with flux or chaos. The poem is an attempt to circumscribe chaos within tight structures. He claimed that he could not invent anything, and in that sense his poems are derivative, because not to derive from a tradition is a symptom of escapism, and escapism is no escape at all: it is self-delusion. Translation is thus a limiting case of his poetic strategy. To rewrite something, to leave it recognizable and yet different from before, was the essence of an artistic success.

The differences between "Tempesta" and a more literal version of the original poem would be scarcely perceptible to a reader not familiar with Montale's poetry; yet Montale's "Tempesta" is not merely a faithful translation, it is an *occasione*, a secular epiphany achieved in a lightning-flash.

Montale may have been attracted by the image of Emily Dickinson's poetry as music played on a spinet with the stylistic purity of great sacred music.[17] He contrasted that light touch with the poetry of Browning and Whitman. But that is another case of Montale venerating something as an ideal and cleaving to its opposite. In "Tempesta" Emily Dickinson's spiritual certainties are defused and transformed into metaphysical uncertainties. Montale took Dickinson's storm symbolism and refashioned it as a vehicle for his own antinomial—perhaps even Manichean—concerns.

NOTES

1 The two essays are "La poesia di Emily Dickinson", first published in *Oggi* [Milan], 1, ix (29 July 1939), 11 and "Emily", *Il corriere della sera*, 4 May 1957. They are reprinted in E. Montale, *Sulla poesia*, edited by G. Zampa (Milan Mondadori, 1976), respectively on pp. 437–41 and 494–99. Quotations are taken from the latter source. It is of course possible that both essays are fakes. Such speculation apart, they both derive very conspicuously from another source. Montale's information was gleaned principally from Conrad Aiken's preface: see *Selected Poems of Emily Dickinson*, edited by C. Aiken (London, Cape, 1924), pp. 5–22. In the 1939 essay Montale acknowledged his source by quoting it.

2 See E. and G. Cecchi, *Emily Dickinson* (Brescia, Morcelliana, 1939).

3 This is the version of the poem which is printed in the *Quaderno di traduzioni* on the page facing Montale's translation. Montale found that version of the poem in Aiken's 1924 edition of Dickinson's poems. The following version is the one included as item 1593 in *The Complete Poems of Emily Dickinson*, edited by T. H. Johnson (London, Faber, 1970), which is now the standard edition of the poems: "There came a Wind like a Bugle—/It quivered through the Grass,/And a Green Chill upon the Heat/So ominous did pass/We barred the Windows and the Doors/As from an Emerald Ghost—/The Doom's electric Moccasin/That very instant passed—/On a strange Mob of panting Trees/And Fences fled away/And Rivers where the Houses ran/Those looked that lived—that Day—/The Bell within the steeple wild/The flying tidings told—/How much can come/And much can go/And yet abide the World."

4 In his review of the Cecchis' book Montale wrote: "fino al brivido freddo che passa sulla calura estiva e al verde fantasma che in 'The Storm' spalanca improvvisamente le finestre in un paesaggio di giudizio universale" ("La poesia di Emily Dickinson", pp. 440–41).

5 "Tempesta" was first published in *Il mondo* [Florence], 1, i (7 Apr. 1945), 9. It is reprinted in E. Montale, *L'opera in versi*, edited by G. Contini and R. Bettarini (Turin, Einaudi, 1980), p. 722.

6 See M. Bulgheroni, "Dickinson/Montale: il passo sull'erba", in *Eugenio Montale: profilo di un autore*, edited by A. Cima and C. Segre (Milan, Rizzoli, 1977), pp. 91–114 (p. 99).

7 See M. Bulgheroni, "Dickinson/Montale", p. 106.

8 The quotation is from "In limine" (E. Montale, *L'opera in versi*, p. 5).

9 See E. Giachery, "Figure di Montale: l'ossimoro", in *Per la lingua di Montale*, edited by G. Savoca (Florence, Olschki, 1989), pp. 45–52 (p. 49).

10 See M. Bulgheroni, "Dickinson/Montale", pp. 98–99; G. Lonardi, "Fuori e dentro il tradurre montaliano", in his *Il vecchio e il giovane e altri studi su Montale* (Bologna, Zanichelli, 1980), pp. 144–63 (p. 147).

11 It is extremely unlikely that Montale was aware of Dickinson's poem before he wrote "Corno inglese", for three mutually dependent reasons. Firstly, "Corno inglese" was one of the "Accordi", so it was a very early poem. Secondly, at that early stage in his writing career (before 1920) Montale's knowledge of English was extremely scant and Dickinson's poem had not been translated into either Italian or French. Thirdly, a claim made as late as 1925 suggests that Montale's interest in Anglo-American literature began after that date (see above, pp. 41 and 73, n. 3).

12 "Corno inglese" contains the embryo of this theme. Although it consists of only one sentence, the poem runs to eighteen lines. It sets out a discord between Nature and the individual. The wind imitates the sound of the cor anglais, blowing through the trees, playing music which echoes in the sky. It blows up a storm on the sea which throws "una tromba/di schiume intorte" onto the coast. Thus the wind, which rises and falls in the rhythm of life and death, orchestrates Nature but cannot animate the individual's "scordato strumento", his out of tune heart. The theme, however, is rather simpler than that of "Tempesta".

13 It appeared in his analysis of the existential shiver in Joyce's "Two Gallants"; see pages 42–44 above.

14 This antithetical approach to reality is much more explicit in Montale's later work, e.g. "Xenia I", 14, ll. 9–12 (*L'opera in versi*, p. 294): "Tu sola sapevi che il moto/non è diverso dalla stasi,/che il vuoto è il pieno e il sereno/è la piú diffusa delle nubi."

15 E. Montale, letter to Silvio Guarnieri (29 Nov. 1965), reproduced in his *L'opera in versi*, p. 939; Montale's italics.

16 E. Montale, *L'opera in versi*, p. 189. As if to underscore this defence against reason, Montale refused to gloss these rather hermetic lines. See his letter of 29 Nov. 1965 to Silvio Guarnieri, in E. Montale, *L'opera in versi*, p. 939: "Marmo manna e distruzione sono le componenti di un carattere: se tu le spieghi ammazzi la poesia."

17 See the 1957 essay on Dickinson: "La Dickinson suona una spinetta, Browning ne aveva forse suonato dieci insieme e il suono d'organo nascerà con

Whitman sebbene la poesia whitmaniana non abbia la purezza di stile della grande musica sacra" ("Emily", p. 498).

Chapter 4

HOPKINS AND THE MATURING OF CLIZIA

Hopkins, Montale and the Critics

Montale's Estimation of Hopkins

Montale kept a war-time notebook, which remains unpublished. It was rescued from the Florentine flood of 1966 and presented to Vanni Scheiwiller in 1968.[1] This notebook, dating from November 1943, contains Montale's transcriptions of eighteen poems by other poets, written in either English, French or Italian. Included in the little anthology were both "Pied Beauty" and "God's Grandeur" by Gerard Manley Hopkins. Montale's translation of "Pied Beauty" was first published five years later, but there is no suggestion that he ever attempted a version of the other poem. Nevertheless, the notebook is conclusive evidence that Montale's interest in Hopkins's poetry dates from at least as early as 1943.

In 1962 Montale expressed surprise at the fact that critics had made little of his technical affinity with Hopkins.[2] He had already mentioned the sprung rhythm connection in relation to T. S. Eliot in 1950:

> Come Gerard Manley Hopkins, come parecchi altri dei migliori poeti moderni passati attraverso Baudelaire, Eliot tenta di investire musicalmente l'atto dell'ispirazione, senza ridurlo a semplice, "aurorale" ineffabilità, senza ridursi allo stato di un automa che diffidi del proprio pensiero e scriva solo in stato di sonnambulismo.[3]

Such a musical conception of poetry should be familiar to readers of Montale; he said himself in a well-known passage of the "Intervista immaginaria", "Ubbidii a un bisogno di espressione musicale."[4] So

Montale recognized that he had a particular way of perceiving poetic inspiration in common with Hopkins. In other words, Montale's favourable estimation of Hopkins's poetry was quite consistent with his own avowled intention to "scavare un'altra dimensione" ("Intervista immaginaria", p. 567) in the Italian poetic language through a form of sprung rhythm.

The Rediscovery of Hopkins in Anglo-American Criticism

Although Robert Bridges had published his edition of Hopkins's poems in 1918, Hopkins's real influence dates from I. A. Richards's essay on him in *The Dial* (1926).[5] This essay is recognized as decisive in such seminal works of Hopkins criticism as those of William Empson in *Seven Types of Ambiguity* (1930) and F. R. Leavis in *New Bearings in English Poetry* (1932).[6] Empson developed a somewhat Freudian analysis of Hopkins's ambiguities in "The Windhover". Leavis placed Hopkins within the Shakespeare–Donne–Eliot–(later) Yeats tradition, ignoring Hopkins's own claims of affiliation with Milton.

Thus by the early 1930s Anglo-American criticism regarded Hopkins as an important and influential modern poet.

Hopkins and the Italian Critics

The introduction of Hopkins to the Italian reading public was due primarily to Benedetto Croce. Croce integrated his own Italian translations of twenty-six of Hopkins's poems into his essay "Un gesuita inglese poeta: Gerard Manley Hopkins" (1936).[7] These twenty-six translations include a version of "Pied Beauty". Escobar's translation of "Rosa mystica" also appeared in 1936 and Sergio Baldi's prose version of "The Wreck of the Deutschland" was published in 1939.[8]

Croce was attracted to the religious aspect of Hopkins's poetry, and deliberately rejected the Modernist thesis of an affinity between the poetry of Hopkins and that of Mallarmé. Commenting on "That Nature Is a Heraclitean Fire", he wrote:

> Ma l'oscurità di questi ultimi versi non è voluta dall'Hopkins per produrre un complesso privo di senso determinante e, con la sua misteriosità, atto a dar luogo a infinite interpretazioni, come presso i mallarmiani e altri tormentati-tormentatori artefici

> francesi e di altri paesi, la cui presunta e vantata ricchezza è povertà. È un'oscurità per effetto di eccessiva condensazione e per mancanza di passaggi nella quale il suo pensiero è rimasto impigliato. La sua tendenza generale è alla chiarezza espressiva.[9]

Montale later drew attention to what he held to be the limits of Croce's analysis of Hopkins in an important critical essay which linked the names of Hopkins and Hölderlin, thereby equating the metaphysical tendency of the two poets but refraining from judging either on the basis of religious orthodoxy:

> È stato osservato che ponendo il principio dell'arte come totalità, e non piú come primordiale lirismo, il Croce rischiava di inclinare verso quella teoria della simpatia immedesimata (dell'*Einfühlung*), verso la quale egli era stato sempre indulgente.
>
> Ebbene io credo che questo dono di immedesimazione (legato fatalmente al gusto e al carattere) sia sempre stato alla base dei giudizi critici che il Croce ha dato su poeti e scrittori. E credo che questo sia il punto piú forte, il vero punto di resistenza della sua critica. A volte l'immedesimazione gli riesce impossibile; come nel caso del Kleist, questo strano poeta perfettamente traducibile, che spinge l'obiettivazione del suo mondo fino a un'apparente freddezza e gratuità (e certo la figura dell'uomo Kleist incapace di comporre in armonia i suoi dissidi doveva riuscire ostica al Croce); e come nel caso del Pirandello, che per lui doveva appartenere alla classe degli pseudopoeti filosofanti, il che era parzialmente vero. Simpatia ebbe invece Croce per alcuni poeti religiosi come il difficilissimo Hopkins perché il sentimento religioso come materia d'arte ebbe sempre in lui pronto riconoscimento; ma scarsa comprensione per la poesia di Hölderlin mostra il saggio crociano compreso nei *Discorsi di varia filosofia* (vol. I).[10]

Montale seems to have read Hopkins as he read Hölderlin, that is to say, as a visionary and almost untranslatable poet.

Affinities between Hopkins and Montale

In the wake of Montale's expression of surprise at the lack of critical awareness of his affinities with Hopkins, several Italian critics have discussed the relationship between the work of the two poets. These critics include Gilberto Lonardi and Laura Barile.[11] Lonardi's discussion considers "Pied Beauty" and "La bellezza cangiante" as poetic objects in themselves. Barile's essay, which is much longer than Lonardi's brief note on the subject, discusses some of the affinities between Hopkins and Montale, the translation itself and some areas of possible influence.

Barile's essay is an appropriate starting-point for further research into the Hopkins–Montale connection. She argues from Montale's claim of technical affinity to a much deeper affinity between the work of the two poets:

> La loro vera consonanza è ben piú profonda e sta proprio nelle intenzioni espressive degli autori, nella loro posizione di fronte alla realtà, o natura che sia: mistico e pronto a riconoscervi i segni della Grazia l'uno, e laico ma altrettanto sensibile alla metafisica e alle sue suggestioni l'altro. E, ambedue, situati in quel crinale, in quel territorio di frontiera che separa la poesia dalla musica, arte "pura" per eccellenza.[12]

Not only is there an important affinity between the two poets: according to Barile, Hopkins's poetry provided a type of role-model for Montale's "metaphysical" phase:

> Il decennio 1937–1947 (anche se la lettura di Hopkins da parte di Montale va anticipata di qualche anno) registra la scintilla di un incontro che sprigiona altissimo fuoco di immagini, sensi e forme che, fondate su una sintonia preesistente, confermano il cammino montaliano di quegli anni in direzione metafisica: Montale trova in Hopkins ali, per cosí dire, al "folle volo" in senso metafisico tra *Occasioni*, *Finisterre* e *La bufera*; ali che solo un accesso mistico, un visionario di fede adamantina poteva fornire, anche se nella dimensione, estranea di Montale, di una religiosità legata ad una Chiesa; ma ugualmente basata sul tema del sacrificio.[13]

Barile's arguments are stimulating and convincing. There are, however, some other interesting affinities between Hopkins's and Montale's poetics for which Barile does not argue.

Beyond their unquestionable technical affinities, Montale and Hopkins shared a fascination with the sea. As Catherine Phillips observes in her essay introducing the 1987 edition of Hopkins's poems, "Twice his [Hopkins's] periods of poetic aridity were broken by the news of shipwrecks, calling from him two of his longest poems, 'The Wreck of the Deutschland' and 'The Loss of the Eurydice'."[14] There is thus in Hopkins's poetics a fundamental link between the sea and death. But death for Hopkins carries with it no commonsense nuance of finality. "The Wreck of the Deutschland" represents an attempt on his part to express a central Christian belief, that death is life and life is death.

Montale's dedication to the sea is principally represented by the "Mediterraneo" section of *Ossi di seppia*, though the sea is an important context for much of his poetry.[15] In Montale's symbolic landscape the sea is a vibrant force which casts its rubbish on the coast, the extremity of tired earth. The life of the sea is more alluring and more real than life on land, where the sun scorches the parched earth in the glare of the meridian. A symbolic demarcation is apparent in *Ossi di seppia* between land and sea in terms of death and life. Life on earth in *Ossi di seppia* increasingly resembles a metaphysical hell where the shades cast no shadows and there is no theological hope of escape or salvation. Life, for Montale in *Ossi di seppia*, seems to be essentially damnation. Therefore sea and land, life and death are subjects for Montale's early antinomial imagination. Likewise, in "The Wreck of the Deutschland" the nuns drown and that is their passing into eternal life. Hopkins contemplates the tragedy as a Christian mystic. Drowning for Montale is quite a different matter. The sea is the context of his "Crisalide" ("sommersa" in an earlier draft of the poem), Arletta—a girl who, according to Montale, died in her youth.[16] Arletta, the submerged girl of *Ossi di seppia*, undergoes a fictional death in Montale's poetry and through that process becomes the first of his visiting messengers.

The sea is a symbolic presence in both Hopkins's and Montale's poetry; that is one basis of symbolic affinity between their poetics. Their particular uses of the symbolism, while similar on a superficial level (for example, the sea for both of them has a connotation of death), are nevertheless quite distinct and different.

As we have seen, Barile has claimed that both Hopkins and Montale are "situati in quel crinale, in quel territorio di frontiera che separa la poesia dalla musica, arte 'pura' per eccellenza". Incontrovertibly Hopkins is a poet who was particularly sensitive to the power of music. Writing to Canon Dixon about "The Wreck of the Deutschland" in 1875, he described his own experience of the creative process thus: "I had long had haunting my ear the echo of a new rhythm which now I realized on paper".[17] This self-conscious concern with language which integrates musical elements of discourse into the poetic act has a correspondence in Montale's "Intervista immaginaria", where he writes about obeying "un bisogno di espressione musicale" and breaking with the language of the Italian poetic tradition in order to dig deeper into the language in search of his own voice:

> Ubbidii a un bisogno di espressione musicale. Volevo che la mia parola fosse piú aderente di quella degli altri poeti che avevo conosciuto. Piú aderente a che? Mi pareva di vivere sotto a una campana di vetro, eppure sentivo di essere vicino a qualcosa di essenziale. Un velo sottile, un filo appena mi separava dal *quid* definitivo. L'espressione assoluta sarebbe stata la rottura di quel velo, di quel filo: una esplosione, la fine dell'inganno del mondo come rappresentazione. Ma questo era un limite irraggiungibile. E la mia volontà di aderenza restava musicale, istintiva, non programmatica. All'eloquenza della nostra vecchia lingua aulica volevo torcere il collo, magari a rischio di una controeloquenza.[18]

On a critical level this linguistic self-consciousness of composition has made Montale's post-*Ossi di seppia* texts very fruitful areas of research for textual scholars.

The Texts

Sonnets in English and Italian

Hopkins seems to have been as aware of the differences between the Italian and English languages as was Montale. He was critical of verse translations:

> I should be very glad to see your [Robert Bridges's] prose of Michelangelo's sonnets and also your verse, for though I do not like verse-renderings (according to the saying *Traduttore traditore*), yet I think you could do them if anyone can. I have seen something of them, in particular a most striking one beginning—
>
> Non ha l'ottimo artista alcun concetto.[19]

Two years later Hopkins elaborated on the differences between an Italian and an English sonnet in a letter to Canon Dixon:

> The reason why the sonnet has never been so effective or successful in England as in Italy I believe to be this: it is not so long as the Italian sonnet; it is not long enough, I will presently say how. Now in the form of any other work of art the intrinsic measure-

ments, the proportions, that is, of the parts to one another and to the whole, are no doubt the principal point, but still the extrinsic measurements, the absolute quantity or size goes for something. Thus supposing in the Doric Order the Parthenon to be the standard of perfection, then if the columns of the Parthenon have so many semidiameters or modules to their height, the architrave so many, and so on these will be the typical proportions. But if a building is raised on a notably greater scale it will be found that these proportions are no longer satisfactory, so that one of the two things—either the proportions must be changed or the Order abandoned. Now if the Italian sonnet is one of the most successful forms of composition known, as it is reckoned to be, its proportions, inward and outward, must be pretty near perfection. The English sonnet has the same inward proportions, 14 lines, 5 feet to the line, and the rhymes and so on may be made as in the strictest Italian type. Nevertheless it is notably shorter and would therefore appear likely to be unsuccessful, from want not of comparative but of absolute length. For take any lines from an Italian sonnet, as

> Non ha l'ottimo artista alcun concetto
> che un marmor solo in se non circonscriva.

Each line has two elisions and a heavy ending or 13 syllables, though only 10 or, if you like, 11 count in the scanning. An Italian heroic line then and consequently a sonnet will be longer than an English sonnet in the proportion 13:10, which is considerable. But that is not all: the syllables themselves are longer. We have seldom such a delay in the voice as is given to the syllable by doubled letters (as *ottimo* and *concetto*) or even by two or more consonants (as *artista* and *circonscriva*) of any sort, read as Italians read. Perhaps the proportions are nearer 4:3 or 3:2. The English sonnet is then in comparison with the Italian short, light, tripping and trifling.[20]

Hopkins's sonnets are not, however, "short, light, tripping and trifling" compositions, as we shall see in the case of "Pied Beauty".

"Pied Beauty"

"Pied Beauty" is dated "St Beuno's, Tremeirchion. Summer '77." It is marked "Curtal Sonnet: sprung paeonic rhythm." Hopkins elaborated on his terminology in a preface:

> Nos 1 and 25 are Curtal sonnets, that is they are constructed in proportions resembling those of the sonnet proper, namely 6 + 4 instead of 8 + 6, with however a half-line tailpiece (so that the equation is rather 12/2 + 9/2 = 21/2 = 10 1/2).[21]

It is far from being a typical Victorian sonnet. Hopkins had very little regard for the stock-in-trade devices of Victorian sonneteers:

> By the by, inversions—As you say, I do avoid them, because they weaken and destroy the earnestness or in-earnestness of the utterance. Nevertheless in prose I use them more than other people, because there they have great advantages of another sort. Now these advantages they should have in verse too, but they must not be seen to be due to the verse; that is what is so enfeebling (for instance the finest of your sonnets to my mind has a line enfeebled by inversion plainly due to the verse, as I said once before "Tis joy the falling of her fold to view"—but how it would be mended I do not see). As it is, I feel my way to their use. However in a nearly finished piece I have a very bold one indeed. So also I cut myself off from the use of *ere, o'er, wellnigh, what time, say not* (for *do not say*), because, though dignified, they neither belong to nor ever cd arise from, or be the elevation of, ordinary modern speech. For it seems to me that the poetical language of an age shd be the current language heightened and unlike itself, but not (I mean normally: passing freaks and graces are another thing) an obsolete one. This is Shakespeare's and Milton's practice and the want of it will be fatal to Tennyson's Idylls and plays, to Swinburne, and perhaps to Morris.[22]

"Pied Beauty" is direct, without inversions. The text reads as follows:

Glory be to God for dappled things—
  For skies of couple-colour as a brinded cow;
    For rose-moles all in stipple upon trout that swim;
Fresh-firecoal chestnut-falls; finches' wings;
  Landscape plotted and pieced—fold, fallow, and plough;
    And áll trádes, their gear and tackle and trim.

All things counter, original, spáre, strange;
  Whatever is fickle, frecklèd (who knows how?)
    With swíft, slów; sweet, sóur; adázzle, dím;
He fathers-forth whose beauty is pást change:
                Práise hím.[23]

To describe the poem as direct, however, is not to detract from its complexity. "Pied Beauty" is a "curtal" sonnet consisting of ten lines with a tailpiece (made up of two monosyllables). There are end-rhymes which may be represented schematically thus: ABC ABC DBCDC. Hopkins aspired to write English sonnets which were not trite but vigorous.

Hopkins's sonnet departs from his thesis that the English sonnet should be longer than it customarily is, but is true to at least some of his principles. The rhyming words are monosyllables: "things":"wings", "cow":"plough":"how", "swim":"trim":"dim": "Him", "strange":"change". Each line ends with a punctuation mark of some kind (there are in all seven semi-colons, three commas, two dashes, two full stops and one colon). As Hopkins wrote poetry primarily to be declaimed, these punctuation marks are to be taken as pause marks for the reading voice. The end-rhymes are supplemented by internal assonances, which may, as Barile has suggested, recall Hopkins's study of Welsh poetry. The broad diphthong /au/ acts as a pedal note for the music of the poem: "cow" → "trout" → "coal" → "fallow" → "plough" → "counter" → "how" → "sour". There is also an intense alliterative process at work, as in "couple-colour" (line 2), "Fresh-firecoal chestnut-falls" (line 4), "fold, fallow" (line 5), "trades [...] tackle [...] trim" (line 6), "fickle, freckled" (line 8), "swift, slow; sweet, sour" (line 9), "fathers-forth" (line 10). To these we may add three pairs of double consonants: "dappled"/"stipple" (lines 1, 3), "falls"/ "fallow" (lines 4, 5) and "plotted"/"adazzle" (lines 5, 9). As we shall see, the double consonant as a structural element is one which Montale seizes upon in his version. Finally, Hopkins insinuates a phonetic element into the meanings of words by giving an alliterative list of antonyms: "swift, slow; sweet, sour; adazzle, dim" (line 9). This combination of phonetics and semantics is documented in his early diaries.[24]

"La bellezza cangiante"

Montale's translation was first published in 1948 with the title "Bellezza cangiante";[25] it acquired the definite article in the *Quaderno di traduzioni*. The definitive version reads as follows:

Gloria a Dio per le cose che ha spruzzate:
i cieli bicolori, pezzati come vacche,
la striscia roseo-biliottata della
trota in acqua, il tonfar delle castagne
—crollo di tizzi giovani nel fuoco—
e l'ali del fringuello; per le toppe
dei campi arati e dissodati, e tutti
i traffici e gli arnesi, e tutto ch'è
fuor di squadra, difforme, impari e strambo,
tutto che muta, punto di lentiggini
(chissà come?) di fretta o di lentezza,
di dolce o d'aspro, di lucore o buio.
Quegli le esprime—lode a Lui—ch'è sola
bellezza non mutabile.

Montale's was not the first Italian translation in print: Croce had published his prose translation in 1936, as we have seen, and Sergio Baldi had published a verse translation in 1940.[26] Croce's translation reads as follows:

> Gloria a Dio per le cose variegate—pei cieli di accoppiati colori come una vacca chiazzata; per le macchie rosee che screziano la trota nuotante; per le cascate di castagne dal colore di carbone appena acceso; per le ali del fringuello; per il paesaggio a macchie e a toppe, parco, terra brulla, campo arato; e per tutti i mestieri, e i loro arnesi, strumenti e attrezzi.
>
> Tutte le cose contrastanti, originali, disparate, strane; tutto quello che è cangiante, che varia (chi sa come?) col rapido il lento, col dolce l'agro, con l'abbagliante l'opaco, Colui le produce la cui bellezza è di là dai mutamenti: lode a lui![27]

Croce's prose translation has the virtue of being exceptionally literal, and thus is unquestionably the work of a careful scholar rather than a creative artist. Montale probably found it a useful crib.

Montale takes his title from Croce, though it is not a simple case of appropriation. Croce's prose translation gives the eighth line as "tutto quello che è cangiante, che varia (chi sa come?)". Montale takes "cangiante" from there and translates "freckled" as "punto di lentiggini".

Unlike his procedure in translating the three Shakespeare sonnets, Montale does not retain the formal structure of Hopkins's curtal sonnet. Montale's sonnet runs to fourteen lines, though the last line is a *settenario* (the others are of hendecasyllable length except the second line, which is a *settenario doppio*). It is extremely unlikely that Montale was aware of Hopkins's letters which discuss the differences between Italian and English sonnets. A poet's instinct seems to have led him to translate Hopkins's form, the "curtal" sonnet, into a relatively conventional Italian form. Montale dispenses with the rhyme-scheme of "Pied Beauty" and changes the syntactic structures of Hopkins's poem by introducing five *enjambements*. That is a technique which Montale had also used in his Shakespeare *rifacimenti* as a way of achieving a velocity in Italian comparable to that of English. The effect of the first *enjambement* is to produce a strong caesura after "acqua" (line 4), linking a chain of assonance from "vacche" (line 2) to "castagne" (line 4). The second *enjambement* (lines 6–7) highlights the sounds of the adjectival past participles "ar*a*ti" and "dissod*a*ti", which point back towards "spruzz*a*te", "pezz*a*ti" and "biliott*a*ta", and forwards towards "muta", "fretta" and "lentezza". Montale does not neglect the list of antonyms (lines 11–12): he connects them through alliteration ("dolce"/"d'aspro") and through assonance ("fretta"/"lentezza", "lucore"/"buio"). He takes what is quite a minor feature of Hopkins's poem—the double consonants—and uses it extensively, as Hopkins had observed that Italian poets do. There are in fact twenty-two double consonants in "La bellezza cangiante". They are mainly /zz/, /tt/ and /ll/, and they culminate in the final *settenario*, specifically in the word "be*ll*ezza', which receives especial stress from the *enjambement*. The use of double consonants as opposed to single consonants is a way of shortening Italian vowels, thus clipping words in something approaching English fashion.[28]

Montale translates "dappled" as "spruzzate" (line 1), in contrast to Croce's "variegate". Montale's word, gaining a syllable on Croce's, fits the hendecasyllable and echoes the "spruzzo di metallo" of his own poem "Barche sulla Marna" (1938).[29] "Bicolori" is a *hapax legomenon* chosen instead of Croce's literal but awkward "di accoppiati colori" on the grounds of velocity. The "striscia" (line 3) of the trout is part of the *Ossi di seppia* idiolect, appearing there twice, once in "Corno inglese" ("dove strisce di luce si protendono/come aquiloni al cielo") and again in "Marezzo" ("Tutto fra poco si farà piú ruvido,/fiorirà l'onda di piú cupe strisce").[30] Montale's uses of "fringuello" (line 6), "arati" (line 7) and "arnesi" (line 8) all follow Croce, and none of the three suggests important Montalian resonances.

The point worth stressing in relation to Montale's translation of "Pied Beauty" is the degree of affinity between his and Hopkins's conceptions of the sonnet and the relative velocities of English and Italian. Montale seems to have sensed what Hopkins was doing in his curtal sonnet, and indeed why he was doing it. His reworking of the curtal sonnet into something very like an Italian sonnet suggests that he recognized the form of the Italian sonnet lurking in the Hopkins poem.

Affinity and Influence

"Inscape" and "Poesia dell'oggetto"

Croce, unlike Montale, observes the division which Hopkins made in "Pied Beauty" at the end of the sixth line. As Barile has noted, the poem obeys the rhetorical rules of a sermon. The sestet consists in an imitation of Nature, which includes the four elements in synecdoche (skies, trout, firecoals and landscape). The second part consists in a meditation on the vignette of Nature, articulating a cognitive process through the instressed language which is finally transformed into a hymn. The process, as practised by Hopkins, takes as its model St Ignatius Loyola's *Spiritual Exercises*.[31]

Hopkins, through his exercises in word-painting and perhaps through the influence of Pater (his tutor at Oxford), had begun to develop an original theory in his *Journal* (1866–75). His experiments in word-painting induced him towards the concept of "inscape". "Inscape", according to Hopkins, was the distinctive internal form of objects. There are numerous references to the term in his *Journal*, and it is apparent that it denoted an intuition on the part of the individual relating to objects of the natural world. It is analogous to, and derived from, the *principium individuationis* of Duns Scotus.[32]

According to Scotus, the universal manifests itself in the individual, and as the objects of our perception are necessarily individuals it follows that we can attain knowledge of universals or abstract ideas only through a process of induction based on our knowledge of individuals. The internal form of an individual, when it appears to the observer, appears as a manifestation, intimating the perfect form. In the thinking of Duns Scotus as in the thinking and poetry of Hopkins, this Platonism is tempered with Christianity. Consequently, Hopkins's "inscapes" manifest the divinity in creation.

For Hopkins a poem expresses the inscapes of objects as a cognitive process rather than a representational one, and this cognitive process is central to the act of artistic perception. Consequently the language of his poems is charged with emotional and intellectual elements which combine to produce what he calls "instress". It is "instress" which gives expression to the "inscape", and this shifts the focus of critical attention from a real object to what might be called a poem-object. Words come to be treated as objects. In his *Journal* Hopkins wrote notes on the incantatory power of words and constructed etymologies on the basis of alliteration.[33] Thus Hopkins's interest in words is rooted in the syllable or even the phoneme, and he conceives of the syllable as a musical beat or pulse which might be prolonged or shortened as appropriate to the "instress".

This process of presenting an objective situation, a moment trapped in a poetic still and followed by instressed contemplation, should be familiar to readers of Montale. In fact it would be an accurate statement of the poetics underlying the motet "La speranza di pure rivederti", but for the structural detail that there the objective situation comes at the end of the poem.[34] The poetic significance of the liveried servant with the two jackals on a leash in Modena is not that the animals are on a leash; it is rather that on an objective level the sight of these strange animals prompts Clizia's return to the poet's memory (as Montale later explained tongue in cheek).[35] On a textual level the word "guinzaglio" rhymes with "barbaglio", a keyword which in Montale's poetics of the time announced an epiphany. So we may conclude that Montale was using words themselves by the mid-1930s for incantatory effect rather than solely as signifiers of external objects.

In linking the musical and cognitive aspects of poetry in theory (for instance, in the "Intervista immaginaria") and in practice (as in the *mottetti*) Montale did little more than reiterate an article of faith first expressed in his *Quaderno genovese*:

> *Linee di una poesia impressionistica* — Fusione completa, inscindibile, di psicologia e *paesismo* (non-io, insomma), come nella vita ci avviene sempre. La natura dev' essere poi trasformata, sezionata,

> capovolta magari; colta cioè negli elementi soli che operano sulla sensibilità poetica, all'atto della pura intuizione. È l'occhio freddo che abbraccia e fotografa tutto; il momento fantastico-lirico sceglie fra la realtà, trasforma e assimila. Poesia insomma che colga della vita *il momento*, considerato nella esistenza nostra come sola realtà semplice irredutibile e inconvertibile. Non-io visto a traverso lo specchio prismatico dell'io. Poesia doppia, matrimonio della fantasia con la materia (?) esterna. Il ritmo assecondi la creazione *nervosamente*: non trascurare il suono di una lettera. Le parole dipingano e suggeriscano: diano l'idea. La musica dia il sentimento.[36]

That act of intuition, posited by Montale in 1917, which connects the observer with the objects of observation in a complete fusion, forms the nucleus of his poetics. The analogy of the photograph which captures a particular moment is slightly provocative. Photographic realism is not Montale's aspiration, but rather a starting-point from which he proceeds to express the interaction of the object with the individual observer through the medium of music. The words, considered semantically, present the sentimental bond between that reality and the individual.

The foregoing accounts of "inscape" and "poesia dell'oggetto" demonstrate that there are interesting similarities between the two theories. Nevertheless, there is no causal connection between them. Montale expressed his protean theory in 1917, well before he could have been aware of Hopkins's poetry. Therefore it does not provide ground on which to build a case for "influence". Montale, when he read Hopkins's poetry, saw the striking similarities between Hopkins's and his own work. In short, Montale read Hopkins as a predecessor.

Affinity

Laura Barile has argued that Hopkins was an important influence in the development of Montale's poetics between 1937 and 1948.[37] "Influence" is a nebulous term, but stripped to its essentials it must surely denote an element of appropriation of the first writer's work in the second writer's poetry. The appropriation might involve formal devices, thematic matter, symbolism, style and so forth. The question is, in the present case, can Hopkins's influence be detected in Montale's war-time poetry? Clearly the "poesia dell'oggetto" method used in the *mottetti* is not an example of such influence. There may, however, be other instances.

Barile has correctly shown that the area of greatest Montalian resonance in "Pied Beauty" is the phrase "Fresh-firecoal chestnut-falls" (line 4), which Montale enlarges to "il tonfar delle castagne/ —crollo di tizzi giovani nel fuoco—" (lines 4–5).[38] There are two aspects of this translation which might attract the reader's attention. Firstly, Montale usually reduces an original in his translations, but in this case he enlarges on one specific part of the text. Secondly, he separates the two images which Hopkins, through an absence of punctuation marks, had fused together.[39]

The noun cognate with *tonfare*, meaning "thud", "bang", "splash" or less commonly "fall", has a long and consistent history in Montale's poetry. *Tonfo* appears ten times in the poems of *L'opera in versi* written between 1924 and 1974, while the verbal form *tonfare* appears three times. What is more suggestive than these statistics, from an exegetical point of view, is the context of the noun's first appearance. The poem in question, although written in 1923, was first published in *L'opera in versi* (1980). It is, in effect, a reservoir of later Montalian pith, and it merits quotation in full:

> Scendiamo la via che divalla
> tra i grovigli dei dumi;
> ci guiderà il volo di una farfalla
> in faccia agli orizzonti rotti dai fiumi.
>
> Serriamoci dietro come una porta
> queste ore di esistenze e di groppi in gola.
> Nostalgie non dette che piú c'importano?
> Anche l'aria d'attorno ci vola!
>
> Ed ecco che a uno svolto ci appare
> di colpo la riga argentea del mare;
> buttano ancora l'àncora le nostre vite anèle.
> Ne intendo il tonfo—Addio, sentiero! Ed ora
> mi sento tutto fiorito non so se d'ali o di vele...[40]

The "tonfo" in this early poem is the climax of a downward progression, where the protagonist follows the flight of the butterfly down the street surrounded by an exciting dynamism in nature, until suddenly the silver line of the sea appears in an existential epiphany. Montale's reasons for not including this poem in *Ossi di seppia* are quite clear. Although it contains his symbols of the parched earth and the vibrant sea, and although it almost conforms to the structure of the Montalian epiphany at this stage of his poetic development, its conclusion violates his poetics of sacrifice. "Fiorito", while it is a wonderfully ambiguous word with nuances stretching from "decked with flowers" to "mildewed", suggests in this context a successful escape from "le nostre vite anèle", and escapism is never admitted into Montale's "official" poetry without a counterweight of irony.

But the poem has two claims to importance. It acted as a reservoir of motifs and established the form of its existential epiphany. Arsenio follows this downward itinerary where the "ore/uguali" (lines 9–10)—which correspond to the "ore di esistenze" of "Scendiamo la via che divalla" (line 6)—are shattered by "un ritornello/di castagnette" (lines 10–11) rather than by the sudden glimpse of the sea.[41] The nature of the shocks is different in the two poems (one auditory and the other visual), but their function is the same: they are cues for Montale's epiphany. This technique developed in the course of the *mottetti*, where the signifiers became as important as the signifieds. The development in technique ran parallel to a development in metaphysics. The two jackals on a leash were a *senhal* invoking Clizia, and Clizia, by the time of Montale's "La bellezza cangiante", had been transformed from a sunflower into a visiting angel and thence into a sacrificial victim, a female counterpart of Christ.[42] The "tonfo" of "Scendiamo la via che divalla" and the "ritornello di castagnette" were recalled, whether consciously or not, in the "tonfar delle castagne" in line 4 of "La bellezza cangiante". Thus Montale's departure from literal translation in this part of Hopkins's poem was motivated by echoes of his own earlier work. "Influence" may not be an accurate definition of that process.

Influence

Gerard Manley Hopkins is a poet mentioned consistently in Montale's critical writings throughout the 1940s, 1950s and 1960s. In a 1951 "Intervista con se stesso" discussing contemporary Italian poetry Montale wrote:

> Un'antologia della poesia italiana del Novecento che fosse fatta con criteri d'imparzialità potrebbe dare molte sorprese. Finora

> non era possibile farla: non era né possibile né augurabile il criterio stesso dell'imparzialità. Dovevano prevalere ragioni di scuola o di programma. Coloro che odiano il decadentismo si rassicurino: l'Italia d'oggi non ha poeti propriamente decadenti. Non ha avuto un Valéry, non ha un Benn, un Eliot, un Auden, uno Char. Non ha grandi ortopedici e sperimentatori. Ma ha avuto ed ha poeti che possono valere, io credo, un Apollinaire o un Antonio Machado o, se vogliamo risalire, addietro, un Hopkins; *poeti in cui il meglio del simbolismo francese* (che fu in poesia ciò che in pittura fu l'impressionismo) *si innesta in forme italiane assai originalmente*. Bisogna però aggiungere che la recente poesia italiana è minacciata d'esaurimento. Ed è propriamente il suo lato classico che sembra in pericolo.[43]

Montale may well have been talking about himself and equating himself with Hopkins. In any case, Montale's 1943 notebook contained his transcription of "God's Grandeur" along with that of "Pied Beauty". "God's Grandeur" begins:

> The world is charged with the grandeur of God.
> It will flame out, like shining from shook foil;
> It gathers to a greatness, like the ooze of oil
> Crushed.

There is a corresponding passage in Hopkins's *Sermons*: "All things are charged with love, and charged with God, and if we Know how to touch them give off sparks and take fire, yield drops and flow, ring and tell of Him."[44] Montale had already applied this sort of imagery to the emanations of Clizia in the *mottetti*, and while there is no extant translation of "God's Grandeur" among Montale's papers, what is of interest in the context of 1943 and the development of Montale's private mythology is its sestet:

> And for all this, nature is never spent;
> There lives the dearest freshness deep down things;
> And though the last lights off the black West went
> Oh, morning, at the brown brink eastward, springs—
> Because the Holy Ghost over the bent
> World broods with warm breast and with ah! bright wings.

The bright wings of the dove, symbol of the Holy Spirit, cannot have been far from Montale's mind when he wrote "Giorno e notte" (1943),[45] where Clizia was the "perigliosa/annunziatrice dell'alba". Twenty years later Montale described this dawn messenger in terms which may suggest a religious comparison:

> Ma chi è costei? Certo, in origine, donna reale; ma qui e altrove, anzi dovunque, *visiting angel*, poco o punto materiale. Non è necessario attribuirle la piuma che vola [line 1], quasi si fosse distaccata in anticipo dalle sue ali (sebbene non sia impossibile). Piuma, luccichío dello specchio [line 3] e altri segni (in altre poesie) non sono che enigmatici annunzi dell'evento che sta per compiersi: l'istante "privilegiato" (Contini), spesso la visitazione. E perché la visitatrice annunzia l'alba [line 16]? Quale alba? Forse l'alba di un possibile riscatto, che può essere tanto la pace quanto una liberazione metafisica. In sé la visitatrice non può tornare in carne ed ossa, ha da tempo cessato di esistere come tale. Forse è morta da tempo, forse morirà altrove in quell' istante. Il suo compito di inconsapevole Cristòfora non le consente altro trionfo che non sia l'insuccesso di quaggiú: lontananza, dolore, vaghe fantomatiche riapparizioni (vedi "Iride" pubblicata nel '43 e inclusa nella seconda edizione di *Finisterre*, pubblicata dal Barbèra), quel tanto di presenza che sia per chi lo riceve un memento, un'ammonizione. La sua fisionomia è sempre corrucciata, altera, la sua stanchezza è mortale, indomabile il suo coraggio: se angelo è, mantiene tutti gli attributi terrestri, non è ancora riuscita a disincarnarsi (cfr. con "Voce giunta con le folaghe", scritta qualche anno dopo). Tuttavia è già *fuori*, mentre noi siamo *dentro*. Era *dentro* anche lei (cfr. "Nuove stanze", nelle *Occasioni*), ma poi è partita (cfr. "La primavera hitleriana") per compiere la sua missione.[46]

Thus, perhaps under the influence of Hopkins, the vision of the holy dove coming to redeem "the bent/World", which was in darkness, enters into the *chiaroscuro* symbolism of Montale's private mythology in the form of Clizia, his visiting angel. Clizia's "beatification" may have taken place under the auspices of Hopkins's influence. "Beatification" is not a word to use lightly, especially in relation to Montale's poetry.

In the *mottetti* Montale had used darkness or shadow as a symbol of death:

> Lontano, ero con te quando tuo padre
> entrò nell'ombra e ti lasciò il suo addio.
> (*L'opera in versi*, p. 136)

Darkness and death are, of course, also cognates in Hopkins's poetry. Hopkins wrestled with the idea of extinction in "That Nature Is a Heraclitean Fire":

> Million-fuelèd, nature's bonfire burns on.
> But quench her bonniest, dearest to her, her clearest-selvèd
> spark
> Man, how fast his firedint, his mark on mind, is gone!
> Both are in an únfathomable, all is in an enormous dark
> Drowned. O pity and indignation! Manshape, that shone
> Sheer off, disseveral, a star, death blots black out.[47]

Darkness is the background to Montale's war-time poetry. "La bufera" closes with the sombre omen of Clizia clearing the hair from her forehead, waving and entering into the gloom:

> Come quando
> ti rivolgesti e con la mano, sgombra
> la fronte dalla nube dei capelli,
>
> mi salutasti—per entrar nel buio.[48]

The gloom ("buio"), Montale explains in a letter to Silvio Guarnieri (29 November 1965), is many things: distance, separation, even uncertainty as to whether Clizia was still alive.[49] In "Giorno e notte" Clizia had been the "inconsapevole Cristòfora", the unwitting messiah, who announces the dawn in the East. In "Iride", the most enigmatic of Montale's war-time poems, Clizia undergoes a metaphysical transformation which, according to Barile, had Hopkins's poetics as its foil.

The first three stanzas of "Iride", which constitute about half the poem, form a single sentence.[50] The very beginning, with its four pairs of double consonants, may suggest the music of "La bellezza cangiante". That, of course, is only a superficial correspondence. The fourth line, however ("schiocchi di pigne verdi fra la cenere"), continues the tradition of Montale's sacrificial symbolism in a way that finds a clear parallel in Hopkins's poetry. The second stanza:

> questo e poco altro (se poco
> è un tuo segno, un ammicco, nella lotta
> che me sospinge in un ossario, spalle

al muro, dove zàffiri celesti
e palmizi e cicogne su una zampa non chiudono
l'atroce vista al povero
Nestoriano smarrito);

(*L'opera in versi*, p. 239)

presents Clizia in terms of Hopkins's philosophy by describing her "segno" (her "sign" or "sake") as a nod, or a wave of the hand. In "Iride" Montale still catches glimpses of Clizia, but the reference to himself as the "poor lost Nestorian" is indicative of a shift in his relationship with Clizia, and indeed a shift in his whole metaphysical structure.[51]

It is not that Montale had suddenly become a heretic. His artistic vision had never—unlike Hopkins's—been one compatible with Christianity. The point is that for Barile's argument to hold (that is, for Montale's metaphysics in the 1940s to have developed under the influence of Hopkins's poetry), we must accept that Hopkins's adamantine faith inspired Montale's sacrificial—mystical perhaps but certainly not Christian—view of the world. It is an interesting argument, but it is ultimately a matter of speculation.

Montale, Hopkins and Hölderlin

In one of his later musings on poetry and theology Montale wrote:

> I Greci avevano risolto il problema in altro modo: inventando gli Dei, divinità *ad hoc* fatte a loro misura. Non diverso il pensiero di Hölderlin che credeva all'esistenza di divinità terrestri, viventi in *incognito* tra di noi. Ma non è facile incontrarne qualcuna; solo ai poeti è concessa tale possibilità. Ed è questo ancor oggi *l'unico modo di avere un'esperienza concreta del divino*.[52]

Thus Montale attributes a sacramental function to poetry, positing an aesthetic religion to which only poets have access through communion with terrestrial divinities. This is an article of faith with roots in his early work, and one which has little or nothing to do with Hopkins's Christianity. Montale's position is worked out more rigorously in the *mottetti*, alluded to in the presence of the lost Nestorian in "Iride" and transmuted into an emblem in his postwar poetry. The *mottetti* establish Clizia's metamorphosis from a sunflower into a visiting angel. The significance of Hopkins in relation to the *mottetti* rests in the terms of Clizia's "beatification".

The tokens of Clizia's presence correspond to those which announce the Divinity in Hopkins's work. As has been mentioned above, in Montale's work the sudden dazzle and the flash, the "barbaglio" and the "fulgore", are both indices of Clizia's presence, especially in the *mottetti*.[53]

Clizia's only hope of success is through failure. Her *raison d'être* is thus the same as Hopkins's description of Christ. Hopkins had written in a letter to Dixon: "Whereas he would have wished to succeed by success [...] nevertheless he was doomed to succeed by failure."[54] In Montale's metaphysics what relates Christ to Clizia is the idea of sacrifice, and the relation alluded to in "Iride" is consummated in "La primavera hitleriana", which is the apotheosis of the sunflower myth:

> Guarda ancora
> in alto, Clizia, è la tua sorte, tu
> che il non mutato amor mutata serbi,
> fino a che il cieco sole che in te porti
> si abbàcini nell'Altro e si distrugga
> in Lui, per tutti.
>
> (*L'opera in versi*, p. 249)

In attributing these messianic qualities to Clizia, Montale fuses together three disparate strands of his metaphysics as expressed in the first collection. The sunflower myth, in which the sunflower turns its head to meet the sun, started as a brief poem, "Portami il girasole", where the flower appeared as a barely fetishized object.[55] In that poem the flower was "impazzito di luce" (line 12), as butterflies and moths are in the later poems.[56] In the "Silvae", and specifically in "La primavera hitleriana", the sunflower (recalled in the poem's epigraph) is transmuted into a symbol and identified with Clizia, who destroys herself in the *other* sun. Clizia's act of self-annihilation is the perfect instance of sacrifice. Yet in *Ossi di seppia* it was always the poet's *io* whose lot it was to sacrifice himself for the good of others.[57] In the "Silvae" Clizia has become the world's redeemer, taking on in the process the divine attributes associated with the sea in *Ossi di seppia*.[58] Underpinning the identification of Clizia with Christ, therefore, is the theme of sacrifice, a theme latent in Montale's own earlier poetry, and one which he develops further in the course of translating Hopkins and a number of other writers (such as Melville and Hudson).

That much at least is clear, but there are questions remaining unanswered. Why, for example, is the woman identified with Christ and cast as a victim whose sacrifice might in some way give grace to the world? Part of the answer must begin with the poetics of the *dolce stil novo*. The influence of *stilnovismo* on Montale's poetics in the *mottetti* phase is considerable. Clizia stands, at that stage, in the tradition of the *donna angelicata*, of Beatrice and of Laura. In the "Silvae"—specifically in "Voce giunta con le folaghe"—Montale follows Dante again rather than Petrarch in having Clizia act as intermediary between himself and his dead father; there the encounter is reminiscent of Dante's with Cacciaguida. That, however, is an identification of Clizia with Beatrice and not with Christ.

Thus by the mid-1940s Montale had passed beyond latter-day *stilnovismo*, possibly under Hopkins's influence, to the point of communicating with Clizia through artistic perception, because she had become an earthly divinity, in the fashion of Hölderlin's divinities, living *incognito* and disdaining communication with all except poets.

NOTES

1 See *Mantova per Montale: immagini e documenti*, edited by V. Scheiwiller (Milan, All'insegna del Pesce d'oro, 1983), document 20.

2 See Montale's preface to Gösta Andersson's Swedish translations of his poems [1960], in his *Sulla poesia*, edited by G. Zampa (Milan, Mondadori, 1976), pp. 87–91: "Piú serrato è l'intreccio delle rime e delle assonanze ed è strano che nessuno abbia fatto il nome di Gerard Manley Hopkins. A modo mio cercavo il mio *sprung rhythm*" (p. 89).

3 E. Montale, "Invito a T. S. Eliot", in his *Sulla poesia*, pp. 457–65 (p. 461).

4 E. Montale, "Intenzioni (intervista immaginaria)", in his *Sulla poesia*, pp. 561–69 (p. 565).

5 See *Hopkins: The Critical Heritage*, edited by G. Roberts (London, Routledge and Kegan Paul, 1987), pp. 140–45.

6 W. Empson, *Seven Types of Ambiguity* (London, Chatto and Windus, 1930), pp. 224–26; F. R. Leavis, *New Bearings in English Poetry* (London, Chatto and Windus, 1932), p. 165.

7 B. Croce, "Un gesuita inglese poeta: Gerard Manley Hopkins" [1936], reprinted in his *Poesia antica e moderna* (Bari, Laterza, 1966), pp. 423–48.

8 Both were published in *Frontespizio*, "Rosa mystica" in October 1936 and "The Wreck of the Deutschland" in March 1939.

9 B. Croce, "Un gesuita inglese poeta", p. 438.

10 E. Montale, "L'estetica e la critica" [1962], in his *Sulla poesia*, pp. 128–43 (pp. 136–37).

11 See G. Lonardi, "Fuori e dentro il tradurre montaliano", in his *Il vecchio e il giovane e altri studi su Montale* (Bologna, Zanichelli, 1980), pp. 144–63 (pp. 149–51); L. Barile, "Sparviero o procellaria? Una versione di Montale da Hopkins", in her *Adorate mie larve: Montale e la poesia anglosassone* (Bologna, Mulino, 1990), pp. 15–50.

12 L. Barile, "Sparviero o procellaria?", pp. 15–16.

13 L. Barile, "Sparviero o procellaria?", pp. 17–18.

14 *Gerard Manley Hopkins*, edited by C. Phillips (London, Oxford University Press, 1987), p. xv.

15 Carpi relates Montale's fascination with the sea to that of other Ligurian poets: "Montale non avrà certo tradotto meccanicamente (e forse neppure avuto direttamente presente) quel concetto di tradizione e di legge nel dare corpo al mito poetico del mare: ma sarà piuttosto che con questo mito poetico ha concretato in una precisa forma poetica di coscienza il bisogno di rispondere ad una contraddizione radicata socialmente ed ha espresso quindi (a livello specifico, ma non separato, per intenderci) una condizione riconducibile a quella che aveva motivato la costruzione ideologica boiniana." See U. Carpi *"La voce": letteratura e primato degli intellettuali* (Bari, De Donato, 1975), pp. 156–60 (p. 160).

16 Montale claimed that Arletta was a real person who had died in her youth. She is the "tu" of "La casa dei doganieri" (see "Annetta", in E. Montale, *L'opera in versi*, edited by G. Contini and R. Bettarini [Turin, Einaudi, 1980], pp. 490–91). The lady in question, Anna degli Uberti, spent her summer holidays at Monterosso between 1920 and 1924, and although Montale did not meet her after 1924 she lived to be fifty-five years of age (despite what Montale claimed), dying in Rome in 1959. See "Montale e il *Corriere*", a supplement to *Il corriere della sera*, edited by F. Roncoroni (27 June 1986), p. 21.

17 G. M. Hopkins, *Poems and Prose*, edited by W. H. Gardner (Harmondsworth, Penguin, 1984), p. 186.

18 E. Montale, "Intenzioni", p. 565. It is perhaps indicative of the literary nature of Montale's revolt that his words should echo those of Verlaine, "Prends l'éloquence et tords-lui son cou." The phrase is quoted by Laforgue in a letter to Charles Henry (July 1884), and this may be Montale's source. See also M. Hamburger, *The Truth of Poetry* (London, Weidenfeld and Nicolson, 1969), p. 51.

19 Letter to Bridges (14 Aug. 1879), reprinted in *Gerard Manley Hopkins*, p. 239. According to Phillips (p. 394), there are no known verse translations of Michelangelo's poems by Bridges, though nos 35 and 64 of "The Growth of Love" as printed in the *Poetical Works* were based on *madrigali* by Michelangelo. The version of "Non ha l'ottimo artista" to which Hopkins alludes is J. A. Symonds's "The Lover and the Sculptor".

20 Letter to Canon Dixon (29 Oct. 1881), in *Gerard Manley Hopkins*, pp. 246–47.

21 See *Gerard Manley Hopkins*, p. 109.

22 Letter to Bridges (14 Aug. 1879), in *Gerard Manley Hopkins*, pp. 239–40.

23 *Gerard Manley Hopkins*, pp. 132–33.

24 See *Gerard Manley Hopkins*, p. 185: "[Oxford, 1863] Flick, fillip, flip, fleck, flake: *Flick* means to touch or strike lightly as with the end of a whip, a finger etc. To *fleck* is the next tone above flick, still meaning to touch or strike lightly (and leave a mark of the touch or stroke) but in a broader less slight manner. Hence substantively a *fleck* is a piece of light, colour, substance etc. looking as

though shaped or produced by such touches. *Flake* is a broad and decided *fleck*, a thin plate of something, the tone above it. Their connection is more clearly seen in the applications of words to natural objects than in explanations. It would seem that *fillip* generally pronounced *flip* is a variation of *flick*, which however seems connected with *fly, flee, flit*, meaning to fly off. Key to meaning of *flick, fleck* and *flake* is that of striking or cutting off the surface of a thing; in *flick* (as to flick off a fly) something little or light from the surface, while *flake* is a thin scale of surface. *Flay* is therefore connected, perhaps *flitch*."

25 In *La fiera letteraria* [Rome], 3, xxviii–xxix (10 Oct. 1948), 1. In the same year it appeared in Montale's *Quaderno di traduzioni* (Milan, Mondadori, 1948), p. 53. It is now most conveniently located in E. Montale, *L'opera in versi*, p. 723.

26 In his "Nota su una traduzione da Hopkins", *Letteratura* [Florence], 4, ii (Apr–June 1940), iii–17. Within three years of the appearance of Montale's *Quaderno di traduzioni* another creative writer, Beppe Fenoglio, was engaged in translating Hopkins's poems. He translated eight of them between October and November 1951, but the translations were not published in his lifetime. One of his translations was a version of "Pied Beauty".

27 B. Croce, "Un gesuita inglese poeta", p. 430.

28 For an extensive treatment of the differences between English and Italian phonology see F. B. Agard and R. J. Di Pietro, *The Sounds of English and Italian* (Chicago, University of Chicago Press, 1965; Midway reprint 1973), especially §2.6 (pp. 10–13).

29 See E. Montale, *L'opera in versi*, p. 173.

30 See E. Montale, *L'opera in versi*, pp. 11, 88.

31 See St Ignatius Loyola, *Spiritual Exercises*, translated by T. Corbishley, SJ (London, Burns and Oates, 1963), pp. 12–13: "The person who gives another the method and outline for meditation or contemplation must faithfully recount the historical subject of such a contemplation or meditation, just running over the headings in a brief and summary explanation; the reason for this is that when the person making the contemplation is given the basic facts of the story and then goes over it and thinks about it for himself, any discovery he makes which sheds light on the story, or brings it home to him more, will give him greater delight and more benefit of soul. Such discoveries may be due to his own reflection or to the divine action, but they are better than if the giver of the exercises had gone into great detail and expounded at length the significance of the story. Nor does the soul's full satisfaction come from wide knowledge so much as from the personal appreciation of and feeling for things."

32 According to Croce, "Un gesuita inglese poeta", pp. 428–29, Hopkins's choice of Duns Scotus as his philosophical influence is symptomatic of his intellectual independence, as the preferred philosopher of the Jesuits is St Thomas Aquinas.

33 For an example see n. 24 above.

34 E. Montale, *L'opera in versi*, p. 138.

35 See E. Montale, *L'opera in versi*, pp. 904–09.

36 E. Montale, *Quaderno genovese*, edited by L. Barile (Milan, Mondadori, 1983), pp. 24–25; Montale's italics.

37 See L. Barile, "Sparviero o procellaria?", pp. 32–47.

38 Croce's version reads "per le cascate di castagne dal colore di carbone appena acceso", which is, as Benjamin would have it, the accurate transmission of inessential content.

39 L. Barile, "Sparviero o procellaria?", p. 18 quotes a phrase from Hopkins's *Selected Poems*, "Chestnuts as bright as coals or spots of vermilion", which she interprets as the symbol of an epiphany in Hopkins's poetry, a lightning-flash which reveals itself as a sign of divine grace, or (as she adds in more Montalian terms) "il punto in cui le cose rivelano il loro segreto".

40 E. Montale, *L'opera in versi*, p. 777. It is not clear whether the poem underwent any revisions between 1923 and 1980.

41 E. Montale, *L'opera in versi*, pp. 81–82.

42 See E. Montale, "Intenzioni", p. 568: "In chiave, terribilmente in chiave, tra quelle aggiunte, c'è 'Iride', nella quale la sfinge delle 'Nuove stanze', che aveva lasciato l'oriente per illuminare i ghiacci e le brume del nord, torna a noi come continuatrice e simbolo dell'eterno sacrificio cristiano. Paga lei per tutti, sconta per tutti." Elsewhere Montale made it clear that this enigmatic figure is Clizia; see his *L'opera in versi*, p. 962.

43 E. Montale, "Confessioni di scrittori (interviste con se stessi)" [1951], in his *Sulla poesia*, pp. 569–74. The quotation comes from p. 572 and the italics are mine.

44 *The Sermons and Devotional Writings of Gerard Manley Hopkins*, edited by C. Devlin, second edition (London, Oxford University Press, 1967), p. 195.

45 First published in *Parallelo* [Rome], 1, i (Spring 1943), 27; collected in E. Montale, *La bufera e altro* (Milan, Mondadori, 1957), p. 23 and in his *L'opera in versi*, p. 201.

46 Letter to Glauco Cambon (16 Oct. 1961), in E. Montale, *Sulla poesia*, pp. 91–92 and his *L'opera in versi*, pp. 945–46; Montale's italics.

47 *Gerard Manley Hopkins*, pp. 180–81.

48 Lines 19–22 (E. Montale, *L'opera in versi*, p. 189). Montale claimed that this was an actual memory of the real woman who became Clizia (*L'opera in versi*, p. 939). There are, however, literary precedents, as will be demonstrated in Chapter 6.

49 E. Montale, *L'opera in versi*, p. 939: "Il buio è tante cose; distanza separazione, neppure certezza che lei fosse ancora viva."

50 For "Iride", first published in May 1945 and dated 1943–45, see E. Montale, *L'opera in versi*, p. 961.

51 The Nestorius in question was the Patriarch of Constantinople in 428 AD who asserted that Christ had distinct divine and human persons. For Montale's version of the Nestorian heresy see his "Intenzioni", p. 568: "il Nestoriano [è] l'uomo che meglio conosce le affinità che legano Dio alle creature incarnate, non già lo sciocco spiritualista o il rigido e astratto monofisita."

52 E. Montale, "Lettera da Albenga" [1963], in his *Auto da fé: cronache in due tempi* (Milan, Saggiatore, 1966), pp. 349–50 (p. 350); my italics at the end.

53 See "La speranza di pure rivederti", "Ecco il segno; s'innerva" and "Perché tardi? Nel pino lo scoiattolo", in E. Montale, *L'opera in versi*, pp. 138, 140 and 142.

54 The letter is quoted by L. Barile, "Sparviero o procellaria?", p. 30.

55 E. Montale, *L'opera in versi*, p. 32.

56 See "Vecchi versi" and "La primavera hitleriana" (E. Montale, *L'opera in versi*, pp. 111–12 and 248–49).

57 See for example "In limine" or "Casa sul mare" (E. Montale, *L'opera in versi*, pp. 5, 91–92).

58 The idea of Clizia coming not as a divine messenger but as a divinity is effectively the Williamite heresy, which posits Christ's second coming in feminine form. See U. Carpi, *Il poeta e la politica* (Naples, Liguori, 1978), p. 341 for a discussion of the Williamite heresy in relation to "Elegia di Pico Farnese".

Chapter 5

HERMAN MELVILLE: THE SACRIFICE OF THE INNOCENT

MONTALE, MELVILLE AND *BILLY BUDD*

Herman Melville died in 1891 leaving *Billy Budd* incomplete. Melville's early literary fame had been eclipsed by that stage, and the unfinished manuscript was tidied away by his widow. It was rediscovered and published in 1924.[1] The ballad "Billy in the Darbies" closes the novel. Montale included his translation of "Billy in the Darbies" ("Billy in catene") in the 1948 *Quaderno di traduzioni*. This translation was, however, only a minor revision of a translation already completed in 1941.

Montale had taken steps to ensure that he would be commissioned to translate *Billy Budd* for Vittorini's *Americana*. Pavese, having made the first Italian translation of *Moby Dick*, had expected the commission for *Billy Budd*, and complained to Vittorini when he did not receive it. Vittorini explained his predicament in a letter to Pavese: "Caro Pavese, mi dispiace che ti sia seccato di Melville. Ma è Montale che lo fa, e ha insistito tanto a farlo [...] e io gli sono troppo amico."[2] Montale's *Billy Budd, gabbiere di parrocchetto* was duly first published in Vittorini's *Americana* anthology (1941). It was then published separately in 1942 by Bompiani with a brief translator's introduction. Montale was proud of his translation. He wrote in 1949, on the subject of the Italian war-time translations: "Avevano [...] un carattere di spiccata serietà artistica, degna di una tradizione di traduttori e rifacitori genialmente infedeli che va dall'Apuleio del Firenzuola, all'Omero del Monti, al *Viaggio sentimentale* del Foscolo, fino, *si parva licet...*, al *Billy Budd* del sottoscritto e al *Piccolo campo* di Vittorini."[3]

Montale's insistence on having the commission to translate *Billy Budd* suggests that he discerned some degree of affinity between the novel and his own poetry. There are indeed several symbolic, thematic and metaphysical affinities between the work of Melville and Montale. As was also the case with Hopkins, both Melville and Montale bring the sea into their work, not merely as a physical reality but as a symbolic presence. In the sea, time and space are relative, marginalized. Captain Ahab (in *Moby Dick*), by the light of his pewter lamp, attempts to encounter Moby Dick with the help of his sea charts, and in his presentation of the scene Melville hints at the symbolism of the chart:

> While thus employed, the heavy pewter lamp suspended in chains over his head, continually rocked with the motion of the ship, and for ever threw shifting gleams and shadows of lines upon his wrinkled brow, till it almost seemed that while he himself was marking out lines and courses on the wrinkled charts, some invisible pencil was also tracing lines and courses upon the deeply marked chart of his forehead.[4]

The chart is as much a cipher of Ahab's fate as of the sea. Fate itself is a preoccupation in the work of both writers. The following are Ishmael's musings on the mat-maker:

> I was the attendant or page of Queequeg, while busy at the mat. As I kept passing and repassing the filling or woof of marline between the long yarns of the warps, using my own hand for the shuttle, and as Queequeg, standing sideways, ever and anon slid his heavy oaken sword between the threads, and idly looking off upon the water, carelessly and unthinkingly drove home every yarn; I say so strange a dreaminess did there then reign all over the ship and all over the sea, only broken by the intermitting dull sound of the sword, that it seemed as if this were the Loom of Time, and I myself were a shuttle mechanically weaving and weaving away at the Fates. There lay the fixed threads of the warp subject to but one single, ever returning, unchanging vibration, and that vibration merely enough to admit of the crosswise interblending of the other threads with its own. This warp seemed necessity; and here, thought I, with my own hand I ply my own shuttle and weave my own destiny into these unalterable threads. Meantime, Queequeg's impulsive, indifferent sword, sometimes hitting the woof slantingly, or crookedly, or strongly, or weakly, as the case might be; and by this difference in the

> concluding blow producing a corresponding contrast in the final aspect of the completed fabric; this savage's sword, thought I, which thus finally shapes and fashions both warp and woof; this easy indifferent sword must be chance—ay, chance, free will, and necessity—nowise incompatible—all interweavingly working together. The straight warp of necessity, not to be swerved from its ultimate course—its every alternating vibration, indeed, only tending to that; free will still free to ply her shuttle between given threads; and chance, though restrained in its play within the right lines of necessity, and sideways in its motions directed by free will, though thus prescribed to by both, chance by turns rules either, and has the last featuring blow at events.[5]

Ahab's chart and Ishmael's mat do not belong to Montale's poetic memory; nonetheless, the burden of random fate is one as keenly felt in Montale's work as in Melville's.

Montale encountered Melville's work cumulatively, reading *Billy Budd* as a development out of the earlier books:

> In lui [Melville] quel senso oscuro e condannato che il puritano Hawthorne moderò e contenne in una onorevole carriera letteraria non priva di compromessi, si solleva a soffi biblici, esplode talora con violenza manichea; ed è quel sentimento che dopo aver serpeggiato nei suoi libri piú inquieti, da *Redburn* fino a *Pierre*, ed essersi disteso nel grande affresco di *Moby Dick*, trova infine in *Billy Budd* una sintesi breve ma perfettissima. Da questo punto di vista *Billy Budd*, cosí sostenuto e illuminato dai libri che lo precedono, rappresenta il fiore e il coronamento dell'opera melvilliana.[6]

Montale felt closer to Melville than to Hawthorne or Poe because of the tension between Melville's Biblical allusions and his Manichean impulse. According to Montale's reading of the text, *Billy Budd* is "tutto insieme epopea e racconto d'avventura, dialogo platonico, saggio critico intinto di spiriti rivoluzionari e dramma: dramma sacro che rappresenta il sacrificio per eccellenza, il sacrificio cristiano della Croce".[7]

Billy Budd does have each of the characteristics here attributed to it by Montale. It is the story of Billy the innocent and attractive foretopman, who sails on *The Rights of Man* and whose innocence and beauty arouse the vengeance of Claggart. Claggart sets out to destroy Billy and succeeds in framing him on a charge of incitement to mutiny. Billy and Claggart are summoned to the Captain's cabin for a face-to-face confrontation. Billy Budd strikes Claggart, who falls dead. Billy is now guilty of the murder of a superior. The captain, De Vere, the only witness to the event, while he sides with Billy, decides that Billy must be sacrificed in order that De Vere shall be able to maintain his own authority. So Billy is condemned to execution. The novel closes with the poem "Billy in the Darbies".

Reading Billy Budd's execution in Messianic terms calls for some explanation. In the 1940s Montale was obsessed by the notion of sacrifice. Clizia's fate in his poetry has three interesting cognates in Montale's reading of English texts. Billy Budd, Hopkins's tall nun in "The Wreck of the Deutschland" and W. H. Hudson's Rima are all innocent sacrificial victims. Montale described Melville's treatment of this sacrificial theme as "un grande argomento in mano di un forte poeta che in esso riassume e incentra tutti i fantasmi, tutti gl'idoli e i segreti di un'intera vita".[8] That is the key to Montale's reading of Melville. He commented on Melville's treatment of the sacrifice theme towards the end of the introduction to *Billy Budd*: "In *Billy Budd* la vita che esprime con pari violenza il bene e il male, il giusto e l'ingiusto, tenta, ma non riesce, di chiarire a se stessa il suo mistero."[9] The essence of the sacrificial theme *secundum* Melville is distilled in "Billy in the Darbies", and Montale's decision to include his translation of the ballad in the 1948 *Quaderno di traduzioni* indicates his abiding interest in the fate of Billy Budd. Just why that should be so will become apparent in the following pages.[10]

The Texts

"Billy in the Darbies"

Melville's "Billy in the Darbies", as it appears in the *Quaderno di traduzioni*, reads thus:

> Good of the Chaplain to enter Lone Bay
> and down on his marrowbones here and pray
> for the likes just o' me, Billy Budd. —But, look:
> through the port comes the moonshine astray!
> It tips the guard's cutlass and silvers this nook;
> but 'twill die in the dawning of Billy's last day.
> A jewel-block they'll make of me tomorrow,

pendant pearl from the yard-arm-end
like the eardrop I gave to Bristol Molly—
oh, 'tis me, not the sentence they'll suspend.
Ay, ay, all is up; and I must up too,
early in the morning, aloft from alow.
On an empty stomach now never it would do.
They'll give me a nibble—bit o' biscuit ere I go.
Sure, a messmate will reach me the last parting cup;
but, turning heads away from the hoist and the belay,
heaven knows who will have the running of me up!
No pipe to those halyards. —But aren't it all sham?
A blur's in my eyes; it is dreaming that I am.
A hatchet to my panzer? all adrift to go?
The drum roll to grog, and Billy never know?
But Donald he has promised to stand by the plank;
so I'll shake a friendly hand ere I sink.
But—no! It is dead then I'll be, come to think.
I remember Taff the Welshman when he sank.
And his cheek it was like the budding pink.
But me; they'll lash in hammock, drop me deep
fathoms down, fathoms down, how I'll dream fast asleep.
I feel it stealing now. Sentry, are you there?
Just ease these darbies at the wrist,
and roll me over fair.
I am sleepy, and the oozy weeds about me twist.[11]

"Billy in the Darbies" is a ballad of thirty-two lines. Melville's metrical structure works as a type of sprung rhythm based on iambic pentameter. The metre establishes a sobbing quality in Billy's lament, for example:

> Ay, ay, all is up; and I must up too,
> early in the morning, aloft from alow.
> On an empty stomach now never it would do.
> They'll give me a nibble—bit o' biscuit ere I go.
> (lines 11–14)

Melville's end-rhymes do not conform to any specific pattern, but only two end-words are without corresponding end-rhymes. Melville is also a master of alliteration, as in "*B*ut 'twill *d*ie in the *d*awning of *B*illy's last *d*ay" (line 6). There is play on "Budd/But" in line 3, and this introduces the rhetorical function of "but" in the poem. "But" appears seven times, and the repetition serves to indicate Billy's mental anguish. The world is going to carry on *but* it will carry on without him; the moonlight illuminates his last night *but* it will die in the dawn. The rhetorical power and the anguish of this sevenfold "but" is such that it casts a nuance of inevitability over the poem. Billy has to die because of circumstances arising out of Claggart's malfeasance; his fate is sealed and his time is almost come. Against this fatalism are poised two Biblical allusions. The first one, in "Sure, a messmate will reach me the last parting cup" (line 15), is a relatively obvious allusion to the Passion. The second one, in "I am sleepy, and the oozy weeds about me twist" (line 32), is a less obvious allusion to Jonah 2. 5: "The waters compassed me about, even to the soul: the deep closed me round about, the weeds were wrapped about my head." Thus "Billy in the Darbies" seems to be a microcosm of Montale's reading of the novel, an unresolved tension between morbid resignation and Biblical allusion.

"Billy in catene"

The following is Montale's translation of "Billy in the Darbies":

Billy in catene

Il cappellano è entrato nella cella,
s'è curvato sull'ossa midollose e ha pregato
per quelli come me. Ma guarda, Billy,
il chiar di luna viene ed inargenta
la daga del guardiano e il mio cantuccio.
(Morrà lui pure all'ultima alba di Billy Budd).
Un gioiello faran di me domani,
un bel pendant di perle e dal pennone,
come il par d'orecchini che un giorno detti a Molly.
Sospenderanno me, non la sentenza!
Ahi ahi, ché tutto è pronto e domattina
presto risalirò fra le mie gabbie.
E sarà questa volta con lo stomaco vuoto
o forse mi daranno
da rosicchiare un pezzo di galletta
ed un compagno m'offrirà un grappino.
E Dio sa chi dovrà tirarmi in alto
torcendo il capo dalla cerimonia!
Neppure avrà bisogno di fischietto...

Ma forse è una finzione,
un brutto sogno fatto ad occhi aperti.
Me n'andrò alla deriva, suonerà
la chiamata pel grog senza di me?
Donald m'ha garantito d'essere sulla plancia.
Gli stringerò la mano prima di andare giú.
(Ma ora mi ricordo che allora sarò morto).
Mi sovviene il gallese Taff quando dette il tuffo.
La sua guancia era come il garofano in fiore.
Ed io... io sarò avvolto in un'amaca, e giú,
sempre piú giú, in un fondo sonno sarò calato.
E il sonno viene. Sei tu sentinella?
Allenta un poco le manette, ch'io
mi sporga appena.
Ho sonno e l'alghe viscide faranno
presto ad attorcigliarsi su di me.[12]

In keeping with his usual translation practice, Montale retained the basic form of Melville's ballad in his translation, though the translation runs to thirty-five lines instead of thirty-two. The metre of Montale's text is essentially hendecasyllabic, though hendecasyllables are periodically replaced by hypermetric lines. Montale used this metrical variation as an expressive device. The opening lines illustrate the point:

Il cappellano è entrato nella cella,
s'è curvato sull'ossa midollose e ha pregato
per quelli come me. Ma guarda, Billy,
il chiar di luna viene ed inargenta
la daga del guardiano e il mio cantuccio.

The opening perfect hendecasyllable is followed by a hypermetric line which runs on to a caesura in line 3. The extra syllables in the second line linger in Billy's words as the image of the chaplain praying for Billy lingers in the condemned youth's mind. The next hypermetric line ("Morrà lui pure all'ultima alba di Billy Budd", line 6) is a further reflection by Billy on his mortality. In lines 9, 13 and 24 Montale combined two *settenari* to produce fourteen-syllable lines. Of the short lines two (lines 14 and 20) are *settenari* while one (line 33) is a five-syllable line.[13] Another hypermetric line in which Billy manifests his awareness of imminent death (line 26) begins a short section of text characterized metrically by its unsteadiness, in which Billy recalls the image of the Welshman Taff, whose complexion was as of a budding carnation and conjures up the image of Billy's own death.

Montale dispensed with rhyme as a principle of organization in his translation. In line 3 Melville had played on the /d/ and /t/ sounds of "Budd" and "But": "for the likes just o' me, Billy Budd. —But look". Montale dropped "Billy Budd" from his line but preserved an echo of Melville's word-play in the juxtaposition of "me" and "ma": "per quelli come me. Ma guarda, Billy". Montale's text also generates word-play of its own. Some of this emerges incidentally from literal translation (for instance, "galletta"/ "gallese", lines 15, 27), while other instances of word-play are deliberate Montalian strategy (such as "Taff"/"tuffo", line 27).

Montale avoided Melville's recurrent use of "but": he used "ma" only three times (lines 3, 20 and 26). Avoiding "ma" in line 6, Montale used "pure" instead, thus catching nuances which approximate to both "but" and "also" in English.

The narration of the ballad in Montale's translation is more spare than it is in Melville's poem. Montale removed the judgement of value ("Good of the Chaplain [...]"), the description ("Lone Bay"), the colloquial expression ("for the likes just o' me") and Billy's name from the first sentence, and the result is a prose sentence divided between three lines:

> Il cappellano è entrato nella cella,
> s'è curvato sull'ossa midollose e ha pregato
> per quelli come me.

Melville's two infinitives ("to enter" and "pray") became three past participles ("entrato", "curvato" and "pregato"), which interlock in a chain of assonance. Montale's tendency to exclude the inessential continued in the removal of "through the port" and the adverb "astray" from line 4 and the present-tensed verb "to tip" from the next line. Melville's second sentence is dislocated through hyperbaton. Montale's second sentence is again prose:

> Ma guarda, Billy,
> il chiar di luna viene ed inargenta
> la daga del guardiano e il mio cantuccio.

Whereas Melville's third sentence tended towards the verbose ("but 'twill die in the dawning of Billy's last day"), Montale's is compact and presented in parenthesis: "(Morrà lui pure all'ultima alba di Billy Budd)." In spite of the relative verbosity and compactness of the two lines, Montale's is no shorter than Melville's in terms of scansion—a point which serves to emphasize again the relative speeds of the two languages. Montale's fourth sentence hugs close to the hyperbaton of Melville's sentence. The translation could not be closer to a word-for-word literal version were it not for the two modifications which Montale introduced, "il par d'orecchini" for "the eardrop" and the removal of the locative adjective "Bristol". Montale's fifth sentence features more of his editorial procedure: Melville's apostrophe and colloquial or paronomastic nuances ("oh, 'tis me, not the sentence they'll suspend") became prose ("Sospenderanno me, non la sentenza!"), though Montale did preserve the pun. The nautical terminology of Melville's fifth sentence ("aloft" and "alow") became "fra le mie gabbie" in Montale's version.[14] Montale completely excised the colloquial "now never it would do" from the sixth sentence, and his thirteenth line (a *settenario doppio*) is slightly dislocated to allow for assonance with emphasis on "volta" and "vuoto". Melville's metonymic Biblical nuance at the end of his next sentence ("the last parting cup" proffered from below) is more mundane in Montale's version: "un grappino"—in this case Montale reduces the metonymy to a primary object. He inverted the two lines of the seventh sentence, producing two hendecasyllables (lines 17–18) with a recurrent /a/ vowel sound: "s*a*" → "dovr*à*" → "tir*a*rmi" → "*a*lto" → "c*a*po" → "d*a*lla" → "cerimon*ia*". In the next sentence Montale made no attempt to translate the nautical term "halyard", and his syntax differs from Melville's in that Melville's sentence ("No pipe to those halyards") does not contain a verb whereas Montale's does ("Neppure avrà bisogno di fischietto...").

There is a series of elliptical sentences without verbs in this section of Melville's poem, which effectively begins the second part, in which Billy's fatigue begins to overcome his powers of reasoning. Montale avoided the ellipsis and translated in prose sentences—compare Melville's lines:

No pipe to those halyards. —But aren't it all sham?
A blur's in my eyes; it is dreaming that I am.
A hatchet to my panzer? all adrift to go?
The drum roll to grog, and Billy never know?

with Montale's:

Neppure avrà bisogno di fischietto...
Ma forse è una finzione,
un brutto sogno fatto ad occhi aperti.
Me n'andrò alla deriva, suonerà
la chiamata pel grog senza di me?

Montale even translated the object "drum roll" by a reference to its function rather than making the literal translation and leaving the interpretation of a naval drum-roll to the reader. He here achieved the clarity of prose in four hendecasyllables and a *settenario*, and in so doing used only one word ("pel") which belongs more properly to poetry than to prose. Melville's "so I'll shake a friendly hand" (line 23) loses the adjective in Montale's translation ("Gli stringerò la mano", line 25). "But—no! It is dead then I'll be, come to think" (line 24) gave Montale an opportunity to indulge his taste for paradox: in the translation Billy remembers the future—"(Ma ora mi ricordo che allora sarò morto)" (line 26). Having used the verb *ricordarsi* here for "come to think", Montale avoided the same verb in the next sentence ("I remember Taff [...]") and instead used the more poetic alternative *sovvenire*. Melville's personification of sleep and its stealthy advance ("I feel it stealing now", line 29) in Montale's translation become almost clinical prose ("E il sonno viene", line 31). In Melville's poem Billy is in the "darbies" in both the title and line 30. Montale instead has Billy in "catene" ("chains") in the title and "manette" ("handcuffs" or "bonds") in line 32. "Catene" and "manette" are near-synonyms; the point is that Montale decided against using the same word twice.

To what extent does this translation help Montale to achieve "un'altra dimensione" in Italian?[15] "Billy in the Darbies" is a ballad, and more pertinently it is a ballad on the boundary between lyric and narrative poetry. Montale wrote in 1957:

> Il verso è oggi tollerabile solo come espressione di sentimenti lirici. Ciò è avvertibile persino nella poesia piú terrestre, la

> dialettale, l'ultima in cui dettero frutto la satira o il racconto verseggiato (dal Porta al Tessa). Si aggiunga che il verso narrativo, in Italia e fuori, tende sempre piú a farsi prosa: la forma esteriore, l'illusione ottica degli "a capo" non è ormai che semplice allusione, nostalgia degli schemi tradizionali.[16]

"Billy in the Darbies" is, in effect, a literary "racconto verseggiato", and Montale, from the evidence of his translation, treated it as such. Thus Melville's dislocated and inverted syntax becomes standard prose syntax in Montale's version. For Montale, rhyme in such a translation would be a matter of illusion, a pretence that narrative is lyric, and so rhyme—even imperfect rhyme—is entirely eschewed. Montale uses the translation, then, to explore the prose possibilities of an Italian poetic form, without completely removing the poetry. The linguistic register of the translation is standard Italian. There are occasional poetic forms, such as *pel* for *per il* and *sovvenire* as an alternative to *ricordarsi*, but Montale's fundamental strategy was to understate the poetry of the ballad in order to concentrate the lyricism into the smallest units of text. The lyric concentration of "Billy in catene" depends for its efficacy on the wider context of Montale's poetry.

Billy Budd's Contexts

"Billy in catene" contains very few Montalian keywords; in other words, there is very little evidence of intertextual connections between "Billy in catene" and Montale's own poems. But Montale did translate the "oozy weeds" of the last line as "l'alghe viscide". *Melmoso* would probably be a closer equivalent to "oozy" than *viscido*. *Viscido*, according to the Sansoni-Harrap dictionary, translates "viscid", "slimy", "oily" or "unctuous", and is thus reasonably accurate.[17] The significance of the word *viscido* in the context of Montale's own work is that it is the adjective which qualified Arsenio's roots.[18] The reference back to Arsenio is vital, because Arsenio (1927) and Billy have several important things in common.[19] Arsenio followed a descending itinerary to his destination, which is the sea. Billy Budd will be hanged before his downward journey into the sea takes place. Billy will sink to join the dead, but before the downward motion he will rise on the butt of a gibbet, up for one last time to his familiar cages ("gabbie").[20]

Billy's seafaring routine was essentially circular, rising every day to the cages and returning down to deck. Arsenio, too, had a life whose dynamics were quite circular. Arsenio's opportunity for escape from the circle has been described by Philip Horne as occasioned by a "propitious obstacle": Arsenio's "propitious obstacle", the image used "to suggest the imminent possibility of breaking out and flying free from the cycle of repetitive activity", is the tangle of seaweed ("il viluppo dell'alghe").[21] It is a fascinating coincidence that the tangle of seaweed, which for Horne represents Arsenio's "propitious obstacle", is the image which ushers Billy Budd into the kingdom of the dead.

Given the connection established between Billy Budd and Arsenio, it is worth developing it a little further. What is Arsenio's status in Montale's poetics? Frederic Jones's theory is incisive but may perhaps be expanded upon. Jones has written:

> If then we were to speak in stilnovistic terms of the efficacy of Arsenio, we might argue that he becomes a "cosa nova" in a magico-humanistic sense, just like an earlier "galantuomo" who salvaged the boats of the "estroso fanciullo", Sbarbaro, in "Epigramma", when, driven by chance, they floated dangerously away. From *Le occasioni* onwards, however, this role is completely taken over by women, notably Clizia, and male redeemers wholly disappear.[22]

Arsenio's mission is redemptive, and he is thus a precursor of Clizia; but he is not the last male character to be cast in that role. Billy Budd is the intermediary figure who allows Montale to make the transition from Arsenio to Clizia. In *Le occasioni* Clizia is a *donna angelicata,* but not even in the "Elegia di Pico Farnese" (1938) is she cast as a redeemer, a sacrificial victim. She develops into that role in the course of *La bufera,* that is to say, in poems written after Montale's translation of *Billy Budd*. Billy, like Arsenio, is bound for the sea. Clizia's destiny is different: she burns herself out in the sun.

The sea, in Montale's poetry, is often the home of the dead. The sailor, Billy Budd, first has to undergo a ritual death as the Hanged Man. The Hanged Man motif introduces an interesting textual infidelity which appears between lines 7 and 9 of Montale's translation. Montale translated the following lines:

> A jewel-block they'll make of me tomorrow,
> pendant pearl from the yard-arm-end
> like the eardrop I gave to Bristol Molly

as:

> Un gioiello faran di me domani,
> un bel pendant di perle e dal pennone,
> come il par d'orecchini che un giorno detti a Molly.

Melville's singular "eardrop" became a "par d'orecchini". Why? Melville's eardrop has metaphorical power connoting—as it explicitly does—the hanged man on the gibbet. The image seems to enter into Montale's poetic memory.

The "orecchini" image appeared contemporaneously in the translation of "Billy in the Darbies" and in Montale's own poetry.[23] "Gli orecchini" (1940) is one of his pseudo-Shakespearean sonnets and has attracted considerable attention from scholars.[24] It reads as follows:

> Non serba ombra di voli il nerofumo
> della spera. (E del tuo non è piú traccia.)
> È passata la spugna che i barlumi
> indifesi dal cerchio d'oro scaccia.
> Le tue pietre, i coralli, il forte imperio
> che ti rapisce vi cercavo; fuggo
> l'iddia che non s'incarna, i desiderî
> porto fin che al tuo lampo non si struggono.
> Ronzano èlitre fuori, ronza il folle
> mortorio e sa che due vite non contano.
> Nella cornice tornano le molli
> meduse della sera. La tua impronta
> verrà di giú: dove ai tuoi lobi squallide
> mani, travolte, fermano i coralli.
>
> (*L'opera in versi*, p. 194)

It is a poem with a context of war and death:

> Le èlitre [line 9] sono gli aerei di guerra visti come funesti insetti. Due vite [line 10], la tua e la mia ma anche in generale le sorti dei singoli individui. Meduse [line 12], ombre nello specchio, parti-

> colare realistico. Il personaggio è tanto assente da sembrar quasi morto. Emerge dallo specchio e porta ancora gli orecchini di corallo. Niente alleati verso il nord. Verrà di giú [line 13] dal nero dell'inconoscibile. Il volo [lines 1–2] è il tuo. E di chi potrebbe essere? La spugna [line 3], simbolo di ciò che cancella, ma anche particolare realistico.[25]

The *tu* is almost certainly a woman and probably Clizia (though "identification" is scarcely relevant), and she appears in the mirror ("la spera") at the end of the poem wearing the coral ear-rings. The end of the sonnet, in fact, is rich in marine imagery (such as the jellyfish and the corals), which suggests a connection with "Billy in the Darbies". Montale frequently used objects from the natural world in his poetry but they are rarely used as gratuitous descriptions. As an observer, Montale invested the physical objects with symbolic significance. The relation, of course, between the object and its symbolic nuance is arbitrary, and generally to probe the nature of the connection in the poet's mind would be arrant speculation. On this occasion, however, there is a case for suggesting a literary dimension to the relationship between object and symbolic nuance. Molly's eardrop in "Billy in the Darbies" represents Billy's fate in symbolic terms: the swinging ear-ring is a miniature of Billy on the gallows. Thus the ear-ring acquires a connotation of tragedy, of the slaughter of an innocent. Tragedy is also the context of "Gli orecchini". D'Arco Silvio Avalle has written in relation to the latter poem:

> Il calare della notte [...] ha tutti i segni nefasti della catastrofe imminente; guerre, persecuzioni, stragi, la fine del mondo. In questo momento tragico l'unico bene che si difende è quello della memoria e del destino individuale; esso deriva dalla presenza, invisibile per gli altri, degli oggetti piú legati al paesaggio sentimentale del nostro passato, quei *petits riens* che garantiscono un minimo di sopravvivenza nei momenti solenni della storia, e si concreta, come sempre nella poesia montaliana, in pochi dettagli scelti come a caso.[26]

Avalle's last words are important. Montale chose his little details "come a caso". The significance of the "orecchini" seems to reside in the objects themselves. Clizia (or whoever it may be) appears in the mirror (which is as much sea as it is mirror—hence the jellyfish); she emerges, wearing the ear-rings, from the depths into which Billy has sunk, to continue his redemptive mission in Montale's poetics.[27]

Arsenio, Billy Budd and Clizia

Montale's translation of *Billy Budd* is an important text in its own right. It was the first Italian translation of Melville's last novel, and Montale was proud of that fact. It is also important in the context of the relationship between Montale's translations and his own work. Montale translated the novel at the beginning of the Second World War, but held his version of "Billy in the Darbies" in sufficiently high esteem to include it in the *Quaderno di traduzioni* seven years later.

I have put forward arguments to suggest that Montale's reading of Billy's fate links that fate implicitly with the destiny which Clizia lives out in his poetry during the 1940s. Billy is also a soul brother of Arsenio, Montale's major *persona* of the 1920s. In other words, Billy Budd was interpreted by Montale as belonging to the matrix of the sacrificial theme he announced in the liminal poem of *Ossi di seppia* ("Va, per te l'ho pregato, —ora la sete/mi sarà lieve, meno acre la ruggine...")[28] and developed in terms of altruistic abnegation and even ritual sacrifice, as in the concluding stanza of "Crisalide":

> Il silenzio ci chiude nel suo lembo
> e le labbra non s'aprono per dire
> il patto ch'io vorrei
> stringere col destino: di scontare
> la vostra gioia con la mia condanna.
> È il voto che mi nasce ancora in petto,
> poi finirà ogni moto. Penso allora
> alle tacite offerte che sostengono
> le case dei viventi; al cuore che abdica
> perché rida un fanciullo inconsapevole;
> al taglio netto che recide, al rogo
> morente che s'avviva
> d'un arido paletto, e ferve trepido.[29]

Therefore, rather than seeing Billy Budd as a figure who merely influences Montale's subsequent poetics, I would suggest that it does more justice to Montale as a reader to interpret the Billy Budd phase as a step in a continuum which runs from before Arsenio to after Clizia.

NOTES

1 See H. Melville, *Billy Budd, Sailor and Other Stories*, edited by H. Beaver (Harmondsworth, Penguin, 1967), p. 8. There are substantial variants to Melville's text. The 1924 text, edited by Raymond Weaver and known as the "reading text", was published as *Billy Budd, Foretopman* (London, Constable). Weaver revised his edition in 1928, and it is from the 1928 text that Montale made his translation (hence Montale's title, *Billy Budd, gabbiere di parrocchetto*). A further edition followed in 1948. F. B. Freeman produced a "literal text" (Cambridge, Mass., Harvard University Press, 1948), and this was revised in 1953 by Elizabeth Treeman, whose edition (Cambridge, Mass., Harvard University Press) was published with *Corrigenda*. In 1962 Harrison Hayford and Merton M. Sealts produced two versions of the text, one containing all known variants and styled the "genetic text", the other based on this and known as the "reading text". The latter is now the standard reading text; it carries the title *Billy Budd, Sailor: An Inside Narrative*. For further information, see Beaver's edition, pp. 51–53 ("A Note on the Text") and the note on *Billy Budd* in H. Melville, *Pierre, Israel Potter, The Confidence Man, Tales and Billy Budd*, edited by H. Hayford (Cambridge, Cambridge University Press, 1984).

2 See C. Pavese, *Lettere*, edited by L. Mondo and I. Calvino, 2 vols (Turin, Einaudi, 1966), II, 552.

3 E. Montale, "Buon anno senza perle ai traduttori mal pagati!", *Corriere d'informazione* (28–29 Dec. 1949), 1. *Piccolo campo* was the title of Vittorini's translation of *God's Little Acre* by Erskine Caldwell.

4 See H. Melville, *Moby Dick* (New York, Random House, 1926), p. 197 (Ch. 44).

5 H. Melville, *Moby Dick*, pp. 213–14 (Ch. 47).

6 Montale's introduction to his translation of *Billy Budd* (Milan, Bompiani, "Tascabili" reprint, 1984), p. xxii.

7 Montale's *Billy Budd*, pp. xxii–xxiii.

8 Montale's *Billy Budd*, p. xxiii.

9 Montale's *Billy Budd*, p. xxiii.

10 For a different reading of "Billy in the Darbies" in relation to Montale's poetic development, see R. Orlando, "Il tema del prigioniero in Montale: note sulla traduzione della *Storia di Billy Budd*", *Italianistica*, 21 (1992), 107–14. Orlando sees "Billy in catene" as a possible forerunner of "Il sogno del prigioniero".

11 The only substantial difference between this version and the one established in the "reading text" by Hayford and Sealts occurs in line 20, where their version replaces "panzer" with "hawser".

12 This is the version printed in E. Montale, *L'opera in versi*, edited by G. Contini and R. Bettarini (Turin, Einaudi, 1980), p. 724. The variants between the texts are as follows (Amer = *Americana*, edited by Elio Vittorini; Gor = the 1984 reprint of Montale's *Billy Budd*, with an introduction by Claudio Gorlier): 1 nella cella] nella baia solitaria [Amer]; 3 per quelli] per quelli, [Gor]; 16 un

grappino] un grondino [Amer]; 19 Neppure avrà bisogno] E non avrà bisogno [Amer and Gor]; 23 la chiamata] l'adunata [Amer]; 28 il garofano] un garofano [Amer and Gor]; 32–33 Allenta un poco le manette, ch'io / mi sporga appena] Allenta un poco le manette e poi / fa ch'io m'affacci un poco alle murate [Amer and Gor].

13 This five-syllable line is a revision of a hendecasyllable for the 1948 *Quaderno di traduzioni*. See the variants in n. 12 above. In the *Americana* variant the first line was hypermetric.

14 There is a element of cultural equivalence here. *Gabbia* is a noun which has nautical connotations of its own ("crow's nest" or "foretop").

15 See "Intenzioni (intervista immaginaria)" [1946], in E. Montale, *Sulla poesia*, edited by G. Zampa (Milan, Mondadori, 1976), pp. 561–69: "Ho continuato la mia lotta per scavare un'altra dimensione nel nostro pesante linguaggio polisillabico, che mi pareva rifiutarsi a un'esperienza come la mia" (p. 567).

16 E. Montale, "Parliamo della poesia" [1957], in his *Sulla poesia*, pp. 126–28 (p. 126).

17 See *Standard Italian and English Dictionary*, edited by V. Macchi et al. (Florence–Rome, Sansoni; London, Harrap, 1970).

18 See "Arsenio", in E. Montale, *L'opera in versi*, p. 82: "Cosí sperso tra i vimini e le stuoie / grondanti, giunco tu che le radici / con sé trascina, viscide, non mai / svelte [...]."

19 It is conceivable that Montale read *Billy Budd* before he wrote "Arsenio", but it is very unlikely.

20 Up-and-down motion is familiar in Montale's poems, sometimes in relation to water, e.g. in the following *osso breve*: "Cigola la carrucola del pozzo, / l'acqua sale alla luce e vi si fonde. / Trema un ricordo nel ricolmo secchio, / nel puro cerchio un'immagine ride. / Accosto il volto a evanescenti labbri: / si deforma il passato, si fa vecchio, / appartiene ad un altro... / Ah che già stride / la ruota, ti ridona all'atro fondo, / visione, una distanza ci divide" (E. Montale, *L'opera in versi*, p. 45); though not inevitably in relation to water, e.g. in the following *mottetto*: "Il fiore che ripete / dall'orlo del burrato / non scordarti di me, / non ha tinte piú liete né piú chiare / dello spazio gettato tra me e te. / / Un cigolío si sferra, ci discosta, / l'azzurro pervicace non ricompare. / Nell'afa quasi visibile mi riporta all'opposta / tappa, già buia, la funicolare" (*L'opera in versi*, p. 148). The movement has the status of a topos in Montale's own work. The presence of the topos in "Billy in the Darbies" provides a further affined link between the ballad and Montale's poetics.

21 See P. Horne. "Further Notes towards a Reading of Montale's 'Arsenio'", in *Journal of the Association of Teachers of Italian*, 37 (Autumn 1982), 11–18 (p. 16).

22 F. J. Jones, "The Mythological Status of Arsenio in Montale's Ideology", *Journal of the Association of Teachers of Italian*, 38 (Spring 1983), 73–77 (p. 75).

23 The word *orecchini* does not appear anywhere in the poems of *L'opera in versi* other than in the two under discussion. "Gli orecchini" was first published in *Prospettive* [Rome], 4, xi–xii (15 Dec. 1940), 21, and was subsequently published in *Finisterre* and *La bufera e altro*.

24 D'Arco Silvio Avalle dedicated eighty pages to this sonnet in his *Tre saggi su Montale* (Turin, Einaudi, 1970 and 1972), pp. 9–91.

25 Letter from Montale to Silvio Guarnieri, in his *Commento a se stesso*, edited by L. Greco (Parma, Pratiche, 1980), pp. 45–46.

26 D'A. S. Avalle, *Tre saggi su Montale*, p. 84.

27 Montale claims to have thought of the "orecchini" as clasp ear-rings rather than pendants: "Gli orecchini non erano a pendente ma a fermaglio, di un genere che spesso richiede mano estranea" (letter to Avalle, quoted in Avalle's *Tre saggi su Montale*, p. 66n). Montale's "explanations" do, however, have to be treated with great caution: "Va molto bene tutto, ti do l'*imprimatur*. Liuba è una invenzione. Credo che fosse già cittadina inglese e residente a Londra ai tempi delle persecuzioni. Non l'ho vista partire, non so nulla del suo eventuale bagaglio. *Quindi ciò che ho detto a Guarnieri non vale nulla*" (another letter to Avalle, dated 1 Mar. 1972 and quoted on p. 95n of *Tre saggi su Montale*; my italics). Given that Montale wrote the sonnet while translating *Billy Budd*, Bristol Molly's eardrop may well be a significant literary context to "Gli orecchini".

28 "In limine", ll. 17–18 (E. Montale, *L'opera in versi*, p. 5).

29 Lines 71–83 (E. Montale, *L'opera in versi*, p. 87).

Chapter 6

W. H. HUDSON AND THE *AUTO DA FÉ*

HUDSON, MONTALE AND THEMATIC AFFINITY

La vita della foresta, Montale's translation of *Green Mansions* by W. H. Hudson, was finally published by Einaudi in 1987 as the twenty-third volume in a series of "scrittori tradotti da scrittori".[1] Various sections of Montale's manuscript are missing, and the lacunae in the text have been filled with translations by Rossana Bonadei.

Montale translated a large number of novels and short stories by English and American writers during the 1930s and 1940s, but the circumstances of *La vita della foresta* differ from those of the other translations in one important respect: this translation was not commissioned by a publisher. Between 1938 and 1945 Montale worked as a full-time translator, employed on more or less successive commissions from publishing houses in Italy. The commissions did not come automatically, and there was at times an element of competition between translators for specific assignments, owing to the fact that many anti-Fascist writers in Italy had become translators as they could not write for the newspapers.

The absence of a commission for *La vita della foresta* explains the work's status as a posthumous publication. The translation was still incomplete in 1945, when Maria Martone's version was published by Allegranza of Milan as *Verdi dimore*.[2] Another translation, that of Aldo Camerino, followed almost immediately, published by Bompiani.[3] As late as December 1945 Giulio Einaudi was prepared to publish Montale's *La vita della foresta*, but there were still pages to be revised. In any case, Montale appears to have lost interest in having the translation in print.

W. H. Hudson

W. H. Hudson (1841–1922) grew up in Argentina, where his devout English parents had moved after their farming attempts in the United States had failed. He spent much of his childhood in the woods and the countryside observing plants, birds, animals and insects. Later he worked as a field naturalist, receiving irregular commissions from North American and English academics. In 1871 he moved to London, where he worked occasionally for the Zoological Society and became more committed to the idea of a writing career.[4]

In London he felt alienated from industrial society, preferring public parks to literary circles—he missed the comfort of being close to nature. In his melancholy view, man generally was losing contact with nature, so he set about writing letters, articles, pamphlets and books on ecological issues like the protection of the Argentine albatross and the killing of birds for sordid enterprises such as ladies' fashions and the private collection industry.

Green Mansions

Hudson's novel *Green Mansions* was published in London in 1904,[5] and was followed by a new edition of his *The Purple Land that England Lost*, which had not been well received by critics on its first publication in 1885. Both novels were reviewed enthusiastically in the *Saturday Review* and were reprinted regularly over the following quarter-century. Galsworthy, who wrote a preface for the first American edition of *Green Mansions* in 1915, was one of Hudson's friends, as were D. H. Lawrence, Arnold Bennett, Elizabeth Hunt, Walter De La Mare, Thomas Hardy, Joseph Conrad, Ford Madox Ford and Edward Garnett. Virginia Woolf (in an anonymous essay dated 1919) included Hudson together with Conrad and Hardy as writers who had prefigured Modern Fiction.[6] Conrad, referring to *Green Mansions*, wrote in a letter, "The other volum [*sic*] I've been reading with a surprised admiration. It shall be an abiding delight—I see that much. But I don't pretend to have seen *everything* as yet. The sheer interest in themes and bookmanship stands as yet in the way of deeper appreciation. One must read oneself *into* the true quality of the book."[7]

Hudson's critical fortunes were ephemeral. In the 1930s Ford Madox Ford, having intended to include Hudson in an article on great twentieth-century novelists, found he had to plead his case with the editor of *The American Mercury*. His editor was not convinced, and Hudson was condemned to the status of a minor or eccentric novelist.

Hudson's work was almost unknown in Italy before translations of *Green Mansions* appeared in the 1940s. Emilio Cecchi had dismissed him in the 1920s as a "banditore di un ritorno alla Natura, o di qualche altra panacea contro i mali del nostro tempo sconsacrato".[8] Had the war-time translation industry not evolved, Hudson might well have remained unknown to Italian readers and to Montale.

Hudson's novel, set in the uncharted jungles of South America, relates how, as a young man, Abel Guevez de Argensola is forced into exile by revolution in Venezuela. He travels through the jungle in search of gold. Eventually he settles among the Parahuari and frequents a nearby forest, where superstition keeps the "Indians" from hunting the plentiful wildlife. One day he discovers the object of their superstition, Rima, an orphan girl who lives in the forest with her grandfather Nuflo. Her strange language sounds like the song of a bird, and she befriends all the creatures of the forest. The love between Abel and Rima ends in tragedy when Rima returns ahead of him from a visit to her distant birthplace and is burned alive by the Parahuari, who subsequently suffer Abel's bloody retribution.

Critics have found Rima's putative ancestors within English literature, in romantic and evolutionist traditions. Bonadei quotes Fairchild's views on Rima's similarity to Southey's Mooma in *A Tale of Paraguay* and Lady Morgan's Luxima in *The Missionary*. She also notes Rima's kinship with Mowgli and Peter Pan.[9]

As a means of assessing his artistic sympathies and affinities with Montale, the plot is less important than Hudson's philosophy of nature and society, his imagery and his treatment of themes, which Montale appears to have found suggestive.

The Themes

Within the English-reading public, a market for books of naturalist interest had been created by Darwin's work. This was the niche into which Hudson's first essays and books fitted. Between 1888 and the turn of the century, drawing on his experience as a field naturalist in South America, he published *Argentine Ornithology* (1888), *The Naturalist in La Plata* (1892) and *Idle Days in Patagonia* (1893). After years of poverty and relative obscurity, *The Naturalist in La Plata* established his reputation as the finest writer on Nature of his time.

He had grown up reading and re-reading Gilbert White's *Natural History and Antiquities of Selborne*. Once in England, he made a pilgrimage to White's grave at Selborne.[10] White was his first influence as a scientific observer of nature, but Hudson's poetic instinct for nature was nurtured by his experience of bird-song as a youth and by his reading of English poets. Soon after his discovery of Gilbert White he experienced the idea of poetry as a celebration of nature, as he became acquainted with eighteenth-century poets such as James Hurdis (1763–1801), James Thomson (1700–48) and Robert Bloomfield (1766–1823). Celebration here meant minute observation of naturalist detail, couched in mildly archaic language. In "The Seasons" by Thomson, Hudson found a poem where the poet described the mating behaviour of birds as Hudson himself had observed it:

> First, wide around
> With distant Awe; in airy Rings they rove,
> Endeavouring by a thousand Tricks to catch
> The cunning, conscious, half-hearted Glance
> Of their regardless Charmer. Should she seem
> Softening the least Approvance to bestow,
> Their Colours burnish, and by Hope inspir'd
> They brisk advance; then, on a sudden struck,
> Retire disorder'd; then again approach;
> In fond rotation spread the spotted Wing,
> And shiver every feather with desire.[11]

The flight and song of birds continued to hold a poetic fascination for Hudson in his own writing. In *Green Mansions* the singing of birds in the forest is a leitmotiv which announces the approach of Rima.[12]

Minute observation of nature, acute fear of its destruction, romantic melancholy and bitter polemic against the perceived ills of society are thus essential elements of Hudson's view of the world. These elements converge in "The London Sparrow", a poem published in 1883:

> I from such worlds removed to this sad world
> Of London we inhabit now together
> [...] a desert desolate
> of fabrics gaunt and grim and smoke-begrimed
> by goblin misery haunted; scowling towers
> and castles of despair.[13]

Although Hudson wrote poetry, he recognized that he had no great talent for it and directed most of his creative energy into evocative prose.

When they could afford to, Hudson and his wife travelled around the English countryside on bicycles. These wanderings facilitated the research for the second phase of his naturalist career, which began with *Lost British Birds* (1894). He campaigned for legislation against the indiscriminate and widespread slaughter and/or confinement of wild birds in Britain. In his informative writing he hoped to change attitudes and to mobilize public opinion against the vested interests which were destroying the world's wildlife population.

Travelling around England Hudson also turned his eye to society. In "The Poetic Spirit" he wrote:

> The naturalist's mental habit of always trying to get at the reason and hidden significance of things is apt to become a worry when he begins to look closely at his fellow-creatures with the object of finding out what they really are or what the character of this particular human family or herd is compared with that of some other herd which he has studied and thinks he knows.[14]

In the same essay, after describing a rock pipit living beside a colony of herring gulls and still managing to preserve its autonomy despite the close presence of deadly enemies, Hudson goes on to discuss the imaginative faculty of Cornish people. He argues that popular religion has extinguished all spark of imagination in West Cornwall:

> A mightier change was to come later, when Wesley made his descent on the county about the middle of the eighteenth century

> and converted the people wholesale to Methodism. This was in many ways the very worst form of religion for a people of the temper and character of the Cornish, but it suited them exactly at the time it came to them—a dull and stagnant period in their history when the Church was indifferent. They were a highly emotional race and were in a starved condition, hungry for some great excitement, some outlet for their repressed natures, some excuse for a mad outburst, and this gave it them—these wonderful gatherings of miners, fishermen and labourers on the land, in the old disused theatres under the wide open sky, listening to that mysterious supernatural man who had it in his power to call down God to them. That same God who had been growing further removed from their lives and dimmer in their minds for years and for generations, until He was little more than one of the Cornish giants or supernatural monsters believed in by the "old people"—now once more an awful stupendous reality, a gigantic kite hovering on broad black wings over their congregated thousands, his burning, rapacious eyes fixed on them, while from time to time he made his little tentative swoops to set them fluttering and screaming. For they were like terrified fowls and chickens in a farmyard, each expecting and dreading to be made a victim—each knowing that his miserable soul might not be saved until the winged terror fell upon him to grip and bury its crooked lacerating talons in his flesh. And when the stoop and grip came he rolled on the ground bellowing and shrieking to the accompaniment of groans and sobs and piercing cries of those around him. Dreadful as this was, and horrible and loathsome to witness by any person of a decent or reverent mind, it was yet a joy to them and gave them what they wanted—a glorious emotional feast. [...] I rejoice, and all who have any respect and love for humanity will rejoice, that in Cornwall at all events these exhibitions are declining.[15]

Hudson's imagery in this extract from his social criticism is the most engaging part of the scene. The climax of his argument against the Fundamentalist experiment in West Cornwall departs from bird imagery and concerns itself with Nonconformist chapels, which are "a blot and disfigurement to the village and to God's earth".[16] "Children," he wrote, "were sent to these chapels on a Sunday morning while their mothers cooked dinner and their fathers rested. Surrounded by drab interiors and interminable sermons, one can but say that if any imagination, any sense of beauty, any feeling of wonder and reverence at the mystery of life and nature had survived in their young minds it must inevitably perish in such an atmosphere."[17]

More generally, on nature and society, Hudson had written in his first novel, *The Purple Land that England Lost*:

> O civilization, with your million conventions, soul- and body-withering prudishness, vain education for the little ones, going to church in best black clothes, unnatural craving for cleanliness, feverish striving after comforts that bring no comfort to the heart, are you a mistake altogether? [...] We had only to conquer Nature, find out her secrets, make her our obedient slave, then the earth would be Eden, and every man Adam and every woman Eve. We are still bravely marching on, conquering Nature, but how weary and sad we are getting![18]

This "noble savage versus compromised civilization" motif was one of Hudson's articles of faith, one which underlies the themes of *Green Mansions* and one which may have held a certain attraction for Montale during his period of intense metaphysical development in the late 1930s and early 1940s.

Montale's conviction that salvation is only for the élite had been a postulate of his metaphysics since the 1920s.[19] Carpi, in a book on poets and politics, has cited an essay written by Montale in 1945, in support of an argument extending Montale's "religious" élitism to politics.[20] The essay is "L'Italia rinunzia?", in which Montale contrasted the anti-Fascist "intellighenzia vera e propria" with the "folle che si recavano [a Piazza Venezia] in stato di perpetuo delirio coatto".[21] Carpi continues his argument beyond politics to show that Montale's élitism applies not just to religion and politics but to a more general belief in the dignity and superiority of the intellectual, whether in the context of popular religion, Fascism or consumer society—systems in which the individual and especially the intellectual-critic are apt to be marginalized.[22]

Much of Carpi's argument is based on an analysis of "Elegia di Pico Farnese", a poem which he reads as a reorganization of Montale's literary ideology. In terms of ideological content there are in this poem some important points of convergence between the metaphysics of Montale and of Hudson. The "trapasso dei pochi tra orde d'uomini-capre" is an example of the topology of the few versus the many, evoking Montale's description of the crowds in Piazza Venezia in a state of perpetual and convulsive delirium, and the haggard intellectuals.[23] The term "uomini-capre", with its negative connotations of lasciviousness and irrationality, suggests the militant irrationality and the fear of chaos which Montale opposed in the complex structure of his poem and in his 1945 article. Triumphalism and militant irrationality were also the basis of Hudson's opposition to the Methodism of Cornwall, and the conclusion of his description reads like a calque of Montale's poem: "Dreadful as this was, and horrible and loathsome to witness by any person of a decent or reverent mind, it was yet a joy to them and gave them what they wanted—a glorious feast."

Both Montale and Hudson were witnesses to a kind of Dionysian religious festivity, and both based their division between the hordes and the élite on a broadly religious distinction.

The "Elegia di Pico Farnese" presents two different types of experience. Firstly, there are the pilgrims with whom the poem opens, singing their litanies in procession. The three stanzas of pilgrim chanting punctuate the poem. The second type of experience is of a subtler kind. The "Elegia" is one of the few poems for which Montale left a record of his intentions and motivations. In a letter to Bobi Bazlen he wrote of the second intercalated stanza:

> Nelle grotte (delle isole di cui sopra) c'è il segno del Pesce [lines 28–29] che credo uno dei piú antichi segni cristiani; comunque si esprime il dubbio che la simbologia cristiana (la foresta verde) dimezzi la vita e che Cristo abbia bisogno di essere continuato forse malgré lui. Se puoi, anche mutando tutto, fai una canzonetta sincretistica dove dio e phallus appaiono mescolati equivocamente; è il senso di tutto il meridionale. Senso però che il Poeta (sic) non approva che con molte riserve [lines 27–31].[24]

Montale's intention in the poem was thus to make a distinction between what he held to be the equivocal processions and pageantry of religious observance, which had their roots in the Middle Ages, and the type of religious experience of which Clizia is a messenger. Carpi has noted a subtle contrast in terms of light: the Fish twinkles or glimmers ("luccica il Pesce", lines 28–29) but the sunflower shines ("il seme del girasole / se brilla", lines 49–50).[25] The Fish and the sunflower represent respectively the equivocal god/phallus symbol and Clizia.

Montale is more forthright earlier in the poem. He establishes the distinction in the stanza which follows the description of the pilgrims:

> Oh la pigra illusione. Perché attardarsi qui
> a questo amore di donne barbute, a un vano farnetico
> che il ferraio picano quando batte l'incudine
> curvo sul calor bianco da sé scaccia? Ben altro
> è l'Amore e fra gli alberi balena col tuo cruccio
> e la frangia d'ali, messaggera accigliata!
> (lines 33–38)

In the first draft the "ferraio picano" (line 35) was "l'alacre ferraio", but Montale suppressed the adjective of value in favour of the adjective of place to suit the poem's internal logic. The expert craftsman, the white heat of the metal and the ring of the anvil were all juxtaposed to the "amore di donne barbute" and the "orde degli uomini-capre", as positive to negative.

"Elegia di Pico Farnese" engaged two aspects of passion. On the one hand there is passion approaching frenzy represented by the "orde d'uomini-capre" and the "vano farnetico" which is the "amore di donne barbute". The emphasis in the first half of the poem is on this aspect of passion. This first half seems to be descriptive, but a closer analysis reveals nuances which are part of Montale's strategy. The dawn scene is not joyful ("Nell'alba triste", line 5). A tawny dog ("un cane lionato", line 7) enters the "umido orto / tra i frutti caduti all'ombra del melangolo". The "frutti caduti" have a talismanic power whose significance becomes explicit after the second intercalated stanza. The talismans accumulate between the first two intercalated stanzas, in the "occhi confidenti / dei maiali" and the "archivolti tinti di verderame". The talismans suggest the sleep of Reason and the triumph of neglect. The windfalls have not been collected and are left for a dog's sport, the archivolts have been neglected and are tainted with verdigris, and during Reason's slumber the pigs keep watch. Montale's verdict is copper-fastened in the terse apostrophe, "Oh la pigra illusione." On the other hand, there is a more ascetic view of passion, signalled by Montale's subtle judgement on the sleep of Reason.

Read in a political context the object of criticism is clearly Fascism.[26] According to this thematic reading, Fascism was not so much a dream in Reason's presence as a nightmare in Reason's slumber. But the poem had more than a political focus. Its metaphysical context is the almost Nietzschean conflict between the cults of Dionysus and Orpheus. The hordes of goat-men are representatives of Dionysus, creatures whose minds entertain no doubts.

These sentiments were much in sympathy with Hudson's as he expressed them in various essays and books. Montale may or may not have known Hudson's essay "The Poetic Spirit", which is contained in *The Land's End* (it is an interesting aside that Montale's *Finisterre*, published in 1943 as an appendix to *Le occasioni*, was made up of poems written between 1940 and 1942, during which period he decided to translate *Green Mansions*). It is beyond question, however, that Montale would have been attracted to Hudson's distaste for populism. This distaste found expression, *inter alia*, in the opening pages of *Green Mansions*. The anonymous frame-narrator sounded a clear division in the Prologue between "the things which excited other men—politics, sport and the price of crystals" and Mr Abel's world, "the world of nature and the spirit".[27] This is the novel's fundamental premiss. The story of Abel, an incarnation of the Wandering Jew,[28] is a subjective tale of the emotions and the imagination. In Hudson's work Montale would also have found a poetic fascination with birds, which in *Green Mansions* transforms itself into the symbol of the bird-woman.

The bird theme, common to the two writers, in both entails obsessive symbolism, probably growing out of childhood experiences. Two of Montale's "unofficial" texts are valuable for an insight into the genesis of the bird theme in his work.

His "Lettera levantina" is a long early poem.[29] Its subject is hunting, and it involves various themes which appear again in his later poetry and prose. The dominant theme, the evocation of childhood experiences and pursuits, was treated with a mawkishness uncharacteristic of Montale's work, and this is the most probable reason for its omission from *Ossi di seppia*. It is however a text which has exegetical value in relation to his poetry in general.

In the fifth stanza the first-person narrator relates how as an adolescent in the Levant he climbed crags before dawn to join his tanned companions. Together, stealthily, they prepared their arquebuses. He waited in a bush for the arrival of a flock of wild doves from the valley below. Slowly he took aim at the leader of the flock and let fly:

> Lentamente miravo il capo-fila
> grigio sopravanzante, indi premevo
> lo scatto; era la bòtta nell'azzurro
> sécca come di vetro che s'infrange.

Il colpito scartava, dava all'aria
qualche ciuffo di piume, e scompariva
come un pezzo di carta in mezzo al vento.
D'attorno un turbinare d'ali pazze
e il súbito rifarsi del silenzio.[30]

This picture of Montale the adolescent hunter is not one that is familiar from his "official" poetry, indeed it is an apparent inversion of his status as a poet for whom naturalist observation is almost a *sine qua non* for the making of poetry.

That is another interesting parallel with W. H. Hudson. Hudson, in his childhood, along with his elder and stronger brother Edwin, provided meals for his family by shooting birds. Hudson wrote in *Far Away and Long Ago*: "We could shoot for the table all the year round, for no sooner was it the ducks' pairing and breeding season than another bird-population from their breeding ground in the arctic and sub-arctic regions came on the scene—plover, sandpiper, godwit, curlew, whimbrel—a host of northern species that made the summer-dried pampas their winter abode."[31] Later, working as a field naturalist, Hudson hunted for a living to supply dead birds for natural history museums. It was against the background of this experience that he campaigned in England for the rest of his life for the protection of birds, and made his literary name.

This type of childhood memory was matched in the case of both writers by its antithesis. Power over the destiny of birds is balanced by fear. Luperini, in an appendix to his book *Montale o l'identità negata*, has published a story written by Montale in the early 1940s (that is, while he was translating *Green Mansions*) and not included in *Farfalla di Dinard*. This story, "Una spiaggia in Liguria", written and twice rewritten between 1943 and 1945, also takes a hunting expedition as its subject.[32] The narrator tells how as an adolescent he is accompanied by two friends, Tugnin and Gresta, on a boat journey, trying (unsuccessfully) to hide his seasickness from them. His companions leave him on an island, where he is to wait until dawn with a rifle and other useless baggage from the boat, while they continue fishing. The boy-man narrator considers shooting at birds, even though he has never used such a large weapon before. The birds, however, go to ground. Suddenly he hears a shot, and a moment later he is confronted by a strange creature, part-bear, part-pig, part-cat with human eyes. Terrified, he shoots into the air and the badger disappears.

Hudson, in his autobiographical writing, also recalls nocturnal adventures:

> I used to steal out of the house alone when the moon was at its full to stand, silent and motionless, near some group of large trees, gazing at the dusky green foliage silvered by the beams; and at such times the sense of mystery would grow until a sensation of delight would change to fear, and the fear would increase until it was no longer to be borne, and I would hastily escape to recover the sense of reality and safety indoors, where there was light and company.[33]

Fear, in the cases of both Hudson and Montale, acts as a type of corrective to their attitudes towards nature. Their isolation brings with it reflection on their own actions, and this reflection leads both writers to a greater sense of appreciation of nature's beauty and caducity, because of their feelings of shame and loss. This transformation of hunters into protectors and observers is a common thread in the poetics of Montale and Hudson. There is a large element of guilt and shame in Montale's relationship with nature. In one of the stories in *Farfalla di Dinard*, a chance nocturnal visit by a bat in a hotel room suggests to the male character (Montale himself very thinly disguised) that the bat is his father returned from death to chastise him:

> "Strano" lui continuava tenendo d'occhio il conchiglione. "Tu non sai che il pipistrello è l'unica bestia che io ho ucciso. Mi dicevano ch'era impossibile colpirlo, per via del suo volo irregolare. Basta un pallino a farlo scendere, basta un foro nelle sue ali vischiose. Ma chi ce la fa, chi ce la fa a mettere a segno quel pallino? Spararono tutti, due, tre, quattro persone e nessun pipistrello cadde, anzi ne vennero fuori degli altri, piú numerosi. Pareva ci prendessero in giro. Poi sparai io, quasi a caso; era la prima volta che tiravo un colpo col calibro dodici. E il pipistrello cadde, sbatté a terra come un fazzolettino mencio, si agitò ancora un poco... e morí."
>
> "Ih, ih, ih!"
>
> "Non sono brutti, sai? In fondo sono dei poveri topini con ali di ragnatelo. Si cibano di zanzare, non fanno male a nessuno. E il mio, disgraziatamente non era morto, sussultava... come questo. (Ih, ih!) [...] Questo non è neppure il secondo, è il terzo pipistrello importante della mia vita. Il primo lo sai, il secondo... sei tu o quasi, non ti offendere; il terzo è piovuto qui stasera e noi lo

> accogliamo cosí, scagliandogli contro riviste di carta patinata, pantofole, tappeti; fra poco, se è mezzo morto, sarà finito a colpi di scopa. Non so se sia giusto, non so... no so. [...]"
>
> S'era gettato sul letto, aveva infilato il capo fra le coperte ammassate, fino a raggiungere la testa di lei: "E se fosse" le susurrò all'orecchio "se fosse mio padre ch'è venuto a farmi visita?"
>
> Con un grido lei gettò all'aria coperte e cuscini e si rizzò seduta sul letto. Non pensava quasi piú all'anima nera che ancora palpitava nel conchiglione.
>
> "Sei veramente impazzito" gli disse poi fissandolo in volto. "[...] Tuo padre? Perché? Un pipistrello?"
>
> "Non so" diceva lui quasi piangendo. "È l'unica bestia che ho ucciso, con qualche mosca e qualche formica, s'intende. L'unica, e mio padre ne fu molto addolorato. Io credo ch'*egli* torni qualche volta a trovarmi, in un travestimento o nell'altro. 'Ci ritroveremo in qualche luogo' mi disse il giorno prima di morire. 'Sei troppo fesso per tirare avanti da solo. Non ti preoccupare, troverò il modo, ci penserò io.' Ma io l'ho quasi dimenticato: solo qualche volta vedendo svolacchiare una di queste bestie, alzo il dito, prendo la mira e pàffete! la vedo cadere come uno straccetto. E allora il ricordo di lui..."[34]

It is an interesting coincidence that the theme of shame in relation to nature appears in Montale's stories written in the 1940s, shortly after he had begun to translate Hudson's novel.

There is a more startling coincidence. The theme of the bird-woman with angelic qualities, Abel's fleeting companion and inspiration, cannot but suggest Montale's visiting angel. There is even an extratextual connection with Clizia. Montale's taste for anagrams and other lexical games is well documented. How long would it have taken him to realize that Rima's name was an anagram of Irma, the first name of the real woman who became Clizia in his poetry?[35]

A Romance of the Tropical Forest

The Translation

Towards the end of 1945 (that is, during his work on *Green Mansions*) Montale wrote: "Il linguaggio di un poeta è un linguaggio storicizzato, un rapporto. Vale in quanto si oppone o si differenzia da altri linguaggi. E naturalmente il grande semenzaio d'ogni trovata poetica è nel campo della prosa."[36]

In the case of *La vita della foresta* the process of revision had caused him problems from the start. He had originally suggested to his ghost translator, Lucia Rodocanachi, that they collaborate on the work without contacting a publisher, because a publisher would inevitably set them a deadline. The completed manuscript would eventually be sent to a publisher under Montale's name and the two collaborators would share the fee. The proposed method was that the ghost translator would produce a literal translation leaving a gap of one line after each of her lines for Montale's revisions.[37] After several months of operating that system Montale wrote to Rodocanachi: "Sto correggendo *Green Mansions*, ma è una faccenda lunga. Il mio ritmo è cosí diverso che finisco per rifar tutto, senza colpa tua. Bisognerà studiare un'altra forma di collaborazione; ti manderò poi i fogli corretti perché tu possa venirmi incontro next time."[38] The version which Rodocanachi produced was, as Montale had requested, strictly literal.[39] Grignani gives some examples in her essay "A Play of Iridescent Colour". Compare Hudson's original:

> [...] the beams changing to visible flakes as they fall, dissolving into nothing, to be succeeded by others and yet others?

with Rodocanachi's version:

> [...] e come i raggi posandosi si tramutino in visibili lamine per poi dissolversi nel nulla, succeduti da altri sempre rinnovantesi?

Montale's translation is less literal and less faithful:

> [...] mentre i raggi, posandovisi, si sfioccano, cangiano, marezzano e sfumano nel nulla, mentre nuove luci vengono a sostituirli?

So, in order to accommodate his own rhythm, Montale substantially rewrote the manuscript supplied to him by his ghost translator, and in so doing managed to bring into the text echoes of keywords from his other work, such as *cangiare* from "La bellezza cangiante" and *marezzare* from "Marezzo" (in *Ossi di seppia*).

As if to announce a habit of textual infidelity, Montale chose not to translate Hudson's title literally. Instead he took the subtitle, "A

Romance of the Tropical Forest", and substituted *vita* for "romance", leaving *foresta* (rather than *bosco* or the Dantean *selva*) without an adjective.[40] It is not only here that he eschews the obvious adjective + noun rendering: when "green mansions" appears in the text he translates it by a different adjective + noun combination, "verdeggiante asilo".[41]

This type of variation is an example of a more general tendency away from repetition. Hudson, in the fourteenth paragraph of Chapter 5, made liberal use of the verb "to go" and its antonym "not to go" (he used them four times in all):

> Next morning he asked me if *I was going* to the forest of evil fame, and when I replied in the negative seemed surprised and, very much to *my* surprise, evidently disappointed. He even tried to persuade me *to go,* where before I had been earnestly recommended *not to go,* until, finding that I would not, he took me with him to hunt in the woods. By-and-by he returned to the same subject: he could not understand why I would *not go* to that wood, and asked me if I had begun to grow afraid.[42]

The Angelo Bianco (Camerino) version reads as an object-lesson in literal translation:

> La mattina seguente mi domandò se volessi *andare* nella foresta malfamata, e quando risposi di no parve sorpreso, e con *mia* grande maraviglia, evidentemente deluso. Cercò perfino di persuadermi ad *andare* dove, prima, m'aveva tanto raccomandato di *non andare*; ma poi, vedendo che non volevo, mi prese con sé, per *andare* a caccia nei boschi. Poco dopo ritornò allo stesso argomento; non poteva capire perché non volessi *andare* in quel bosco, e mi domandò se cominciassi ad aver paura.[43]

Camerino in fact uses *andare/non andare* five times in the paragraph, unlike Montale, who entirely avoids the generic verb *andare*:

> La mattina dopo mi chiese se *tornavo* alla foresta malfamata e quando risposi di no, con mia sorpresa, parve sorpreso anch' egli e assai deluso. Tentò persino di *farmi mutare idea,* proprio lui che mi aveva finora raccomandato *il contrario*; finché accorgendosi ch'era inutile insistere, *mi condusse* a caccia con sé. Di tanto in tanto ritornava allo stesso argomento: non poteva capire perché non volevo *tornarci* e mi chiese se cominciavo ad aver paura.[44]

Apart from *chiedere* the only verb which Montale uses more than once in the paragraph is *tornare*, and he enhances his variation procedure by alternating *tornare* with *ritornare*.[45]

The evocative descriptions in *Green Mansions* periodically give way to dialogue and apostrophes. Abel's apostrophe to the bell-bird, which is a succinct statement of a Hudsonian article of faith, is a good example:

> O mystic bell-bird of the heavenly race of the swallow and the dove, the quetzal and the nightingale! When the brutish savage and the brutish white man that slay thee, one for food, the other for the benefit of science, shall have passed away, live still, live to tell thy message to the blameless spiritualized race that shall come after us to possess the earth, not for a thousand years, but for ever; for how much shall thy voice be to our clarified successors when even to my dull, unpurged soul, thou canst speak such high things, and bring it a sense of an impersonal, all-comprising One who is in me and I in him, flesh of his flesh and soul of his soul.[46]

The two sentences of the paragraph, addressed to an interlocutor whose "mystic" and "heavenly" attributes serve to remind the reader that he / she is a mediator between human and divine modes of cognition, may strike the reader as archaic because of the "thou" forms ("thy", "thee", "thou canst"), and perhaps as liturgical because of the final cadence ("flesh of his flesh [...]"). The adjectives create an equilibrium; the repeated "brutish" balances "blameless" and "spiritualized", while "clarified" likewise balances "dull" and "unpurged". The paragraph presents few problems for the Italian translator. The following is Montale's version:

> Oh mistico uccello-campana, che appartieni alla celestiale famiglia della rondine e della colomba, del quetzal e dell'usignuolo! Quando saranno scomparsi il bruto selvaggio e il bruto incivilito che ti uccidono—l'uno per cibarsi di te, l'altro a vantaggio della sua scienza—tu continuerai a vivere e a recare il tuo messaggio alla razza innocente, spirituale, che dopo di noi verrà a popolare la terra, non per un millennio, ma per l'eternità; perché qual senso avrà allora per i nostri piú puri successori la tua voce, se tu sai parlare alla mia greve anima impura in modo cosí alto, e sai portarla a comprendere l'Essere impersonale e onnicomprensivo

> ch'è in me com' io sono in lui, carne della sua carne e anima della sua anima![47]

The main semantic difference in Montale's text is the future ("continuerai") which (mis)translates Hudson's "live still". Montale matches the English "thou" with the Italian "tu", and his adjectives (such as "mistico" for "mystic" and "bruto" for "brutal") remain close to Hudson's where they are of Romance provenance. The Germanic adjective "heavenly" is rendered with an uncontroversial Romance equivalent ("celestiale"). Montale finds an opportunity to improve on the original equilibrium of adjectives by balancing "puri" against "impura" where Hudson has "clarified" and "unpurged". "Quetzal" remains "quetzal" in Italian, being a word with origins in the Aztec language. Montale's only real liberty is a nuance which has no equivalent in the original: he has the white man (a term which he translates as "incivilito") kill the bell-bird for *his* science ("per la sua scienza"), suggesting perhaps that science is not free of human motivations which are essentially inimical to the welfare of the bird. Apart from this point, Montale appears to remain close to Hudson's text in this vocative passage. In order to appreciate some of the subtleties of Montale's procedure, however, it is instructive to compare Montale's translation with Camerino's. Camerino translates as follows:

> O mistico uccello della razza celeste della rondine e della colomba, del quetzal e dell'usignuolo! Quando il bestiale selvaggio e il bestiale uomo bianco che ti uccidono, l'uno per mangiarti, l'altro per servire la scienza, saranno morti, vivi ancora, vivi per dire la tua parola alla razza irreprovevole e spiritualizzata che possiederà la terra dopo di noi, non per mille anni, ma per sempre. E che cosa non significherà la tua voce per i nostri successori, purificati, se anche per il mio animo ottuso, greve parli di cose tanto alte, e porti ad esso il senso di un Essere impersonale, che tutto concede, che è in me, mentre io sono in lui, carne della sua carne e anima dell'anima sua![48]

The first difference to note is Montale's composite noun "uccello-campana", which is unusual Italian. Montale used composites (for instance, in "La bellezza cangiante") as a means of increasing the velocity of the language. Camerino's translation is more pedestrian; but "bell-bird" is no less unusual in English than is "uccello-campana" in Italian, and Montale correctly matches the registers between the languages in his translation. Camerino's "razza celeste" for Hudson's "heavenly race" is an accurate translation because English adjective + noun constructions frequently become noun + adjective constructions in Romance languages. Montale's Italian ("celestiale famiglia") contains an echo of the English language but the apparently loose "famiglia" is motivated by the internal logic of Montale's paragraph. Hudson had used "race" twice in his paragraph but the repetition clearly rang false in Montale's ear, so he used "razza" where Hudson used "race" for the second time ("the blameless, spiritualized race"/"razza innocente, spirituale") and avoided it by using "famiglia" in the first sentence. Camerino's second sentence is awkward because he tries to copy Hudson's English syntax in Italian. Montale's sentence is well poised because of his inversion: he moves the compound verb (future in the past) to the beginning of his sentence, thus allowing for a relative clause in parenthesis. His sentence is the most carefully constructed of the three, Hudson's included. Camerino was unable to sustain the length of the sentence and divided it into two. Montale and Camerino translated into different registers. Camerino's linguistic choices were monochrome and bland (for instance, "per mangiarti" = "for food" and "parola" = "message") whereas Montale's were both literary and precise (as in "per cibarsi" = "for food" and "messaggio" = "message"). Hudson's phrase "to possess the earth", which Camerino translates literally ("possiederà la terra"), is a Biblical echo which Montale chose to avoid ("popolare la terra"). There is also evidence in this paragraph of Montale's tendency to gloss with cultivated synonyms rather than translate literally, for example, "not for a thousand years" = "non per mille anni" (Camerino)/"non per un millennio" (Montale), "for ever" = "per sempre" (Camerino)/"per l'eternità" (Montale) and "an impersonal, all-comprising One" = "un Essere impersonale, che tutto concede" (Camerino)/"l'Essere impersonale e onnicomprensivo" (Montale).

Hudson's expressions were Germanic English. Italian could not follow English in that direction, so Montale took the parallel path of Latin. Camerino's translations are accurate standard Italian but they are of little linguistic or philological interest. There is a Latin echo at the end of Camerino's paragraph, where he inverts Hudson's "his soul" ("anima sua"). Montale avoids this echo and takes the less nuanced though quite literal option, "sua anima".

Descriptions of iridescent colours are quite frequent in *Green Mansions* when Abel is observing Rima. The most sustained and evocative of these descriptions occurs in Chapter 6 at the instant before the serpent bites Abel.[49] The final section of the paragraph has the greatest concentration of Montalian resonances:

> Most variable of all in colour was the hair, this being due to its extreme fineness and glossiness, and to its elasticity, which made it lie fleecy and loose on head, shoulders, and back; a cloud with a brightness on its surface made by the freer outer hairs, a fit setting and crown for a countenance of such rare, changeful loveliness. In the shade, viewed closely, the general colour appeared a slate, deepening in places to purple; but even in the shade the nimbus of free flossy hairs half veiled the darker tints with a downy pallor; and at a distance of a few yards it gave the whole hair a vague, misty appearance. In the sunlight the colour varied more, looking now dark, sometimes intensely black, now of an uncertain hue, with a play of iridescent colour on the loose surface, as we see on the glossed plumage of some birds; and at a short distance, with the sun shining full on her head, it sometimes looked white as a noonday cloud. So changeful was it and ethereal in appearance with its cloud colours, that all other human hair, even of the most beautiful golden shades, pale or red, seemed heavy and dull and dead-looking by comparison. (pp. 81–82)

Montale's version reads:

> Anche piú variabili di colore erano i capelli, per questa sciolta, sottile e lucida morbidezza ond' essi, dalla testa, scendevano vaporosi e leggeri sulle spalle e sulla schiena, simili ad una nube soffusa da un alone luminoso, degna cornice e corona di una forma di cosí rara e mutevole beltà. Guardati con piú attenzione, all'ombra, predominava in quei capelli un color di lavagna che s'incupiva qua e là in una tinta violacea; ma anche all'ombra un nimbo piú libero e fluido velava il fondo piú cupo di uno smorzato pallore di lanugini che dava alla capigliatura, a breve distanza, un aspetto vago e nebuloso. Alla luce del sole il colore era ancora piú cangiante e pareva a volte scuro, altre di un nero intenso, poi di una sfumatura incerta e chiara, sparsa alla superficie di un riflesso di colori iridescenti, come si osserva talora nelle piume di certi uccelli. A poca distanza, e col sole che le splendeva in pieno sul capo, non si vedeva infine che una tinta bianca, di nuvola meridiana. Era cosí mutevole ed eterea coi suoi colori di

> nube, che tutte le altre capigliature umane in confronto, anche le piú belle, le piú sfumate e dorate, apparivano pesanti e opache. (p. 80)

In the second sentence Montale follows his earlier procedure of stressing the word *colore*. This time he translates Hudson's passive structure ("the general colour appeared") by an active one ("predominava in quei capelli un color di lavagna"). The image of Rima's hair again recalls the "nube dei capelli" which describes Clizia's hair in "La bufera".[50] "Beltà" (for "loveliness"), with its literary nuances (for example, Petrarch's "questo nostro caduco e fragil bene,/ch'è vento et ombra, et ha nome beltate": *Canzoniere*, CCCL. 1–2), is an unusual word for Montale to use. It does not appear at all in his own poetry but he did use it to translate Shakespeare's "beauty" in Sonnet 22 ("My glass shall not persuade me"/"Allo specchio ancor giovane"). In fact this section of *La vita della foresta* contains several echoes of the lexis of the *Quaderno di traduzioni*. This is particularly true of the adjectives. "Beltà" is qualified by "rara" and "mutevole". Montale used *raro* occasionally in his poetry but "mutevole" is more interesting. It is used twice in this section of text to translate "changeful". "Mutevole" appears only once in *L'opera in versi*—in the translation of T. S. Eliot's "Animula". (The cognate verb *mutare* is, of course, quite common in Montale's own poetry.)[51] "Cangiante" is a semantic equivalent of "mutevole"; indeed "mutevole beltà" and "bellezza cangiante" are both combinations which would accurately translate Hudson's "changeful loveliness" or Hopkins's "Pied Beauty". It is a significant coincidence, especially when one bears in mind that Montale's interest in both Hudson and Hopkins may be traced to the early 1940s.

Montale's revision of Rodocanachi's literal translation, then, displays characteristics such as the avoidance of repetition and subtle nuances in his choices of linguistic register which are also apparent in his translations of poetry. There is, too, a significant linguistic and thematic convergence between *La vita della foresta* and "La bellezza cangiante", texts which we know Montale worked on around the same time.

Sakes and Personal Identity

Some of the linguistic clues which indicate a level of convergence in relation to Montale's translations of Hudson and Hopkins have already been noted by Grignani.[52] On the subject of composites in English and their Italian equivalents she gives the example of "the crystal and yellow fluid in the gem-like shells" (Chapter 20), which Montale translates as "il fluido cristallino di quei gemmei gusci bianchi, azzurri o biliottati di cocciniglia".[53] What stands out here is "biliottati", a term derived from heraldry, but one which is more important in relation to Montale because of the fact that he also uses it in his translation of "Pied Beauty": as we have seen, Hopkins's line "for rose-moles all in stipple upon trout that swim" in Montale's translation becomes "la striscia roseo-biliottata della/trota in acqua".

The point regarding convergence may be supported by other examples. Abel's meeting with the snake (Chapter 6) presents a number of Montale's keywords, as well as concepts related to the changeful beauty contained in Hopkins's poem. The first linguistic clue is Montale's "un barbaglio di colori brillanti" for "a gleam of brilliant colour". The second is "striscia" for "band". Montale uses "striscia" as a singular noun only once in *L'opera in versi*, and that is in "La bellezza cangiante".[54] "Guizzo" is an important word in Montale's idiolect. In the passage from Chapter 6 he uses the cognate verb: "gli guizzava una lingua irrequieta e luccicante" for "the glittering tongue flickered ceaselessly." "Guizzo" is not used in "La bellezza cangiante" but it is used in relation to another trout in "L'estate" (1935):

> Forse nel guizzo argenteo della trota
> controcorrente
> torni anche tu al mio piede fanciulla morta
> Aretusa.[55]

Montale and Hopkins, as was noted in Chapter 4, were both concerned with particularities as a means of establishing identity. According to Laura Barile, Hopkins's theory of "sakes", which he applied in the sonnet "Henry Purcell", is also to be found in Montale's poetry.[56]

The following is Hopkins's own account of his theory of "sakes":

> *Sake* is a word I find it convenient to use: I did not know when I did so first that it is common in German, in the form *sach*. It is the *sake* of "for the sake of", *forsake, namesake, keepsake*. I mean by it the

> being a thing has outside itself, as a voice by its echo, a face by its reflection, a body by its shadow, a man by his name, fame, or memory, *and also* that it is the thing by virtue of which especially it has this being abroad, and that is something distinctive, marked, specifically or individually speaking, as for a voice and echo clearness; for a reflected image light, brightness; for a shadow-casting body bulk; for a man genius, great achievements, amiability, and so on.[57]

"Sakes" are thus attributes of an object, and although they may be either necessary or contingent, they are perceived by observers as defining characteristics of the object. Hopkins, for example, perceived genius in Henry Purcell and took that genius to be a defining characteristic of Purcell's identity, even though such an attribute was contingent rather than necessary.

It is interesting to note that a quite similar theory of particularities and identity appears in *Green Mansions*. Abel, attempting to describe Rima, says:

> To each one of us, as to every kind of animal, even to small birds and insects, and to every kind of plant, there is given something peculiar—a fragrance, a melody, a special instinct, an art, a knowledge, which no other has. And to Rima has been given this quickness of mind and power to divine distant things; it is hers, just as swiftness and grace and changeful, brilliant colour are the humming-bird's.[58]

Montale translates:

> A ognuno di noi, come ad ogni specie di animale, persino agli uccellini e agli insetti, ed ogni specie di pianta, è concesso alunché di particolare, una fragranza, una melodia, uno speciale istinto, un'arte, una conoscenza, che nessun altro possiede. E a Rima è stata concessa sveltezza di mente e la facoltà di prevedere le cose lontane, cosí come la rapidità e la grazia, e il variegato colore sono proprî del colibrí.[59]

Montale's translation is faithful and accounts for everything in Hudson's text with one small but significant exception: where Hudson wrote "just as swiftness and grace and changeful, brilliant colour", Montale removed "brilliant" as an adjective modifying "colour", thereby placing a certain emphasis on the other adjective, "changeful" ("variegato"). "Variegato", the word which Croce used to translate "dappled" in his version of "Pied Beauty", is one of those words—like "cangiante", "marezzo" and "striscia"—which entail the shimmering of light and colour that is essential to the artistic visions of Montale, Hopkins and Hudson.

The point worth emphasizing here is that the connection between "sakes" and personal identity—which, according to Laura Barile, Montale developed under the influence of Hopkins—is also present in *Green Mansions*. The presence of the idea in Hudson's book to some extent weakens Barile's argument, though it certainly does not disprove it; it is a case of a theory being over-determined by data. In other words, Montale may have developed the idea under the influence of Hopkins or Hudson or both, or he may have developed it quite independently of both of them and felt himself vindicated when he found the same idea in their work. The concept was firmly in place in his metaphysics by 1942, as is demonstrated by the poem in memory of his mother:

> La strada sgombra
> non è una via, solo due mani, un volto,
> *quelle* mani, *quel* volto, il gesto d'una
> vita che non è un'altra ma se stessa,
> solo questo ti pone nell'eliso
> folto d'anime e voci in cui tu vivi;
>
> e la domanda che tu lasci è anch' essa
> un gesto tuo, all'ombra delle croci.[60]

What is significant is that it is an aspect of his own poetics and as such provides an element of affinity between his work and that of the other two writers, who are his *de facto* predecessors. The affinity is interesting in relation to Montale's poetry in the 1940s, but it is probably less significant than the next passage of *Green Mansions* to be quoted.

A Context for "Giorno e notte"?

One of the most evocative descriptive paragraphs of *Green Mansions* occurs in Chapter 7:

> Have you ever observed a humming-bird moving about in an aërial dance among the flowers—a living prismatic gem that changes its colour with every change of position—how in turning

> it catches the sunshine on its burnished neck and gorget plumes—green and gold and flame-coloured, the beams changing to visible flakes as they fall, dissolving into nothing, to be succeeded by others and yet others? In its exquisite form, its changeful splendour, its swift motions and intervals of aërial suspension, it is a creature of such fairy-like loveliness as to mock all description. And have you seen this same fairy-like creature suddenly perch itself on a twig, in the shade, its misty wings and fanlike tail folded, the iridescent glory vanished, looking like some common dull-plumaged little bird sitting listless in a cage? Just so great was the difference in the girl, as I had seen her in the forest and as she now appeared under the smoky roof in the candlelight.[61]

The narrator is here addressing the reader, so Hudson uses "you" rather than "thou". The abundance of gerunds in the English text makes literal translation into Italian quite awkward.

Montale's version reads as follows:

> Avete mai osservato un colibrí che si muove in un'aerea danza tra i fiori, viva gemma prismatica che ogni posizione fa cambiare di colore; l'avete visto volgersi e rifletter la luce del sole col collo lucente e con le piume della gola, verdi e dorate e color della fiamma, mentre i raggi, posandovisi, si sfioccano, cangiano, marezzano e sfumano nel nulla, mentre nuove luci vengono a sostituirli? Per le forme squisite, per il mutevole splendore, per le sue rapide movenze e quelle sue soste di aereo equilibrio, la favolosa bellezza d'un essere simile si beffa di ogni tentativo di descriverla. E avete pure osservato quest' essere d'incantesimo, quando si posa a un tratto su un ramoscello, e piegate l'ali eteree e la coda a ventaglio, spento il suo iridescente splendore, diventa uguale a un comune uccellino dalle piume smorte, pigramente appollaiato in una gabbia? Altrettanto grande era la differenza della fanciulla, da quella che avevo scorto nella foresta, a colei che mi appariva ora sotto il tetto affumicato, alla luce della fiamma.[62]

Montale follows Hudson in adopting "avete" for "have you". In the English text, Abel twice appeals directly to the reader ("Have you ever observed [...]?"; "And have you seen [...]?"); in Montale's text Abel addresses the reader three times ("Avete mai osservato [...]; l'avete visto [...]?"; "E avete pure osservato [...]?"). Montale makes this alteration in order to divide the long gerund-based first sentence into sections which are more easily sustained in Italian. The first gerund in the English text (in the first clause of the first sentence) in Italian becomes "che si muove". This solution causes Montale a problem in the parenthesis which follows the first section (in Montale's text there is no parenthesis): having already used a relative clause structure, he now has to deal with an English relative clause structure ("a living prismatic gem that changes its colour with every change of position"). His solution, which avoids using "change" as both a verb and a noun together, is to make "ogni posizione" the subject instead of "viva gemma".

Montale's textual infidelities in this paragraph become an act of possession. From Hudson's text and from the ghost translation Montale constructs a series of internal assonances peppered with keywords from his own poetic idiolect, which cohere as a type of prose-poem.

It is, however, the "piume della gola" and the "piume smorte" which prove to be the most important keywords of the passage in relation to Montale's poetics in the early 1940s. The bird in flight, darting here and there in the play of light, to which Abel likens Rima seems to have more than an incidental kinship with Montale's Clizia in "Giorno e notte" (1943), a poem written while Montale was working on *La vita della foresta*:

> Anche una piuma che vola può disegnare
> la tua figura, o il raggio che gioca a rimpiattino
> tra i mobili [...].[63]

The "comune uccellino dalle piume smorte" in its cage also seems to find an equivalent in the knife-grinder's parrot of the same poem ("giú sul trespolo s'arruffa il pappagallo/dell'arrotino").

The connection between Hudson's Rima and Montale's Clizia as she appears in "Giorno e notte" is reinforced by a later passage of *Green Mansions*. Old Nuflo tells Abel, as they discuss the long journey to Riolama which lies ahead of them:

> It seems to me the same thing whether you have a revolver or many revolvers and carbines and swords, or no revolver—no weapon at all. And for a very simple reason. While Rima is with us, so long as we are on her business, we are protected from above. The angels, señor, will watch over us by day and night.[64]

Montale translates this description of Rima as a guardian angel quite literally, as was his way with passages of dialogue, thus allowing the emphasis to fall on "giorno e notte" by virtue of its position at the end of the sentence:

> Mi sembra che sia la stessa cosa avere una rivoltella o molte rivoltelle e carabine e sciabole, oppure nessuna rivoltella; nessun' arma. E per una ragione molto semplice. Finché Rima è con noi, e fin tanto che facciamo quel che lei vuole, siamo protetti dall'alto. Gli angeli, señor, ci veglieranno giorno e notte.[65]

Given Montale's statement that prose is the seed-bed for his poetry, there is overwhelming evidence here to demonstrate that his translation of *Green Mansions* is an important intertextual context for "Giorno e notte", one of his finest poems of the 1940s. The evidence suggests that the context is more than a casual one.

Clizia and Rima

La vita della foresta is perhaps most important as a descriptive context for Clizia, the *donna angelicata* who is present in Montale's poetry from the *mottetti* onwards but in *La bufera* makes more vivid appearances.

Abel's first encounter with Rima does not occur in visual terms at all. Her approach is announced by a flock of birds whose sound is "as of a coming tempest of wind mixed with shrill calls and cries" ("un confuso rumore come quello che annunzia una bufera di vento, e ad esso si mescolavano acuti richiami e strida").[66] This acts as a type of orchestral introduction to a concerto, or indeed a Wagnerian leitmotiv. Rima's voice then emerges into the texture as "a voice purified and brightened to something almost angelic" ("una voce umana purificata e schiarita fino a sembrare quasi angelica").[67] The second encounter is also an auditory one.

It is the third encounter which is really significant in the identification of Rima with Clizia. Hudson wrote:

> Her hair was very wonderful; it was loose and abundant, and seemed wavy or curly, falling in a cloud on her shoulders and arms. Dark it appeared, but the precise tint was indeterminable, as was that of her skin, which looked neither brown nor white. Altogether, near to me as she actually was, there was a kind of mistiness in the figure which made it appear somewhat vague and distant, and a greenish grey seemed the prevailing colour.

> This tint I presently attributed to the effect of the sunlight falling on her through the green foliage; for once, for a moment, she raised herself to reach her finger to the bird, and then a gleam of subdued sunlight fell on her hair and arm, and the arm at that moment appeared of a pearly whiteness, and the hair, just where the light touched it, had a strange lustre and a play of iridescent colour.[68]

Montale's translation reads as follows:

> Meravigliosi i capelli, abbondanti e sciolti, ma tutti ondati e inanellati, che le cadevano come una nube sulle spalle e le braccia. Parevano scuri, ma il vero colore n'era inafferrabile, e cosí quello della pelle che non poteva dirsi né bruna né bianca. Nell'insieme, benché ora mi fosse molto vicina, c'era come una nebbia in lei, che la faceva apparire vaga e lontana; e un grigio verdastro ne pareva la tinta predominante. Questo colore mi parve effetto della luce del sole che cadeva su di lei attraverso il verde del fogliame; e allorché per un momento si drizzò per avvicinare il dito dell'uccello, un pieno riflesso di luce le cadde sulle braccia e sui capelli, il braccio parve un istante di una bianchezza di perla, e i capelli, proprio dove n'erano sfiorati, ebbero uno strano bagliore e un guizzo di colori iridescenti.[69]

Montale alters the rhythm of the first sentence in his translation, placing the adjective in a position of syntactic emphasis at the beginning of the sentence and then stressing the three past participles, "sciolti", "ondati" and "inanellati". The effect is to heighten the semantic power of the qualities attributed to Rima's hair. The fact that Rima's hair falls "in a cloud" is too much of a coincidence not to be linked to the vision of Clizia's farewell in "La bufera", a poem first published in 1941, that is, before Montale started translating *Green Mansions*:

> Come quando
> ti rivolgesti e con la mano, sgombra
> la fronte dalla nube dei capelli,
>
> mi salutasti—per entrar nel buio.[70]

The translated passage contains several keywords from the Montalian idiolect, despite the fact that it is, for the most part, an accurate and even literal translation of Hudson's text. These keywords include *nebbia*, a word used in positions of syntactic emphasis in the first two collections (and later) but entirely absent from *La bufera* and the *Quaderno di traduzioni*, *tinta*, which occurs in each of the first three collections, *bagliore*, which Montale sometimes uses instead of *barbaglio*, *guizzo* (usually used by Montale in the context of colours changing in water) and *iridescente*, a word not actually used by Montale in his poetry but having obvious connections with "Iride".[71]

AUTO DA FÉ

That the idea of particularities establishing identity should have been present in Montale's work (possibly under the influence of Hopkins) before he discovered a similar idea in *Green Mansions* is not surprising. It serves to confirm an affinity rather than to suggest an influence. There are other examples of images occurring in *Green Mansions* which recall images from Montale's earlier poems.

In Chapter 1 the birds' song falls into Abel's heart like raindrops. There is a faint trace here of "I limoni", where "piove in petto una dolcezza inquieta" (line 17).[72] Likewise Abel, talking about love, says: "for this is love, Rima, the flower and the melody of life, the sweetest thing, the sweet miracle that makes our two souls one." The Montalian trace here is found in the *mottetto* "Ecco il segno": "sangue tuo nelle mie vene".[73] Another *mottetto*, "Infuria sale o grandine?" ("brilla come te/quando fingevi col tuo trillo d'aria/Lakmé nell'Aria delle Campanelle"), has an affinity with Rima's "clear trill of merry laughter" in Chapter 5.[74]

On the other hand, there are words and images from *Green Mansions* which appear in Montale's writing for the first time during and after the period in which he translated the novel. One such word is "cerbottana" ("zabatana"), a type of blow-pipe. "Cerbottana" is a hapax in Montale's poetry appearing in "Nel parco" (1946).[75] Rima's touch also has Montalian ramifications:

> I felt her fingers touching my skin, softly, trembling over my cheek as if a soft-winged moth had fluttered against it; then the slight aerial touch was gone, and she, too, moth-like, had vanished from my side.[76]

Bearing in mind that a moth is not a butterfly, Montale's infidelity is interesting in the context of his later prose:

> Sentii le sue dita che mi scorrevano leggere e tremule sulla guancia, come il volo di *una farfalla* dalle morbide ali; poi anche quel contatto lieve e immateriale cessò, e *come una farfalla* Rima svaní dal mio fianco.[77]

Camerino's translation is a useful foil to Montale's appropriation of Hudson's text:

> Sentii le sue dita toccare la mia pelle, leggere, tremando sulla mia guancia, come se *una falena* dall'ali morbide avesse volato accanto a me; poi il tocco lieve, aereo, scomparve, e anch' essa, *come una falena*, scomparve.[78]

This piece of text provides a further illustration of Montale's translation style, for instance his avoidance of repetition ("cessò" and "svaní" for Camerino's "scomparve"), his nominalization of a verb to achieve precision ("il volo di una farfalla" as against "come se una falena [...] avesse volato") and his rhetorical balance (two adjectives, "leggere e tremule", matched after the semi-colon by two other adjectives, "lieve e immateriale"). But it also shows Montale's creative impulse at work: he translates the passage into the context of his own writing by mistranslating "moth" as "farfalla". There may also be an argument for reading this episode as a prose gloss on his own poetry of roughly the same time.

The butterfly in the passage may suggest the yellow butterfly which appears to the narrator of "Farfalla di Dinard" but not to the incredulous French waitress.[79] At the hour of Rima's death the butterfly image is again present in Montale's text although Hudson's character speaks of a moth:

> And then looking we saw something fall; through the leaves and smoke and flame it fell like a great white bird killed with an arrow and falling to earth, and fell into the flames beneath. And it was the daughter of the Didi, and she was burnt to ashes like a moth in the flames of a fire, and no one has ever heard or seen her since.[80]

After Rima's death, towards the end of Chapter 20 (unfortunately we do not have Montale's translation of the passage but there is no doubt that he had read the chapter), Abel is visited by a moth:

> One night a moth fluttered in and alighted on my hand as I sat by the fire, causing me to hold my breath as I gazed on it. Its fore wings were pale grey, with shadings dark and light written all over in finest characters with some twilight mystery or legend; but the round underwings were clear amber-yellow, veined like a leaf with red and purple veins; a thing of such exquisite chaste beauty that the sight of it gave me a sudden shock of pleasure. Very soon it flew up circling about, and finally lighted on the palm-leaf thatch directly over the fire. The heat, I thought, would soon drive it from the spot; and rising I opened the door, so that it might find its way out again into the cool, dark, flowery world. And standing by the open door I turned and addressed it: "O night-wanderer of the pale, beautiful wings, go forth, and should you by chance meet her somewhere in the shadowy depths, revisiting her old haunts, be my messenger—." Thus much had I spoken, when the frail thing loosened its hold to fall without a flutter, straight and swift, into the white blaze beneath. I sprang forward with a shriek, and stood staring into the fire, my whole frame trembling with a sudden, terrible emotion. [...] A moth that perished in the flame; an indistinct faint sound; a dream in the night; the semblance of a shadowy form moving mist-like in the twilight gloom of the forest, would suddenly bring back a vivid memory, the old anguish, to break for a while the calm of that period. It was calm then after the storm.[81]

The similarities and dissimilarities between this passage and "Farfalla di Dinard" are striking. Both visitors are interpreted as possible messengers ("Farfalla di Dinard": "Passeggiata mattutina, insomma, o messaggio segreto?"), and this is their fundamental kinship. The dissimilarities are in the manner of opposites. Montale's butterfly is bright yellow: "La farfallina color zafferano". (The abruptness of this single adjective, unusual for Montale when describing colours, may be due to the fact that the story was written to comply with newspaper limitations concerning the number of words.) Hudson's moth is more lavishly presented. Montale's readers, however, should be able to note the context of bright yellow as the sunflower myth. The other main difference is quite arbitrary: Abel is warm in his hut with a fire burning, while Montale's narrator is sitting at a table in a cold, windy square in the north of France.

The double incineration in *Green Mansions*, however—first of Rima and then of the moth—, went beyond providing Montale with the outline for a story; it struck to the heart of his symbolism. It is a coincidence, but it is more than a coincidence that Montale should have entitled one of his books *Auto da fé*. In so doing he played on an ambiguity, an *auto da fé* being both an act of faith and a ritual death by burning.[82] It may be instructive to tease out the significance of the *auto da fé* motif in relation to Montale's poetics.

The fascination of Hudson's forest is idyllic; before the journey to Riolama it is an earthly paradise, which contrasts with the boredom of living among the Parahuari.[83] In the absence of Rima and Abel it is invaded by barbarians, and it is transformed into a place of sacrifice when Rima returns alone. The outlines of a conflict between good and evil are clearly presented, in a guise quite similar to the conflict of attitudes in "Elegia di Pico Farnese".[84] Rima's angelic qualities are opposed by the hunting Indians' superstition. Rima befriends all the creatures of the forest and is murdered by the Parahuari because she thwarts their hunting interests. The conflict fits into the pattern of Montale's Few and Many myth, and the sacrifice motif provides both a reinterpretation of earlier symbolism and a vital context for Clizia's mission in "Silvae".

The circumstances of Rima's death run a curious shaft into the underlife of Montale's poetry. The *auto da fé* symbolism is present in the blazing pyre at the end of "Crisalide":

> Penso allora
> alle tacite offerte che sostengono
> le case dei viventi; al cuore che abdica
> perché rida un fanciullo inconsapevole;
> al taglio netto che recide, al rogo
> morente che s'avviva
> d'un arido paletto, e ferve trepido.[85]

"Crisalide" is one of the most important of Montale's earlier poems because it gives expression to much of his mythology. Its importance is heightened by the existence of a first draft which diverges from the published poem in several respects. The final stanza of that first draft reads as follows:

> Che cosa posso dirvi? Torcersi le dita
> per fati inesorabili d'altrui
> è mio destino: al mondo
> ci ha luogo per chi sperpera e per quegli

che raccatta i rottami abbandonati.
Il silenzio ci lega col suo filo,
e le labbra non s'aprono per dire
l'estremo patto ch'io vorrei fermare
col torbido destino: di scontare
la vostra gioia con la mia condanna.
È il voto che mi fruga ancora il petto
—poi finirà ogni moto—:
nel rogo della vostra
vita foss' io il paletto
che si getta sul fuoco e cresce l'ilare
fiamma d'attorno!
E forse non mi è dato.[86]

The symbolism runs deeper in Montale's poetic imagination. Laura Barile has observed that the hearth is the place designated for sacrifice in Montale's poetry even as early as the poem addressed to Giacomino Costa.[87] A cognate image is the vision of wounded little animals in "Lettera levantina" (1923):

ma perché il pensiero
di me e il ricordo vostro mi ridestano
visioni di bestiuole ferite.[88]

Wounded animals and birds and flaming fires are thus all images related to the symbolism of the hunters and the hunted, the many and the few.[89] The essential element of the Montalian sacrifice is fire. Clizia burns herself out in the sun's heat, hope in "Piccolo testamento" smoulders more slowly than a stout log in the hearth—a story that lasts only in its ashes—, and Rima is consumed in a burning tree.[90] Rima's fate is a context, perhaps *the* context, of Clizia's fate. The classical myth of Clytie and Apollo stops short of this development. Montale's use of the myth, however, has much in common with his use of the works that he translated. There is a sense in which Montale presents objective situations in *Ossi di seppia* which he then reinterprets in the course of his writing career. The sunflower is there from the start, but there is no obvious trace of Clytie. The lost nymph is there but she has not been named Arethusa. Why then was Clytie introduced into Montale's poetry, and what is the significance of her sacrifice?

One answer comes in several different parts. According to the myth as it is related by Ovid, Clytie was in love with the sun and was fiercely jealous of Leucothoe. Apollo scorned Clytie because she had revenged herself indirectly on Leucothoe. Clytie withdrew from the company of the other nymphs and was transformed, it was said, into a sunflower:

> Her limbs, they say, became rooted to the earth, and a wan pallor spread over part of her complexion, as she changed into a bloodless plant: but in part her rosy flush remained, and a flower like violet grew over her face. Though held fast by its roots, this flower still turns to the sun, and although Clytie's form is altered, her love remains.[91]

Montale's Clizia is not held by roots. Roots are mentioned in Montale's poetry in relation not to Clizia but to Arsenio:

> Cosí sperso tra i vimini e le stuoie
> grondanti, giunco tu che le radici
> con sé trascina, viscide, non mai
> svelte, tremi di vita e ti protendi
> a un vuoto risonante di lamenti
> soffocati, la tesa ti ringhiotte
> dell'onda antica che ti volge.[92]

Clizia, when she arrives in Montale's poetics, is the summation of a series of images which includes the sunflower and Arsenio's roots. But she is a foil for Arsenio/Montale. She is not rooted and she becomes a messenger, whether woman or bird or butterfly. The poet is the rooted one.[93]

The sunflower, which turns black at the end of summer, the various hearths and the ritual pyre of "Crisalide" and *La vita della foresta* are all variants on fire, the purifying element. From its Dantean context it is the fire which transforms lust into love. Such could be the transformation of the hunter's lust into the observer's love of nature or that which separates the many from the few. The *auto da fé* was, in any case, a value-laden symbol in Montale's poetics which had been smouldering there since his youth, whether as a recurrent nightmare or as an ardent aspiration.[94]

NOTES

1 *La vita della foresta* is edited by M. A. Grignani (Turin, Einaudi, 1987). In addition to Montale's translation it contains two very useful essays, one by

Grignani ("A Play of Iridescent Colour", pp. 303–25), the other by Rossana Bonadei ("W. H. Hudson: un profilo letterario", pp. 327–37).

2 Martone's translation was republished by Mondadori in 1958 and added to Mondadori's Oscar series in 1976.

3 This translation (1945) also carried the title *Verdi dimore;* it was volume 62 in the Corona Collezione Universale Bompiani series. It appeared under the pseudonym Angelo Bianco because of the racial laws. (Camerino also used a variety of other pseudonyms, including Cam, Angelo Bianchi and Marco Lombardi.)

4 Hudson travelled extensively in Britain and Ireland. For an exhaustive account of his travels see D. Shrubsall, "W. H. Hudson's English Country Rambles", *English Literature in Transition, 1880–1920*, 33, i (1990), 64–83.

5 W. H. Hudson, *Green Mansions* (London, Duckworth, 1904). References hereafter are to the New Reader's Library edition (London, Duckworth, 1927).

6 R. Bonadei, "W. H. Hudson", p. 332 refers to this essay, which is to be found in V. Woolf, *The Common Reader* (London, Hogarth Press, 1925), pp. 184–95.

7 Letter to R. B. Cunninghame Graham, 2 July 1904. See *Collected Letters of Joseph Conrad*, edited by F. R. Karl and L. Davies, 3 vols (Cambridge, Cambridge University Press, 1988), III, 149.

8 See M. A. Grignani, "A Play of Iridescent Colour", p. 314.

9 See R. Bonadei, "W. H. Hudson", pp. 333–35.

10 Hudson's biographer describes the visit: "In the churchyard, after long search, he found the little headstone and knelt to put aside the long rank grass half-covering it, 'as when we look into a child's face we push back the unkempt hair from its forehead'." See R. Tomalin, *W. H. Hudson: A Biography* (London, Faber, 1982; Oxford, Oxford University Press, 1984). The quotation is on page 107 of the 1984 edition, to which reference is also made below.

11 Quoted by R. Tomalin, *W. H. Hudson*, p. 65.

12 See, for example, W. H. Hudson, *Green Mansions*, pp. 36–37, 45, 68.

13 Quoted by R. Bonadei, "W. H. Hudson", p. 330.

14 W. H. Hudson, *The Land's End: A Naturalist's Impressions in West Cornwall* (London, Hutchinson, 1908; reissue edited by I. Niall, London, Wildwood House, 1980). The quotation is taken from the 1980 edition (p. 167; Ch. 13), as are the other quotations below.

15 W. H. Hudson, *The Land's End*, pp. 185–86.

16 W. H. Hudson, *The Land's End*, p. 189.

17 W. H. Hudson, *The Land's End*, p. 191.

18 Quoted in R. Tomalin, *W. H. Hudson*, p. 125.

19 See the third stanza of "Casa sul mare", in E. Montale, *L'opera in versi*, edited by G. Contini and R. Bettarini (Turin, Einaudi, 1980), p. 91.

20 See U. Carpi, "L'ideologia di Montale", in his *Il poeta e la politica* (Naples, Liguori, 1978), pp. 271–356.

21 U. Carpi, "L'ideologia di Montale", p. 343.

22 See U. Carpi, "L'ideologia di Montale", p. 277: " [...] la fase piú autentica della polemica montaliana sia rintracciabile non all'avversione a questo o a quel regime, bensí nell'orrore della massificazione che soffoca il libero intellettuale e di cui i regimi stessi (analogamente ai partiti di massa) paiono soltanto varianti accidentali e prive di interesse autonomo".

23 E. Montale, *L'opera in versi*, pp. 175–76 (p. 176).

24 Letter dated 9 June 1939 and printed in E. Montale, *L'opera in versi*, p. 931.
25 See U. Carpi, "L'ideologia di Montale", p. 337.
26 While working on the "Elegia" Montale also had Germany in mind. He wrote to Bazlen: "Scrivimi *subito* che ti pare dell'Elegia. Forse a un pubblico tedesco è piú adatta delle 'Notizie [dall'Amiata]'." See E. Montale, *L'opera in versi*, p. 927.
27 See W. H. Hudson, *Green Mansions*, pp. 3, 4.
28 See W. H. Hudson, *Green Mansions*, p. 312: "A new Ahasuerus, cursed by inexpiable crime, yet sustained by a great purpose."
29 It is dated "febb. giugno 23" and is dedicated "a F. Messina, in copia unica, questo papiro di amicizia... E. Montale 26.7.23." See *L'opera in versi*, p. 1167.
30 E. Montale, *L'opera in versi*, pp. 774–75.
31 W. H. Hudson, *Far Away and Long Ago* (London, Dent, 1918), p. 291 (Ch. 21); quoted in R. Tomalin, *W. H. Hudson*, p. 51.
32 See R. Luperini, *Montale o l'identità negata* (Naples, Liguori, 1984), pp. 211–16.
33 W. H. Hudson, *Far Away and Long Ago*, p. 242 (Ch. 17).
34 E. Montale, "Il pipistrello", in his *Farfalla di Dinard* (Milan, Mondadori, 1960), pp. 145–50 (pp. 148–50).
35 For contributions concerning the various transformations of Irma Brandeis's name in Montale's work see L. Rebay, "Montale, Clizia e l'America", in *La poesia di Eugenio Montale* by various authors (Milan, Librex, 1983), pp. 281–308.
36 E. Montale, "Intenzioni (intervista immaginaria)" [1946], in his *Sulla poesia*, edited by G. Zampa (Milan, Mondadori, 1976), pp. 561–69 (p. 564).
37 Letter of 3 Feb. 1943, quoted by M. A. Grignani, "A Play of Iridescent Colour", pp. 311–12.
38 Letter of 10 June 1943, quoted by M. A. Grignani, "A Play of Iridescent Colour", p. 312.
39 The Rodocanachi manuscript has not been published. I take Grignani as my authority here. She has written: "Le due stesure de *La vita della foresta* si trovano presso il 'Fondo manoscritti di Autori contemporanei' dell'Università di Pavia. La prima, dattiloscritta sul *recto* e sul *verso* di 258 fogli con numerazione a penna facciata per facciata (bianche e non numerate le facciate posteriori dei ff. 191 e 220) risponde ai criteri suggeriti alla Rodocanachi da Montale, che interviene a penna nell'interlinea riformulando interi periodi e colmando le eventuali lacunae in rigo" ("A Play of Iridescent Colour", p. 324). Montale, then, used Rodocanachi's literal version as a crib so that he could avoid consulting dictionaries and concentrate instead on the business of rewriting. In my analysis of Montale's translation I have decided to contrast his work with Camerino's version rather than with Rodocanachi's, on the grounds that Camerino's is also the work of a creative writer and is therefore likely to be interpretive rather than literal. The reason for this method is the following: it is relatively simple to observe where Montale departs from literal translation, so comparison with the Rodocanachi manuscript is of little value; on the other hand, where both Montale and Camerino depart from literal translation, as creative writers are wont to do, it is possible to develop a contrastive analysis on the basis of their different interpretations.
40 Montale's choice of term for the English word "forest" produces a deliberate non-allusion to *Inferno*, I. 1 in the first paragraph of Ch. 5: "quella foresta selvaggia" (*La vita della foresta*, p. 61).

41 W. H. Hudson, *Green Mansions*, p. 61 (Ch. 5); *La vita della foresta*, p. 61.
42 W. H. Hudson, *Green Mansions*, p. 69; my italics except "*my*".
43 W. H. Hudson, *Verdi dimore* (Camerino), p. 93 (Ch. 5); my italics except "*mia*".
44 *La vita della foresta*, p. 69; my italics.
45 *Ri-* forms also occur in Montale's poetry, e.g. "La speranza di pure *ri*vederti" (*L'opera in versi*, p. 138), "Lo sai: debbo *ri*perderti e non posso" (*L'opera in versi*, p. 133), "Poi scendesti dai monti a *ri*portarmi/San Giorgio e il Drago" (from "Molti anni, e uno piú duro", *L'opera in versi*, p. 134).
46 W. H. Hudson, *Green Mansions*, p. 136.
47 *La vita della foresta*, p. 130.
48 W. H. Hudson, *Verdi dimore* (Camerino), pp. 165–66 (Ch. 10).
49 W. H. Hudson, *Green Mansions*, pp. 79–83; *La vita della foresta*, pp. 78–81.
50 E. Montale, *L'opera in versi*, p. 189.
51 For example, "Corno inglese", l. 11, "livido, muta colore [...]"; "La primavera hitleriana", l. 35, "il non mutato amor mutata serbi" (E. Montale, *L'opera in versi*, pp. 11, 249).
52 See M. A. Grignani, "A Play of Iridescent Colour", p. 323.
53 *La vita della foresta*, p. 267.
54 Montale did use the plural noun "strisce" twice in *Ossi di seppia*, once in "Corno inglese" and once in "Marezzo" (*L'opera in versi*, pp. 11, 88). He also used "striscia" as a verb in "Vasca" (*L'opera in versi*, p. 71).
55 E. Montale, *L'opera in versi*, p. 169. "L'estate" has the distinction of being the first poem in which one of Montale's female characters is identified with a figure from classical mythology. (It is true that Esterina in "Falsetto" is likened to "l'arciera Diana", but similarity is not identity.) Arethusa was a nymph pursued by the river god Alpheus in the Peloponnese and changed by Diana into a fountain, which flows under the sea and reappears close to Syracuse. She is the first of a series of mythological presences in Montale's poetry which includes Clytie (Clizia), a water-nymph transformed by Apollo into a sunflower because of her revengeful behaviour, and Iris (Iride), messenger of the gods and goddess of the rainbow.
56 See L. Barile, "Sparviero o procellaria? Una versione di Montale da Hopkins", in her *Adorate mie larve: Montale e la poesia anglosassone* (Bologna, Mulino, 1990), pp. 15–50 (p. 45).
57 *Gerard Manley Hopkins*, edited by C. Phillips (Oxford, Oxford University Press, 1987), p. 237; Hopkins's italics.
58 W. H. Hudson, *Green Mansions*, p. 199.
59 *La vita della foresta*, pp. 187–88.
60 "A mia madre" [1942, published in 1943], in E. Montale, *L'opera in versi*, p. 203; Montale's italics.
61 W. H. Hudson, *Green Mansions*, p. 97.
62 *La vita della foresta*, pp. 93–94.
63 E. Montale, *L'opera in versi*, p. 201.
64 W. H. Hudson, *Green Mansions*, p. 200.
65 *La vita della foresta*, p. 189.
66 W. H. Hudson, *Green Mansions*, p. 36; *La vita della foresta*, p. 37.
67 W. H. Hudson, *Green Mansions*, p. 38; *La vita della foresta*, p. 38.
68 W. H. Hudson, *Green Mansions*, p. 66.
69 *La vita della foresta*, p. 66. Grignani has also drawn attention to that paragraph not only in "A Play of Iridescent Colour", p. 320, but also in the "Appendice"

to her *Prologhi ed epiloghi: sulla poesia di Eugenio Montale* (Ravenna, Longo, 1987), pp. 195–203 (p. 201), and her "La firma stilistica di Montale traduttore", *Autografo*, 15 (1988), 3–20 (p. 16).

70 E. Montale, *L'opera in versi*, p. 189.

71 For *nebbia*, see E. Montale, *L'opera in versi*, pp. 96 ("Incontro", l. 8), 116 ("Bagni di Lucca", l. 12), 150 ("Non recidere, forbice", l. 4). For *tinta*, see *L'opera in versi*, pp. 32 ("Portami il girasole", l. 7), 148 ("Il fiore che ripete", l. 4), 231 ("Dal treno", l. 6). For *bagliore*, see *L'opera in versi*, pp. 76 ("Clivo", l. 32), 145 ("La gondola che scivola", l. 2), 191 ("Su una lettera non scritta", l. 6). For *guizzo*, see *L'opera in versi*, pp. 97 ("Incontro", l. 48), 169 ("L'estate", l. 5), 254 ("L'anguilla", l. 12). For "Iride" see *L'opera in versi*, pp. 239–40.

72 W. H. Hudson, *Green Mansions*, p. 21; E. Montale, *L'opera in versi*, p. 10.

73 W. H. Hudson, *Green Mansions*, p. 238; E. Montale, *L'opera in versi*, p. 140.

74 W. H. Hudson, *Green Mansions*, p. 63; E. Montale, *L'opera in versi*, p. 146.

75 W. H. Hudson, *Green Mansions*, p. 56; E. Montale, *L'opera in versi*, p. 242.

76 W. H. Hudson, *Green Mansions*, p. 186.

77 *La vita della foresta*, p. 175; my italics.

78 W. H. Hudson, *Verdi dimore* (Camerino), p. 220; my italics.

79 See E. Montale, *Farfalla di Dinard*, pp. 240–41.

80 W. H. Hudson, *Green Mansions*, p. 270. Again Montale translated "moth" as "farfalla" (*La vita della foresta*, p. 254) whereas Camerino translated it as "falena" (W. H. Hudson, *Verdi dimore*, p. 309).

81 W. H. Hudson, *Green Mansions*, pp. 289–90.

82 Montale was quite conscious of the ambiguity, as he makes clear in his preface to *Auto da fé*: "Un auto da fé (atto di fede o meglio 'della fede') [...]. E quanto al titolo: se il lettore volesse intenderlo nell'accezione piú nota, sappia che io sono d'accordo con lui perché licenziando queste cronache ho l'impressione di buttarle nel fuoco e di liberarmene per sempre." See E. Montale, *Auto da fé: cronache in due tempi* (Milan, Saggiatore, 1966), p. 11. Even in this apparently "informative" note Montale's language is highly allusive; e.g. the "cerniera" evokes moments of his own poetic past ("Piccolo testamento", in E. Montale, *L'opera in versi*, p. 267) as well as referring directly to the *auto da fé* motif.

83 Montale offered an interpretation of the green forest elsewhere in relation to "Elegia di Pico Farnese": "Nelle grotte [...] c'è il segno del Pesce che credo uno dei piú antichi segni cristiani; comunque si esprime il dubbio che la simbologia cristiana (la foresta verde) dimezzi la vita e che Cristo abbia bisogno di essere continuato forse malgré lui" (E. Montale, *L'opera in versi*, p. 931).

84 See E. Montale, *L'opera in versi*, p. 939: "La Bufera (la poesia iniziale) è la guerra, in ispecie *quella* guerra dopo *quella* dittatura [...]; ma è anche guerra cosmica, di sempre e di tutti" (Montale's italics).

85 E. Montale, *L'opera in versi*, p. 87.

86 E. Montale, *L'opera in versi*, pp. 887–88.

87 For the text of this early poem, see E. Montale, *Tutte le poesie*, edited by G. Zampa (Milan, Mondadori, 1984), pp. 779–80. It is not included in his *L'opera in versi*.

88 E. Montale, *L'opera in versi*, p. 775.

89 The story of Arethusa is a further example of that symbolism. Arethusa, the nymph from Pisa, is pursued by the lustful river god but protected by Dictynna, who covers her in a cloud. When night has fallen, the cloud

condenses and Arethusa sacrifices her nymphal form to be transformed into a stream and sent to flow through the underworld as far as Syracuse. See Ovid, *Metamorphoses*, v. 577–641.

90 E. Montale, *L'opera in versi*, p. 267; W. H. Hudson, *Green Mansions*, p. 269.

91 Ovid, *Metamorphoses*, translated by M. M. Innes (Harmondsworth, Penguin, 1955, reprinted 1970), p. 101 (IV. 264–70).

92 E. Montale, *L'opera in versi*, p. 82.

93 It is tempting to put a biographical construction on this: Montale stayed behind, "rooted", so to speak, working as a translator, a job he claimed to despise, instead of crossing the Atlantic.

94 It should be noted in passing that Jared Becker has drawn attention to Montale's "resilient individuality" in a perceptive reading of "Mediterraneo": "Having described the paltry part of the sea's voice that he has taken as his own, the poet adds, 'a te mi rendo in umiltà' [...]. Yet this obeisance is not, finally, annihilation; rather, it is the coexistence of opposing elements. The persistent difference between the poet and the sea is given expression in the last words of 'Mediterraneo', in which the speaker takes as his identity the image, not of water, but of fire: 'non sono/che favilla d'un tirso. Bene lo so: bruciare,/questo, non altro, è il mio significato.' [...] The metaphor may be self-deprecating, since the spark from a burning brand is a tiny blaze, and one whose duration is perhaps brief. From that point of view there is indeed a 'surrender' on the part of the narrator. But to conclude the sequence by connecting himself with the element that is the contrary of water also testifies to the poet's resilient individuality—not his abject capitulation." See J. Becker, *Eugenio Montale* (Boston, Twayne, 1986), pp. 24–25.

Chapter 7

ACTS OF AMBIGUOUS HOMAGE

Earlier chapters have dealt with writers whom Montale claimed as precursors because their work provided landmarks in his poetic and metaphysical development. The other texts of which the 1948 *Quaderno di traduzioni* is composed consist in individual acts of homage to writers for whom Montale appears to have felt a certain reverence. Apart from Maragall, Milosz and Guillén, the poets in question are William Blake, Thomas Hardy, James Joyce, W. B. Yeats, Dylan Thomas and Léonie Adams.[1] They were further contributors to the tradition which had produced, in Montale's words, "una certa idea della poesia".[2] In some cases there was a thematic attraction which drew Montale to the specific poems. In other cases, where there was no such thematic attraction, there appears to have been a technical feature of the English poem which interested Montale. The following approach groups the poems according to thematic or technical criteria in order to avoid unnecessary repetition.

Il ritorno dei morti: Blake and Hardy

Blake is the sole representative of the eighteenth century in the *Quaderno di traduzioni*. There is at least one superficial reason for Montale's identification with Blake and his desire to claim him as a literary ancestor. In an article on Filippo De Pisis Montale wrote:

> In linea di principio, non siamo tra coloro che diffidano dei pittori che scrivono o dei letterati che dipingono. Il caso di William Blake e di Fromentin (e in epoca piú recente di Viani e di Bartolini) è abbastanza eloquente; i primi due non si sarebbero salvati se si

> fossero ostinati nella pittura, gli altri dimostrano che particolari temperamenti non sono vincolati a un solo mezzo di espressione.[3]

Montale painted as a dilettante, and painting provides a context for some of his poems.[4] While this, however, is only a superficial affinity between Montale and Blake, Montale's translation of "To the Muses" is a more promising point of contact between the two painter-poets, and provides an example of how Montale could rewrite a poem in such a way as to make it entirely his own.

"To the Muses"

The following is the text of "To the Muses" as printed in the *Quaderno di traduzioni*:

> Whether on Ida's shady brow,
> or in the chambers of the East,
> the chambers of the sun that now
> from ancient melody have ceased;
>
> whether in heaven ye wander fair,
> or the green corners of the earth,
> or the blue regions of the air,
> where the melodious winds have birth;
>
> whether on crystal rocks ye rove,
> beneath the bosom of the sea
> wandering in many a coral grove;
> fair Nine, forsaking Poetry;
>
> how have you left the ancient love
> that bards of old enjoyed in you!
> The languid strings do scarcely move;
> the sound is forced, the notes are few!

"To the Muses" is a poem with a precise form. It is composed of four stanzas, each consisting of four lines, which rhyme ABAB. There are two sentences; one is short, occupying only the final two lines, and the other, in consequence, is very long. The first sentence is fraught with grammatical dislocations. Each of the first three stanzas begins with "whether", and in the first stanza there is no verb connecting with this opening word. The grammatical subject appears in the first line of the second stanza, along with the first of two verbs in the indicative mood, which are both governed by this subject. (The two verbs, "ye wander" in line 5 and "ye rove" in line 9, are synonyms.) In suggesting the possible refuges of the nine Muses, Blake includes each of the four elements: fire is represented by "the chambers of the sun" (line 3), earth by "the green corners of the earth" (line 5), air by "the blue regions of the air,/where the melodious winds have birth" (lines 6–7) and water by "the bosom of the sea" (line 10).

Blake uses ten adjective + noun combinations: "shady brow" (line 1), "ancient melody" (line 4), "green corners" (line 6), "blue regions" (line 7), "melodious winds" (line 8), "crystal rocks" (line 9), "coral grove" (line 11), "fair Nine" (line 12), "ancient love" (line 13) and "languid strings" (line 15). "Ancient melody" is the poem's key concept. The noun "melody" is alluded to in the "melodious winds" of the second stanza. The adjective "ancient" is repeated in the fourth stanza in "ancient love", an adjective + noun combination that is virtually synonymous with "ancient melody". Of the other adjectives only "fair" is used twice.

There is an antithesis in Blake's verbs between termination and initiation. Both the first and the second stanzas end with verb structures. In the first a hyperbaton in lines 3–4 pushes "have ceased" to the end of the fourth line. Without the hyperbaton the order would be "the chambers of the sun have ceased from ancient melody." In the second stanza the closing verb structure ("have birth") occurs in conventional syntax. There is another verb of termination in the first line of the fourth stanza ("how have you left"). The interplay of adjectives announces the poem's theme and the verbs sharpen the focus. Termination is the dominant mood: the Muses, beloved of the ancient world, have departed from the modern world.

Montale's translation hugs close to the contours of Blake's poem. It reads as follows:

Alle muse

Siate sull'Ida dalla fronte ombrosa
o nelle stanze dell'Aurora,
le stanze del sole in cui ora
l'antica melodia riposa;

oppure in cielo, bionde,
o nei piú verdi angoli del mondo,
o lungi, nei recessi azzurri d'onde
nascono i venti armoniosi;

o vaganti su rocce di cristallo
sotto il grembo del mare,
perdute tra grovigli di coralli,
voi belle Nove che obliaste i canti;

dove avete lasciato il vecchio fuoco,
delizia d'altri bardi?
Tarde e fioche le corde, il vostro suono
è forzato, le note sono poche![5]

Montale does not follow Blake's rhyme scheme. His first stanza rhymes ABBA ("ombrosa":"Aurora":"ora":"riposa"). Of the remaining rhymes in the poem ("bionde":"onde", "cristallo":"coralli" and "fuoco":"suono") only one pair ("bionde":"onde", lines 5, 7) makes a true rhyme. There are also concealed assonances, such as "*mon*do" → "ar*mon*iosi".

Montale's poem has nuances which represent departures from Blake's text. He translates "the chambers of the sun/that now from ancient melody have ceased" as "le stanze del sole in cui ora/ l'antica melodia riposa". *Riposare* means, *inter alia*, "to rest", "to repose" or "to sleep". It does also have an archaic nuance of *giacere*, but as a translation of "to cease" it is interpretive rather than literal. Montale eschews Blake's repetitions. The key concept, "ancient melody", is translated as "antica melodia" but the "melodious winds" become "venti armoniosi" and the "ancient love" becomes "vecchio fuoco". "Fair", which Blake uses twice, is translated once as "bionde" and once as "belle". Repetition is a structural feature of Blake's poem. Each of the first three stanzas begins with "whether", but there is no such repetition in Montale's translation.

Although Montale keeps to the general outline of Blake's poem, his lines are not of a regular length, as they were in the case of the three "Motivi" from Shakespeare. With one exception Blake confines his semantic expression to regular syntactic lines of poetry, avoiding *enjambement* and caesura. In the "Motivi" from Shakespeare, Montale had slowed down the pace of the final couplets by using *enjambements*, and he adopts the same practice in "Alle muse":

> Tarde e fioche le corde, il vostro suono
> è forzato, le note sono poche!

Montale also takes an independent stand on Blake's verb "to forsake". The choice of *obliare* is an interesting one. *Obliare* is a poetic equivalent of *dimenticare*. It comes from medieval Latin and was used by Foscolo in *Dei seplocri* and by Dante in the *Commedia*. There are more obvious echoes of the *Commedia* in the last two lines:

> Tarde e *fioche* le corde, il vostro suono
> è forzato, le note sono *poche*!

The rhyme "poche":"fioche" occurs in *Paradiso*, XI. 131–33, as Lonardi has observed.[6] It also occurs in *Paradiso*, XXXIII. 119–21.

There is another important difference between "Alle muse" and "To the Muses", and it is one that transforms Blake's poem into a Montalian poem. Montale's poem begins with a verb in the subjunctive mood ("Siate"), which is used as an auxiliary to a past participle ("perdute") in the third stanza. There is a subtle nuance here. Blake had the Muses "wander" and "rove" (two active verbs); Montale has them *lost* (in the passive voice) in the "grovigli di coralli" ("coral grove"), "sotto il grembo del mare". "Grembo" is, of course, a literal translation, but it is also a word with Montalian resonance.[7] It is, however, the nuance of the Muses lost under the sea which is of greater interest. It represents a significant departure from Blake's poem, and is a hint to the reader that a Montalian appropriation is in progress.

The really significant aspect of "Alle muse", in the context of Montale's later work, is the shadowy presence of Arletta. The textual hint comes in the third stanza. The Muses may be

> vaganti su rocce di cristallo
> sotto il grembo del mare,
> perdute tra grovigli di coralli.

Montale's "perdute", as has been mentioned above, represents a departure from Blake's text (it "translates" the verb "wandering").

Montale is thus emphasizing a scenario in which the Muses are "perdute [...] sotto il grembo del mare". Arletta was the name given by Montale to the interlocutor of "Incontro" (1926) in the first draft of the poem.[8] In the final draft of "Incontro" she was addressed as "sommersa" and was called on to perform ritual functions:

> Prega per me
> allora ch'io discenda altro cammino
> che una via di città,
> nell'aria persa, innanzi al brulichio
> dei vivi; ch'io ti senta accanto; ch'io
> scenda senza viltà.

Arletta's activity as a private muse is confirmed in a very late poem, "Morgana" (1977), which draws on the theme and language of "Alle muse":

> Morgana
>
> Non so immaginare come la tua giovinezza
> si sia prolungata
> di tanto tempo (e quale!). [...]
> Hanno detto hanno scritto che ci mancò la fede.
> Forse ne abbiamo avuto un surrogato.
> La fede è un'altra. Cosí fu detto ma
> non è detto il detto sia sicuro.
> Forse sarebbe bastata quella della Catastrofe,
> ma non per te che uscivi per ritornarvi
> dal grembo degli Dèi.[9]

The textual link between "Alle muse" and "Morgana" is "grembo", a keyword with a long history in Montale's poetry. The *tu* of "Morgana" is the same *tu* addressed in "La casa dei doganieri" and in "Incontro", where she is lost beneath the sea like the Muses in "Alle muse". In the late poem Montale returns to the memory of Arletta rather than to "quella della Catastrofe" (Clizia?) in search of his Muse.

"To the Muses" provided a vehicle for a specific phase in Montale's poetry. His appropriation of Blake's poem is not, however, indicative of a relationship of influence between the work of the two poets. Montale was sensitive to Blake's "sfolgorio", which suggests Montale's own "barbaglio" symbolism.[10] He connected

Blake with Emily Dickinson in a 1957 essay, and the basis of the connection is as significant for Montale himself as it is for the other two poets: "Manca, tra le letture della Dickinson, William Blake, ed è strano; poiché tra i due poeti corre qualche affinità nel modo di aggredire felinamente, quasi bestialmente, il mistero della Divinità."[11] But the crucial term there is "affinità": Blake's "influence" on Montale is confined to one poem, which Montale reinterpreted in the light of his own metaphysical development.

The Arletta theme, which entered Montale's poetry in the mid-1920s when he was working on his review of *Dubliners*, is one part of a larger theme in Montale's poetry which might be called "the presence of the dead". This theme is one which also exercised Thomas Hardy's imagination, and it should occasion no great surprise that the Hardy poem which Montale translated concerns the dead.

"The Garden Seat"

Montale mentions Hardy rarely in his critical writings. His only article dealing specifically with Hardy is a 1968 essay published in the *Corriere della sera* but written as the preface for Singh's *Thomas Hardy: Poesie*. Montale's translation of "The Garden Seat", which was first published in the *Quaderno di traduzioni*, is included in Singh's anthology.[12]

Montale regarded Hardy as a paradoxical writer, and given Montale's taste for paradox, that is likely to have constituted a positive estimation: "Il caso di Hardy è piuttosto raro. Non si ha notizia di un prosatore-prosatore che, su altro registro, sia stato tanto poeta-poeta. E, per complicare le cose, la poesia di Hardy tanto piú è poetica quanto piú è prosastica nel linguaggio e nei motivi."[13] Montale's point about poetry and prose in Hardy's work is a restatement of a point which Singh makes in his introductory essay.[14] It does, however, suggest an affinity of method between Hardy and Montale. Montale had laboured, in his poetry, to break out of what he had seen as the mannered conventions of Italian poetry. The observation that Hardy had done something similar in English is tantamount to conspiratorial approval.

Montale is careful to distinguish between language and form. Hardy's poetry may use the language of prose, but that is not to say that it is prose: "Altra stranezza: le forme sono rigidamente chiuse, le strofe impeccabilmente tradizionali: ma di una tradizione che è quella del *song*, del folclore e (cosí hanno detto) della *balladry*. Hardy è riuscito a ingabbiare una grande materia prosastica nel piú fitto reticolo metrico che si possa immaginare."[15] That is another Montalian characteristic. Montale found that tight forms stimulated the imagination, and he railed against Ungaretti and other practitioners of free verse.[16] The ability to fit "una grande materia prosastica" into a "fitto reticolo metrico" is certainly something of which Montale approved.

Montale recognizes the difficulty of transplanting Hardy's poetry into another language:

> L'intricato tramaglio in cui Hardy avvolgeva le sue poesie richiedeva una saturazione di monosillabi quale solo la lingua inglese può consentire. Numerosi sono gli arcaismi, quelli che il dizionario di Oxford registra con la data di nascita e di morte. Ma non mancano i deverbali, le parole che rendono ricco e strano anche il lessico piú comune. Prevale l'intonazione naturalistica, georgica, la minuzia del botanico e del collezionista. Talvolta il poeta acchiappa con la rete dell'entomologo anche le espressioni del meccanico o del contadino.[17]

Clearly the greatest barrier to translation of Hardy's poetry into Italian is the profusion of monosyllables, and the consequent staccato nature of his rhythm. The other problems—archaisms and terms from different linguistic registers—are not so grave.

Montale has reservations about Hardy's monosyllables: "Un'altra difficoltà, almeno per il mio orecchio di straniero, è data dalle rime monosillabiche, troppo numerose e prevedibili. Ma in quanto ho letto su di lui non trovo obiezioni in questo senso; forse ho torto io e la natura della *balladry* imponeva che si pagasse questo scotto."[18] He mentions only one other reservation about Hardy's poetry, and that had been previously expressed by another critic: "Solo punto debole, molti anni fa già osservato da M. Bowra (oggi sir [*sic*] Maurice Bowra), il gusto delle generalizzazioni filosofiche di probabile ascendenza schopenhaueriana: *the Will, the Power*, le cupe forze che aduggiano il suo fondamentale stoicismo."[19] Philosophical generalizations had characterized Montale's very early poetry (the "Accordi" and the poems from before 1919, with the exception of "Meriggiare pallido e assorto"), but he had outgrown them by the time of his mature poetry. Paradoxically, they tend to return in his post-1970 poetry, though in the late poems there is usually a heavy counterweight of irony.

One final affinity to note between the poetry of Hardy and Montale is related to a point made by Montale earlier in the same essay: "Le liriche che egli [Hardy] scrisse negli anni 1912–1913 in memoria della sua prima moglie sono una delle vette della poesia moderna, e non di quella poesia vittoriana alla quale si sarebbe tentati di ascrivere un poeta già operante nel 1870."[20] The Montalian significance of this judgement is that when he wrote the essay he had recently finished *Xenia* II, the second set of poems *in morte di* Mosca, his lifelong companion and latterly his wife.[21] This circumstantial evidence would suggest that in the 1960s Montale had a more specific interest in Hardy's poetry than he had had in the 1940s, when he had translated "The Garden Seat".

The following is the correct text of "The Garden Seat". The version presented in the *Quaderno di traduzioni* has been dogged by typographical errors:

The Garden Seat

Its former green is blue and thin,
and its once firm legs sink in and in;
soon it will break down unaware,
soon it will break down unaware.

At night when reddest flowers are black
those who once sat thereon come back;
quite a row of them sitting there,
quite a row of them sitting there.

With them the seat does not break down,
nor winter freeze them, nor floods drown,
for they are as light as upper air,
they are as light as upper air![22]

Repetition is a key feature of the poem. Apart from the proliferation of monosyllables, there is the fact that the poem is overshadowed by one rhyme ("unaw*are*":"th*ere*":"*air*"). That almost mantric rhyme is underscored by the refrain feature, which Mengaldo has described as a *ritornello*.[23] The final line in each stanza is a repetition of the penultimate line, except in the third stanza, where there is a minor variation. Thus the "mantric" rhyme occurs at the end of exactly half the poem's lines. Not only that, the expression "break down" in the refrain of the first stanza is repeated at the end of the opening line of the last stanza, where it rhymes with "drown". Furthermore, the "down":"drown" rhyme, as Mengaldo has also observed, has a certain inevitability about it because of the *r* just before "down" in "break". So, according to Mengaldo, "b*r*eak *down*" produces "drown". This claim is weakened, however, by Hardy's "black":"back" rhyme in the second stanza. That is also a rhyme where the two words are identical except for one consonant, but there is no floating *l* closely preceding "back".

Mengaldo was trying to establish a link between the thematic determinism which is present in much of Hardy's poetry and the formal strictness of this poem. Indeed he makes the following claim: "Dal punto di vista piú generalmente ideologico m'arrischio a ipotizzare un rapporto fra il determinismo tecnico, se cosí si può dire, di questa lirica e di un po' tutta la poesia di Hardy e il determinismo, il senso nichilistico di una necessità e un fato ineluttabili che dominano, come è ben noto, la concezione del mondo dell'autore."[24] Mengaldo's speculative argument—that a psychological disposition can determine a formal technique—is very interesting. According to that argument, Hardy may have chosen the ballad form because of his taste for nihilism. Whether or not that is the case, there is no doubt that repetition is a characteristic feature of ballads, as it is of most popular art forms. Just how useful that fact is as a tool for interpreting the poem is, however, debatable.

The first stanza introduces past, present and future:

> Its former green is blue and thin,
> and its once firm legs sink in and in;
> soon it will break down unaware,
> soon it will break down unaware.

Three time-scales are present in the first stanza: the seat as it was, firm-legged and green; the seat as it is, "blue and thin" and sinking into the ground; the seat as it will be, broken down. The description of the seat's impending future state is the most interesting. Soon it will "break down". (The seat is consistently referred to by means of pronouns.) The phrasal verb contains both physical nuances (as when a car breaks down) and emotional ones (as when one breaks down and cries); but more interesting than the verb is the adjective "unaware", which draws attention to itself in several ways. Firstly, it is in a position of emphasis at the end of the line; secondly, it is repeated in the following line of the refrain; thirdly, it sets off the chain of "unaware":"there":"air" rhymes; and finally, it attributes to the seat a potential animistic sense of perception (awareness), which is, however, negated by the prefix *un-*. In short, "unaware" is an unusual choice of word, but a word to which Hardy seems to have given an important structural function in the poem.

The second stanza is more quirky than the first. Nightfall, a conventional symbol of death, encompasses both the end of colours and the return of the dead:

> At night when reddest flowers are black
> those who once sat thereon come back;
> quite a row of them sitting there,
> quite a row of them sitting there.

This stanza may well reflect Hardy's reading of Schopenhauer. There is an equation between colours and the dead. Colours can only be perceived by day, while ghosts can only be perceived at night; so who is to say that the ones are more real than the others? Hardy's scepticism, in the final stanza, tends more towards the supernatural than the natural, because the dead become the focus of his attention:

> With them the seat does not break down,
> nor winter freeze them, nor floods drown,
> for they are as light as upper air,
> they are as light as upper air!

Unlike the garden seat, the dead are beyond the influence of the elements, and they are "light" in juxtaposition to the "night", which blots out colours in the second stanza. Hardy's position seems to be that the presence of the dead is more real than the world of everyday appearance.[25]

Montale's translation reads as follows:

Vecchia panchina

> Il suo verde d'un tempo si logora, volge al blu.
> Le sue solide gambe cedono sempre piú.

Presto s'incurverà senz' avvedersene,
presto s'affonderà senz' avvedersene.

A notte, quando i piú accesi fiori si fanno neri,
ritornano coloro che vi stettero a sedere;
e qui vengono in molti e vi si posano,
vengono in bella fila e vi riposano.

E la panchina non sarà stroncata,
né questi sentiranno gelo o acquate,
perché sono leggeri come l'aria
di lassú, perché sono fatti d'aria![26]

The first point to note about the translation concerns its metre. Montale's lines are considerably longer than Hardy's octosyllabic verse. Mengaldo has observed that Hardy's lines are extremely concentrated, unlike Shakepeare's for example, and allow for very little reduction in the process of translation.[27] Moreover, Montale does not attempt the impossible—to find Italian monosyllables to match Hardy's English. Hardy's poem is a very English poem and Montale turns it into a very Italian one, but in that process he does not make substantial alterations to the form. As both Lonardi and Mengaldo have observed, Montale takes the original form as a datum the constraints of which are to be respected in the translation.[28]

His translation oscillates between hendecasyllables, alexandrines and hypermetric lines. He uses hendecasyllables for the refrains in each stanza, though the final stanza is the only one composed entirely of hendecasyllables. That gives the poem a rhythmic regularity. The *enjambement* into the last line, which places a strong stress on "lass*ú*", produces a type of sprung rhythm. The line may be read in either of the following ways:

di lass*ú*, perché *so*no *fa*tti d'aria

(with stresses on the third, sixth and eighth syllables);

di lass*ú*, perché sono *fa*tti d'aria

(with only two stresses, which is to say, as an irregular hendecasyllable).

Montale's method of dealing with Hardy's rhymes is resourceful. He rhymes monosyllables in the opening lines of the first stanza ("blu":"piú"), as if to give some of the flavour of Hardy's monosyllabic rhymes, but after that he avoids *parole tronche*. Mengaldo has observed that the refrains all end in *sdrucciole* rhymes. In the case of the first two stanzas that is quite clear, with "avvedersene" and "posano"/"riposano". Montale's choice of rhyme in the final stanza is more ingenious. He ends the final and penultimate lines with the word "aria" which appears *prima facie* to be a *parola piana*. But Mengaldo has cited several precedents in the Italian poetic tradition which support the use of "aria" as a *parola sdrucciola*. These include Boiardo, Ariosto and Parini.[29] Montale's refrains, unlike Hardy's, do not have a consistent rhyme in common. Mengaldo, however, has defended Montale's technique as a form of innovation:

> A differenza che in Hardy i tre distici di coda non rimano fra loro; ma poiché, secondo un'antica convenzione metrica nostrana che proprio Montale ha rinverdito nel nostro secolo, le coppie o serie di sdrucciole sono considerate equipollenti alle rime, ne deriva che per questa via il traduttore ha "alluso" al tecnicismo del testo di partenza, fornendone un abile equivalente.[30]

Montale does, however, retain a hint of Hardy's rhymes in his own phonic patterns, which mix rhyme and assonance, for example "verde" (line 1), "cedono" (line 2), "presto" (line 3), "avvedersene" (lines 3, 4) → "accessi", "neri" (line 5) → "stettero" → "sedere" (line 6), "vengono" (lines 7, 8) → "leggeri" (line 11). There are several systems of internal rhyme in Montale's poem, such as "s'incurve*rà*":"s'affonde*rà*":"sa*rà*":"sentiranno" (lines 3, 4, 9, 10) and "bl*u*":"pi*ú*":"lass*ú*" (lines 1, 2, 5, 12). Montale uses a large number of *parole sdrucciole* to slow the pace of his syntax, apparently as a cultural equivalent of Hardy's monosyllables: "lògora" (line 1), "sòlide", "cèdono" (line 2), "avvedèrsene" (lines 3, 4), "ritòrnano", "stèttero" (line 6), "vèngono" (lines 7, 8), "pòsano" (line 7), "ripòsano" (line 8) and "arïa" (lines 11, 12).

Montale departs significantly from Hardy's procedure in his treatment of the refrains. In Hardy's poem the lines of each refrain, with one minor exception, are identical; Montale's are all different. The difference is consistent with the variation procedure which we have observed in Montale's other translations. The refrain of the first stanza is the least modified:

> Presto *s'incurverà* senz' avvedersene,
> presto *s'affonderà* senz' avvedersene.

Montale uses two different words to convey Hardy's ambiguous phrasal verb "to break down". *Incurvarsi* catches the nuance of physical collapse in Hardy's verb while *affondarsi* refers back to "sink in and in", which Montale had to leave untranslated in the second line owing to lack of space. The variation in the second stanza is more blatant, though for once probably not so successful:

> e qui vengono in molti e vi si posano,
> vengono in bella fila e vi riposano.

The derived rhyme is unusually feeble by Montale's standards. The variation here seems to have been motivated by habit rather than by more specifically artistic criteria. The final variation is more characteristically Montalian:

> perché sono leggeri come l'aria
> di lassú, perché sono fatti d'aria!

In this refrain Montale moves from literal translation to creative rewriting. The *enjambement* into the last line, a technique which Montale had used elsewhere, is a subtle rhetorical device which slows the syntax of the poem and gives emphasis to Montale's (not Hardy's!) conclusion. Mengaldo has described the rhetorical effect as follows:

> Rigettato asimmetricamente dall'inarcatura all'inizio del verso, e seguito da una pausa che la rima al mezzo marca ulteriormente, il sintagma avverbiale "di lassú" acquista un rilievo che ne esalta il valore espressivo ed iconico (si ha come un momento di sospensione in cui lo sguardo è indotto a volgersi verso l'alto); mentre la rimodulazione del paragone fra la lievità degli ospiti della panchina e l'aria, che trasforma la similitudine in identità di sostanza, logicamente funziona come una *correctio* che dà a quell' identificazione il tono di una sommessa, stupefatta rivelazione (non ho dubbi che una corretta "esecuzione" richieda alleggerimento ed abbassamento della voce e tutt' altro andamento intonativo da quello della frase precedente).[31]

This is one of the more obvious hallmarks of Montale's appropriation of the poem, but there are others.

The title of Hardy's poem is descriptive and without nuance. Montale avoids a literal translation of the title, drops the definite article and replaces the quite objective modifier "garden" with the more emotive adjective "vecchia". Hardy's poem is static and Montale's is not. Hardy wrote, "its former green *is* blue and thin", whereas Montale gives the line a sense of activity by replacing the copula with two indicative verbs: "Il suo verde d'un tempo si *lògora, volge* al blu." In Montale's poem the reader glimpses the ageing process at work on the seat: "le sue solide gambe cedono *sempre piú*." Hardy's poem does not have that kind of activity. Likewise in the second stanza, at night Montale's flowers ("accesi fiori", not merely "red [...] flowers") "*si fanno* neri", while Hardy's "*are* black". Repetition is another symptom of the static quality of "The Garden Seat", and Montale's variation procedure in the refrains changes stasis into action; for example, despite Hardy's many uses of the generic "to sit" (including the noun "seat"), Montale does not once use the verb *sedere* in his translation. Montale's translation is thus much less generic and static than Hardy's original. Hardy's dead are *there* but Montale's dead *make their presence felt*. There is also a hint of the Arletta theme in Montale's verb *affondarsi*, which is not a literal translation of Hardy's "break down", though it does catch the nuance of the legs sinking in.

So what the two poets have in common is a certain scepticism concerning the nature of reality. Hardy's scepticism is evident in "The Garden Seat". The realistic details such as the red flowers are no more real than the nocturnal ghosts, so realism is no more tenable than anti-realism. Reality, Hardy seems to imply, is what we perceive. Hardy may have developed the idea under Schopenhauer's influence or he may equally have found it in a number of other places. Montale had a well-established penchant for anti-realist theories of perception, which is attested to by the *osso breve* "Forse un mattino andando". The realistic details there—the trees, houses and hills—are just images on a screen, held in place by the "inganno consueto". Montale returns to the screen image in the *mottetto* "La speranza di pure rivederti". In both cases the "schermo d'immagini" is the world of appearances rather than of reality. Contini, one of Montale's most faithful and perceptive readers, has drawn attention to his lack of confidence in the world of appearance and to his solipsistic imagination. For Montale the "schermo d'immagini" is only of value when it produces a "segno d'un'altra orbita" (in the terminology of "Arsenio") or, in the *mottetti*, clues of Clizia's presence—in other words, when it heralds an *occasione*.[32]

Communion with the dead, or "il ritorno dei morti", is another aspect of Montale's anti-realism. His conception of the dead is quite distinct from Hardy's, and he works his own into his rewriting of Hardy's poem. The theme was first mooted in the poems added to *Ossi di seppia* in its second edition—in the Arletta myth, which was possibly a legacy from Montale's reading of Joyce.

Homage to Joyce

Montale translated two of Joyce's poems when the reputations of both men were secure. They are slightly unusual choices on Montale's part in that neither of them appears to have a significant thematic connection with his own work. Both poems had been written while Joyce was living in Trieste before he had begun *Ulysses*.[33]

"Watching the Needleboats at San Sabba"

"Watching the Needleboats at San Sabba" is dated "Trieste, 1912" and was published in *Pomes Penyeach* in 1927. It is divided into two four-line stanzas, which rhyme ABAB CDCD. The metrical pattern is thus the same in both stanzas. The following is the poem as it is printed in the *Quaderno di traduzioni*:

> I heard their young hearts crying
> loveward above the glancing oar
> and heard the prairie grasses sighing:
> *no more, return no more!*
>
> O hearts, O sighing grasses,
> vainly your loveblown bannerets mourn!
> No more will the wild wind that passes
> return, no more return.

The title sets a tone of specificity for the poem. The observer is watching "needleboats" rather than any more generic vessel. But the title is somewhat misleading because the poem is primarily an auditory experience and announces itself as such: "I heard their young hearts crying/[...]/and heard the prairie grasses sighing."

The juxtaposition of "heard" and "hearts" in the first line introduces an element of word-play in keeping with the poem's auditory character. There are two unusual composite words in the poem, the first of which, "loveward" (line 2), modelled on words such as "homeward" and "forward", performs a linkage function. It points back to the /rd/ and /rt/ sounds of the first line as well as beginning a pattern of broad-vowel assonance which animates the second line: "l*o*veward ab*o*ve the gl*a*ncing *oa*r".

The second stanza begins with a recapitulation of the motifs of the first—the /rt/ pattern, the broad vowels and the sibilants. The second line of this stanza contains the second unusual composite word, "loveblown", an adjective modifying "bannerets". "Bannerets", the only truly recherché term in the poem, is presumably intended as a diminutive of "banners". Used in that context, it is pure Shakespeare: the *Oxford English Dictionary* records no occurrence of the word in that sense after *All's Well that Ends Well* (II. 3).[34] The wind, which is the real activating principle of the poem, appears explicitly only in the penultimate line, within a pattern of assonance: "No more *w*ill the *w*ild *w*ind that passes [...]." The final line is a variation on the closing line of the first stanza, restating the wind's melancholy message. So the poem shifts from a visual scene (the observer on the coast) into a world in which sound is the dominant sense. This makes translation especially difficult.

Montale's translation was first published in *Il mondo*, where the title was "Guardando i canottieri, a San Sabba". This translation of the title is not entirely literal: Joyce is watching "needleboats", Montale is watching "canottieri" (oarsmen). The title in the *Quaderno di traduzioni* changes the "a" to "di". This is an example of Montale's changing a title as an act of possession. The *Quaderno di traduzioni* version reads as follows:

> Ho udito quei giovani cuori gridare
> spinti da Amore sul guizzante remo,
> l'erbe dei prati ho udito sospirare
> *non torna, non torna piú!*
>
> O cuori, o erbe anelanti, invano gemono
> gonfiate dall'amore le vostre bandierine!

Mai piú il vento gagliardo che trascorre
vi tornerà vicino.[35]

Montale does not follow Joyce's rhyme scheme, but he does build up patterns of rhyme and quasi-rhyme. Some of these are end-rhymes ("gridare":"sospirare" and "bandierine":"vicino"), while others are internal rhymes (such as "cuori":"Amore" in lines 1–2 and "cuori":"amore":"trascorre" in lines 5–7).

Joyce's two composite words, "loveward" and "loveblown", both caused Montale difficulties. In each case he expands on Joyce's neologism in order to explain the sense. Thus "loveward" becomes "spinti da Amore" and "loveblown" becomes "gonfiate dall'amore". The first of these transpositions seems to do violence to the sense of "loveward": if "loveward" follows the structure of "homeward" and "backward", "spinti *verso* Amore" would appear to be the correct literal translation, and in consequence "spinti da Amore" would seem to be the exact opposite of a literal translation.

With two exceptions Montale translated the first line very literally. He replaces the English gerund ("crying") with an Italian infinitive ("gridare"), but this is a grammatical necessity imposed on him by the differences between the two languages; it does not alter the meaning. In the other case ("quei" for "their") there is a semantic shift. There is a similar semantic shift in the second line ("sul" for "above the"), but neither shift is really significant. Joyce's "glancing oar" is matched by an equally elegant adjective + noun construction in "guizzante remo". "Guizzante" is an adjective which belongs to Montale's idiolect and is a loaded term in his poetry. In this instance, however, the translation is literal. Montale's third line is also a literal translation, though he does introduce a hyperbaton which places "ho udito" in the middle of the hendecasyllable. This hyperbaton is motivated by a desire to provide a contrast with the syntactic structure of the first line. Montale begins the second stanza with a hypermetric line which accurately translates Joyce's first line and much of his second. Joyce's sibilant "sighing grasses" is a repetition of his earlier "grasses sighing" (line 3), which exploits the flexibility of the English gerund, demonstrating that it may be used as either a present participle or an adjective. Montale, not having the option of a similar repetition in Italian, decides on an entirely different adjective ("anelanti"), which is preceded by the noun "erbe" in a straightforward grammatical shift (Italian noun + adjective for English adjective + noun). Montale's sixth line is really two *settenari* joined together. The first *settenario* contains his amplification of "loveblown" while the second translates "your [...] bannerets". The last two lines are the least literal in the translation. This may be because Montale confines himself to hendecasyllables and *settenari*. Joyce's "wild" wind becomes "gagliardo",[36] and "passes" becomes "trascorre", which is a verb more usually associated with the passing of time. That is a subtle nuance, of course, which is quite appropriate given the poem's theme. "Vicino" in the final line is not a literal translation but has a structural function (it forms a false rhyme with "bandierine").

On balance, "Guardando i canottieri di San Sabba" is a very close translation of Joyce's poem. "Guizzante" and "bandierine", both words associated with Montale's idiolect, are literal translations of terms in Joyce's poem. Montale hardly intrudes. There are several features of Joyce's poem which minimize the need for a Montalian intrusion. Firstly, the scene (an observer looking out to sea from the coast) is one familiar from Montale's own poetry.[37] Secondly, the wind which animates the poem has an important place in Montale's poetics.[38] Finally, the theme of time passing, with the necessary implication of death, is one which impinges on Montale's own thematic concerns.[39]

"A Flower Given to My Daughter"

"A Flower Given to My Daughter" is dated "Trieste, 1913". The version printed in the *Quaderno di traduzioni* reads as follows:

> Frail the white rose and frail are
> her hands that gave
> whose soul is sere and paler
> than time's wan wave.
>
> Rosefrail and fair—yet frailest
> a wonder wild
> in gentle eyes thou veilest,
> my blueveined child.

Montale again avoids a literal translation of the title. His title reads "Per un fiore dato alla mia bambina", and the version printed in the *Quaderno di traduzioni* is as follows:

> Gracile rosa bianca e frali dita
> di chi l'offerse, di lei
> che ha l'anima piú pallida e appassita
> dell'onda scialba del tempo.
>
> Fragile e bella come rosa, e ancora
> piú fragile la strana meraviglia
> che veli ne' tuoi occhi, o mia azzurro-
> venata figlia.[40]

Montale does not follow Joyce's rhyme scheme, but there are two pairs of end-rhymes ("dita":"appassita" and "meraviglia": "figlia"). Nor does Montale opt for Joyce's taut metrical structure. By adopting a larger metrical frame he moves away from the interlinear translation procedure which he had adopted in "Guardando i canottieri di San Sabba". His first line has an *enjambement* into the second. He follows Joyce's hyperbaton, changing "hands" to "dita", which rhymes with "appassita" ("faded", "withered"). Montale does not repeat one word to match Joyce's repeated "frail", but his two words, "gracile" and "frali", are linked through assonance. "Gracile" is a dactyl, as is "fragile", which in the second stanza twice translates "frail".[41] There is an *enjambement* into the third line, which puts stresses on two more dactyls, "anima" and "pallida". Thus each of the poem's five dactyls stresses a broad /a/ vowel.

Joyce's "rosefrail" is amplified by Montale into "fragile e bella come rosa" (line 5). "Wild" appears again in Joyce's poem as an adjective qualifying "wonder". Montale finds another Italian equivalent for the adjective, translating the collocation as "la strana meraviglia" (line 6). Joyce's other composite word, "blueveined", is the only Joycean composite which Montale transposes into a composite Italian word, "azzurro-venata".

"A Flower Given to My Daughter" is a more difficult poem to translate into Italian than "Watching the Needleboats at San Sabba" because of the way in which Joyce manipulates the resources of the English monosyllable. In "Per un fiore dato alla mia bambina" Montale sets a pattern based on dactyls and broad vowels to establish poetic order. That necessary difference apart, the translation is a very close one.

"A Flower Given to My Daughter" appears to have no direct thematic connection with Montale's own poetry, and his decision to translate it suggests a homage to James Joyce, who had recently died, rather than the more predatory instinct attributed by Luperini to his interest in translating poetry.[42] The more convincing arguments showing that Joyce's prose was of substantially more interest to Montale than his poetry have already been advanced in Chapter 1. Joyce's two poems are weaker and less substantial things than Montale's translations of them.

Love and Absence: W. B. Yeats

Yeats is the only major English-speaking poet translated by Montale to whom he did not devote a critical essay. Montale accepted that Yeats was a great poet but he baulked at Yeats's ideological background:

> Il poeta [T. S. Eliot] resterà certo tra i maggiori del secolo anche se alcuni gli antepongono il cristallino, miracoloso e quasi pazzesco (dal punto di vista ideologico) William Butler Yeats dell'ultima maniera. Ma Yeats era alquanto piú anziano e in lui la distruzione della poesia borghese poteva ancora fondarsi sul mito celtico e in un *engagement* orfico-politico assurdo fin che si vuole ma degno di ispirare grande poesia.[43]

On the subject of *poesia civile* Montale wrote in 1969, thirty years after Yeats's death:

> Se intendiamo per poesia civile quella che celebra l'epifania o i fasti di una *civitas* o addirittura di una stirpe direi che una simile poesia debba considerarsi estinta. Parlo naturalmente dei poeti in do maggiore, restando esclusi quei lirici che tentano di resuscitare nostalgicamente un passato irrecuperabile: l'Elleno di Kavafis o il Celta di Yeats.[44]

Montale clearly had grave reservations about the political motivations of Yeats's poetry, but he had no difficulty in accepting that both he and Yeats belonged to the same Symbolist tradition:

> Sarebbe dunque morta quella poesia pura che, largamente intesa, dovrebbe includere i nomi di Baudelaire e di Hopkins, di Yeats e di Valéry; quella poesia, teorizzata per la prima volta da Edgar Poe, che domanda forte concentrazione espressiva, alto potere di trasfigurazione musicale e una totale compenetrazione dell'idea

> e del significato? Non saprei né vorrei affermarlo ma è certo che in quest' ordine le grandi apparizioni poetiche sono e saranno sempre rare. È dunque legittimo che poeti di natura meno ascetica volgano a una concezione piú lata ma anche piú generica della poesia; e che insomma si torni a credere che è poesia ogni composizione in versi (o quasi versi) che esprima qualcosa di intelligibile e sia condotta a regola d'arte.[45]

Montale's admiration for Yeats concerns the latter's writing rather than his motivations. Montale wrote: "Yeats compone già dal di fuori, ma compone ancora. Ogni sua poesia è un oggetto."[46] According to Montale, Yeats's poetry is the work of "un maestro del verso, un genio della grande tradizione europea che passa attraverso Baudelaire". But this mastery of verse, Montale claims, is problematic: it made of Yeats "un poeta del tutto intraducibile".[47]

"The Indian to His Love"

"The Indian to His Love" is an early Yeats poem; it was first published in 1889 in *Crossways*. The following is the text of the poem as it appears in the *Quaderno di traduzioni*:

> The island dreams under the dawn
> and great boughs drop tranquillity;
> the peahens dance on a smooth lawn,
> a parrot sways upon a tree,
> raging at his own image in the enamelled sea.
>
> Here we will moor our lonely ship
> and wander ever with woven hands,
> murmuring softly lip to lip,
> along the grass, along the sands,
> murmuring how far away are the unquiet lands:
>
> how we alone of mortals are
> hid under quiet boughs apart,
> while our love grows an Indian star,
> a meteor of the burning heart,
> one with the tide that gleams, the wings that gleam and dart
>
> the heavy boughs, the burnished dove
> that moans and sighs a hundred days:
> how when we die our shades will rove,

when eve has hushed the feathered ways,
with vapoury footsole by the water's drowsy blaze.

This poem is one of the best which Montale decided to translate from English. The syntax is exceptionally straightforward: the narrative is almost that of prose; yet Yeats succeeds in casting the poem in a tight metrical structure consisting of four octosyllabic lines per stanza followed in each case by a longer line which resembles an alexandrine. The longer lines which end the stanza are not hexameters because they contain only five metrical feet, so they represent a type of sprung rhythm with several slack syllables, for instance, "*ra*ging at his *own im*age in the en*am*elled *sea*". Each stanza has a definite ABABB rhyme scheme. Syntactic and metrical periods tend to coincide in the poem, there being three caesuras and just one *enjambement*:

the heavy boughs, the burnished dove
that moans and sighs a hundred days.

The poem is dominated by a grammatical figure which consists of noun + verb + preposition + noun. The first four lines conform almost completely to that figure, as do the closing lines. The coherence of sound, imagery and thought is breathtaking. The first stanza contains the seeds of what is to follow. There is extensive anticipation of rhymes, for instance, "is*land*" (line 1) → "hands": "sands":"lands" (second stanza), "dr*eams*" (line 1) → "gleams": "gleam" (line 15) and "*sways*" (line 4) → "days":"ways":"blaze" (fourth stanza). The images equated with the Indian star at the end of the third stanza refer back to the first stanza ("the tide that gleams" → "the enamelled sea" and "the wings that gleam and dart" → "the peahens" and "a parrot"). The poem is an incantation. Repetition builds up the charm in a combination of cadence, interplay of vowels, and alliteration, for example:

The island *dr*eams under the *da*wn
and great boughs *dr*op tranquillity;
the peahens *da*nce on a smooth lawn,
a parrot sways upon a tree,
raging at his own image in the enamelled sea.

The tension running through the poem is that between the heavy quiet boughs of the idealized island, which drop tranquillity ("boughs" appears in three of the four stanzas accompanied by a different adjective on each occasion), and the "unquiet lands" from which the speaker is anxious to depart. The tension is underscored by a characteristic disdain for the living ("we alone of mortals are", "the burnished dove/that moans and sighs a hundred days") and a more positive reference to the dead (in the final three lines). Montale would have had little difficulty in recognizing some of his own preoccupations in Yeats's lyric. Those would include the disdain for the many as against the few, the elemental images equated with the symbol of the Indian star ("the burning heart", "the tide that gleams" and "the wings that gleam and dart"), the "ritorno dei morti" theme and, in the poem's final image ("the water's drowsy blaze"), the characteristically Montalian *barbaglio*.

His translation reads as follows:

L'indiano all'amata

L'isola sogna sotto l'alba,
dai grandi tronchi stilla la pace;
sul prato liscio danzano i pavoni,
un pappagallo dondola su un ramo
e s'infuria specchiandosi in un mare di smalto.

Amarreremo qui la barca vuota,
con le mani intrecciate errando a lungo,
bocca su bocca mormorando teneri
tra l'erbe, tra le sabbie, susurrando
che le terre inquiete sono troppo lontane.

Come soli restiamo fra i mortali,
in disparte, celati fra le grandi ramure,
mentre dal nostro amore si esprime un astro indú,
una meteora dal bruciante cuore,
unita alla marea che luccica, alle ali
che scintillano e razzano,
alle rame pesanti, alla scura colomba
che geme e che sospira cento giorni;
e come vagheranno, quando saremo morti,
le nostre ombre, la sera sui sentieri felpati
smorzando coi passi aerei il sonno abbagliante dell'acque.[48]

For once, Montale gives a literal translation of the title. He does, however, make some structural changes. He combines the third and fourth stanzas, and in so doing divides one of the long lines in two, thus producing two five-line stanzas and an eleven-line stanza. Montale's metrical structure is not as tight as Yeats's. His lines are of various lengths, ranging from a *settenario* ("che scintillano e razzano") to lines of fifteen syllables.

Montale does not attempt to follow Yeats's rhyme scheme; there are, in fact, no end-rhymes in his translation. He does respect Yeats's syntax to some extent. The first stanza is almost a very literal and accurate translation, though Montale does invert the syntax in the third line. The effect of the inversion is to emphasize "danzano" in the middle of the line. This is one of several *parole sdrucciole* which Montale uses in the first stanza. In fact there is a definite pattern to his use of *parole sdrucciole* in the opening lines:

> L'*isola* sogna sotto l'alba,
> dai grandi tronchi stilla la pace;
> sul prato liscio *danzano* i pavoni,
> un pappagallo *dondola* su un ramo
> e s'infuria *specchiandosi* in un mare di smalto.

If, following Mengaldo's analysis of "Vecchia panchina", one accepts "s'infuria" as one more *sdrucciola*, there are five *sdrucciole* in the first stanza alone. Montale uses the *parole sdrucciole* as a means of slowing the pace of his Italian in relation to Yeats's English. He also uses only one *parola tronca* ("indú") where there might have been a temptation to translate "tranquillity" as *tranquillità* rather than *pace*. He compensates by accelerating the pace through *enjambements*, for example:

> susurrando
> che le terre inquiete sono troppo lontane;
> (lines 9–10)

and

> unita alla marea che luccica, alle ali
> che scintillano e razzano,
> alle rame pesanti, alla scura colomba
> che geme e che sospira cento giorni.
> (lines 15–18)

While there are no end-rhymes, Montale's poem has a well-developed pattern of assonance, as in "*i*sola" → "st*i*lla" → "l*i*scio", "s*o*gna" → "tr*o*nchi" → "d*o*ndola" and "l'*a*lba" → "p*a*ce" → "pappagallo" → "ramo" → "mare" → "smalto". He suppresses Yeats's gerund in line 5 ("raging") but echoes it later in the line with "specchiandosi". The only real infidelity in the first stanza is so slight as to appear irrelevant, but it is not irrelevant. Montale resorts to synecdoche in the fourth line, translating "tree" as "ramo". To translate literally (*albero*) would have produced a further *sdrucciola* and would have turned the line from a hendecasyllable into a hypermetric line. But given the profusion of *sdrucciole* and free-verse metre in the first stanza, those can hardly have been the deciding factors in Montale's choice. There is a more probable explanation. "Ramo" and "mare", one line apart, are familiar Montalian words, which formed part of his acrostic sensibility. They are linguistic clues suggesting Clizia's presence, hints in Montale's private language that this translation of Yeats's love lyric is a poem appropriated for Clizia.

Montale's habitual tendency towards variation rather than repetition of individual words manifests itself again in this poem. As we have seen, Yeats had repeated "boughs", varying the adjective on each of the three occasions. Montale uses three different nouns, "tronchi" (line 2), "ramure" (line 12) and "rame" (line 17). His solution to Yeats's repeated "murmuring" is particularly inventive. Italian has not one but two equivalents which translate both the sense and the onomatopoeia of Yeats's gerund, and Montale uses both of them, "mormorando" in line 8 and "susurrando" in line 9. There are a number of mistranslated adjectives in Montale's version, including "vuota" for "lonely" (line 6), "grandi" for "quiet" (line 12) and "felpati" for "feathered" (line 20).

There is another area of Montalian resonance and appropriation in the final stanza of his poem (that is, the third and fourth stanzas of Yeats's). Some of Yeats's words when translated literally produce Montalian resonances, for instance, "to gleam" (*luccicare* and *scintillare*) and "drowsy blaze" ("sonno abbagliante").[49] The last three lines are the most interesting in relation to Montale's appropriation. Yeats's poem has the shades rove *in hora mortis*, with a possible nuance of an action which happens once only; the nuance in Montale's poem could be read as referring to an action which will be habitual—not *in hora mortis* at all but *after* the deaths of the Indian and his love:

> e come vagheranno, *quando saremo morti,*
> le nostre ombre, la sera sui sentieri felpati
> smorzando coi passi aerei il sonno abbagliante dell'acque.

The closing image of the lyric is of the Montalian "ritorno dei morti" once again, at the water's edge, and is reminiscent of "La casa dei doganieri", "Casa sul mare" and other poems associated with Arletta. But while the theme and the waterside location may have drawn Montale to Yeats's poem, the textual evidence suggests that Montale appropriated it for Clizia and not for Arletta, though it is probable that any such attempt to impose a dividing-line between the female figures of Montale's poetry is idle speculation. Montale found what he read as an Arletta reference in Yeats's poem and imported the Clizia reference into that poem in the act of rewriting it.

On Questions of Technique: Adams and Thomas

Léonie Adams's "Lullaby"

Montale's translation, or more precisely his adaptation, of Léonie Adams's "Lullaby" is one of his earlier translations. It was published, with the subtitle "adattamento di Eugenio Montale", together with his translations of two of T. S. Eliot's poems in 1933.[50]

Léonie Adams (b. 1899) described her poetry in the following terms: "Lyric Poetry, in largely traditional forms. At formative period influenced by Elizabethan, early Romantic and, through Yeats largely, Symbolist poetry."[51] So Adams had the poetic background common to many Modernist poets. She published her first two collections in the 1920s, and both volumes had titles likely to commend themselves to Montale's attention, *Those Not Elect* (1925) and *High Falcon and Other Poems* (1929).[52] Léonie Adams received some critical acclaim in the early 1930s and went on from that to a successful academic career at Columbia University.[53]

The poetry of Léonie Adams may have held a certain attraction for Montale. But Adams is not mentioned in any of the essays collected in his *Sulla poesia*. "Lullaby" itself appears to present no thematic affinities with Montale's work.

The following is the text of Léonie Adams's "Lullaby", which was included in her second collection, *High Falcon*:

Hush, lullay,
your treasures all
   encrust with rust.
Your trinket pleasures
   fall
to dust.
Beneath the sapphire arch
upon the grassy floor
is nothing more
   to hold,
and play is over old.
Your eyes
   in sleepy fever gleam,
your lids droop
   to their dream.
You wander late alone,
the flesh frets on the bone,
your love fails
   in your breast.
Here is the pillow.
   Rest.

The poem is a free-verse composition made up of short lines in the manner of a traditional lullaby. As might be expected, there is an abundance of monosyllables, such as the imperatives which begin and end the poem, "Hush" and "Rest". Both those words contain sibilants, and there is in fact a sibilant pedal note throughout the poem: "Hu*sh*", "tr*easures*", "encru*st*", "ru*st*", "pl*easures*", "du*st*", "*sa*pphire", "gr*assy*", "ey*es*", "*sl*eepy", "fle*sh*", "fre*ts*", "fai*ls*", "brea*st*", "re*st*". Many of the rhymes in the poem involve this sibilant pedal: "treasures":"pleasures" (lines 2, 4), "encrust": "rust":"dust" (lines 3, 6), "breast":"rest" (lines 19, 21). There are, however, rhymes which do not involve sibilants: "all":"fall" (lines 2, 5), "floor":"more" (lines 8, 9), "hold":"old" (lines 10, 11), "gleam":"dream" (lines 13, 15), "alone":"bone" (lines 16, 17). All these rhymes are composed either of open vowels or of diphthongs. The first six lines may serve as an example:

Hush, lullay,
your treasures all
  encrust with rust.
Your trinket pleasures
  fall
to dust.

So Léonie Adams's "Lullaby" is a short, simple but well-constructed poem. The finesse of the construction was its most likely attraction for Montale, but that is also what made it rather difficult to translate.

The following is Montale's version, to which he gave the title "Ninna nanna":

Smettila, ninna nanna, arrugginisce
ogni tuo bene;
ogni ninnolo in cenere
        finisce.
Sotto l'arco di zàffiro
e sul terreno erboso
nulla da fare: il giuoco
        è assai noioso!

Nella febbre del sonno
ti scintillano
gli occhi, scendon le pàlpebre
        nel sogno.

Vai solo; tesa all'osso
la carne è rósa.

Muore l'amore in petto.
Ecco il guanciale:
        riposa.[54]

Montale could not have hoped to match Adams's monosyllables or the brevity of her lines because of the differences between the two languages. He does use a free-verse form similar to that of Adams's poem. As we have seen, however, his version does not claim to be a literal translation but an "adattamento".

Montale again makes extensive use of *parole sdrucciole*, apparently as a means of emulating Adams's monosyllables. The following is a list of the *parole sdrucciole*: "smettila" (line 1), "ninnolo", "cenere" (line 3), "zàffiro" (line 5), "scintillano" (line 10), "pàlpebre" (line 11). "Scendon" (line 11) without the apocope would also be a *parola sdrucciola*. The *parole sdrucciole* have the effect of slowing down the pace of the Italian line, making it more reminiscent of the cadence of speech.

The sibilants are not as pervasive in Montale's poem as they are in Adams's, but there is definitely a muted sibilant pedal in "Ninna nanna" composed of the following: "smettila", "arrugginisce" (line 1), "finisce" (line 4), "sotto" (line 5), "sul", "erboso" (line 6), "assai noioso" (line 8), "sonno" (line 9), "scintillano" (line 10), "scendon" (line 11), "sogno" (line 12), "solo", "tesa", "osso" (line 13), "rósa" (line 14), "riposa" (line 17).

"Lullaby", even with its ubiquitous monosyllables, runs to twenty-one lines, whereas "Ninna nanna" has only seventeen. The process of reduction requires some analysis. Montale's first line is a hendecasyllable which translates both Adams's first and third lines. Thus through a process of hyperbaton Montale translated three English lines in two Italian lines. Adams's musical third line is stripped of its redundant elements and translated by a precise verb, *arrugginire*, placed at the end of the opening line. Montale adopts the same procedure for the next three lines of Adams's poem, again reducing them to two Italian lines through a process of hyperbaton. This time the noun + noun compound "trinket pleasures" is reduced to the precise noun "ninnolo". Montale mistranslates "fall" as "finisce" to rhyme with "arrugginisce" in the first line.

The second section of text in Adams's poem runs to five lines while in Montale's version it consists of four. Adams's poem becomes a little obscure in lines 9–11:

> is nothing more
>   to hold,
> and play is over old.

Montale's translation avoids the obscurity but changes the sense:

> nulla da fare: il giuoco
>   è assai noioso!

The next section of text consists of four lines in both poems. The two sets of lines demonstrate nicely some of what might be called essential differences between the two languages:

Your eyes
  in sleepy fever gleam,
your lids droop
  to their dream.

(lines 12–15)

Nella febbre del sonno
ti scintillano
gli occhi, scendon le pàlpebre
    nel sogno.

(lines 9–12)

There is hyperbaton in both versions to a greater or lesser extent. Adams, in placing the adjective + noun construction before the verb ("sleepy fever gleam") achieves a Victorian nuance. Montale excises the adjective + noun construction, though he retains something like the sense of the original—"nella febbre del sonno" ("in the fever of sleep"). His equivalent for "gleam" is accurate (*scintillare*). Montale here found himself at a cutting edge of translation, and his version is faithful to the nature of the Italian language. The second half of Adams's sentence offers more Victoriana: "your lids droop / to their dream." Montale's Italian version avoids the possessive adjectives, leaving a verb, a definite article, a noun, a *preposizione articolata* and another noun ("scendon le pàlpebre / nel sogno").

Montale also removes the possessive adjectives from the second part of Adams's last sentence: "your love fails / in your breast" becomes "Muore l'amore in petto." As before, Montale's verb is more precise and less "poetic" in a Victorian sense. It also gives him the opportunity to place "muore" and "amore" in close proximity, as if to stress by the assonance the close connection in the Italian language between love and death. In short, Montale's poem is more accomplished than Adams's original, but it is quite a different poem.

A Different Kind of Seed-bed

Montale's comment, quoted in the previous chapter, that "il grande semenzaio d'ogni trovata poetica è nel campo della prosa", is well known. The extent to which translation could provide a poetic discovery for his own poetry, however, is more clearly seen in the case of poems to which he was not attracted by thematic affinities. The foregoing analysis has shown that in his "Ninna nanna" virtually every word is important: each word has a function in relation to the other words of the poem. This is also a characteristic of Montale's mature poetry and especially of the *mottetti*, a group of poems written during his period of activity as a translator. To illustrate the point it may be instructive to contrast one of the *ossi brevi* with one of the *mottetti* in the light of Montale's technical solutions to the problems posed by the translation of Léonie Adams's "Lullaby". The following is the last of the *ossi brevi*:

Sul muro grafito
che adombra i sedili rari
l'arco del cielo appare
finito.

Chi si ricorda piú del fuoco ch'arse
impetuoso
nelle vene del mondo; —in un riposo
freddo le forme, opache, sono sparse.

Rivedrò domani le banchine
e la muraglia e l'usata strada.
Nel futuro che s'apre le mattine
sono ancorate come barche in rada.[55]

This poem is representative of the *ossi brevi*. It is written in a free verse which combines hendecasyllables (five in this case) with shorter lines in a random fashion. There are rhymes and half-rhymes, such as "grafito":"finito", "rari":"appare" and "impetuoso":"riposo". There are familiar Montalian objects like a wall, boats and benches. There are noun + adjective combinations, such as "muro grafito", "sedili rari" and "riposo freddo", and an adjective + noun compound, "l'usata strada". These combinations contribute towards a heaviness and lack of vitality in the poem. The obscurity in the second stanza, the fire burning in the veins of the world, seems out of place in the company of the other two stanzas.

Several of the *mottetti* could usefully be contrasted with "Sul muro grafito", but the following is probably the most satisfactory paradigm:

Ecco il segno; s'innerva
sul muro che s'indora:
un frastaglio di palma
bruciato dai barbagli dell'aurora.

Il passo che proviene
dalla serra sí lieve,
non è felpato dalla neve, è ancora
tua vita, sangue tuo nelle mie vene.[56]

There are points of contact between the two poems. The Montalian wall again appears as a type of large screen; there are even veins as before. But this is a very different type of poem. Free verse has apparently been abandoned: the poem is constructed out of five *settenari* and three hendecasyllables. Assonance is at work from the beginning ("*E*cco il s*e*gno; s'inn*e*rva"). It combines with internal rhyme in lines 3 and 4:

un fras*taglio* di p*a*lma
bruci*a*to dai barb*agli* dell'aurora.

Alliteration is worked in too, as in "*b*ruciato dai *b*ar*b*agli dell'au*r*o*r*a". There are end-rhymes—"s'indora":"aurora":"ancora" (lines 2, 4, 7); "proviene":"vene" (lines 5, 8)—but there are also internal rhymes, such as "lieve":"neve" (lines 6, 7). Apart from possessive adjectives (three in the final line) there are no adjective + noun combinations. The punctuation, *enjambements* and caesuras suggest that some of the hendecasyllables are quasi-hendecasyllables, that the line-breaks could very easily come elsewhere. The poem could equally have appeared in the following form:

Ecco il segno;
s'innerva sul muro che s'indora:
un frastaglio di palma
bruciato dai barbagli dell'aurora.

Il passo che proviene
dalla serra sí lieve,
non è felpato dalla neve,
è ancora tua vita,
sangue tuo nelle mie vene.

This restructuring of the poem brings into focus Montale's wordplay and his interest in anagrams and acrostics. "Neve" comes out from within a line and appears at the end in contrast to "vene", another word which uses the same letters. Those three letters, *e*, *n* and *v*, come to dominate the second stanza ("proviene", "lieve", "nelle"), and they also refer back to the verb removed from the first *settenario*, "s'innerva".

Words have vitality in this poem by virtue of their shape and their sound. In the second stanza "passo", "serra", "dalla" and "nelle" seem to conform to a structure of consonant + vowel + double consonant + vowel. In the first stanza "segno", "muro" and "palma" follow a similar pattern based on rhythm. There may be no adjective + noun combinations but there is a different structure instead. It is introduced in the first stanza—"sul muro che [+ verb]"—and repeated in the second: "Il passo che [+ verb]". The image of blood in the veins is an integral part of this poem. The words "sangue" and "vene" appear quite natural in the final line because they have grown out of the linguistic seeds provided in the first line by "segno" and "s'innerva" (both the identical consonants and the internal rhythm of the words connect the ones with the others).

It may be objected that while the above observations on the *osso breve* and the *mottetto* are sustainable, they have little or no bearing on "Ninna nanna". Up to a point that would be a valid objection: there is no specific connection. Given that the *mottetto* is a more sophisticated piece of writing than the *osso breve*, however, and that in the intervening period Montale had begun translating from English and Spanish, there is the basis for an argument which would seek to demonstrate that the practice of translation sharpened Montale's creative ability by making him more aware of the linguistic resources of Italian. His *mottetti* have a complex linguistic unity reminiscent of his 1933 translation of Léonie Adams's "Lullaby". He described that work as an "adattamento": it is a reduction of the American poem to an essential Italian form, and Montale's adaptation is a more coherent unit than Adams's poem. There is a similar relationship between the *osso breve* "Sul muro grafito" (1925) and the *mottetto* "Ecco il segno" (1938). As we have seen, the same objects (the wall and the veins) appear in both, but whereas the *osso breve* is a relatively loose piece of *vers libre*, in the later poem the objects are treated in a manner which had been refined to a significant extent, and I would contend that the refining process had been, at least partly, influenced by Montale's experience of translation.

Dylan Thomas's "Poem Fifth"

Montale met Thomas met twice, once in Florence and once in Oxford, and dedicated an essay to him in 1954.[57] He acknowledges that Thomas possessed "uno straordinario dono verbale", which resulted in "difficult" poetry. He describes Thomas as "un compendio di un buon secolo e mezzo di poesia inglese, da Shelley a Joyce, attraverso Hopkins ed Eliot". This judgement suggests a basis for affinity between the two poets because Montale had attempted to appropriate that English tradition as a literary ancestor to his own poetry.

Montale was aware of Thomas's claim to have been saved from Swinburne by Hopkins: "Di lui [Thomas] fu detto che Hopkins lo aveva salvato da Swinburne: cioè che il demone del Verbo lo salvò dai rischi di un troppo scoperto abbandono sentimentale e sensuale." He connects Thomas with both Hopkins and Blake, two English poets to whom he felt attracted, and whose work he chose to translate:

> È un grande poeta Dylan? La questione resta aperta, per lui e per quasi tutti gli inglesi moderni (Yeats escluso, che ha già un posto altissimo). Ma non può negarsi che quel suo blakiano scrivere "per amor dell'Uomo e in lode di Dio" abbia trovato accenti e punte laceranti. Forse è un errore volerlo comprender troppo; fondamentalmente era un analogista a sfondo religioso, che non avrebbe scritto un rigo se si fosse davvero chiarito razionalmente. In ciò Dylan fu veramente "moderno" in tutti i sensi, buoni e men buoni, e chi lo ama non lo vorrebbe diverso.

Montale's conclusion concerning Dylan Thomas throws his precise estimation of Thomas's poetry into some doubt. On several occasions Montale defined poetry as "a dream in reason's presence", and this definition seems to have been normative rather than descriptive. Therefore, to claim that Thomas would not have written a line if he had used reason rather than analogy as the basis of his thinking is not necessarily a positive judgement on Montale's part.

Montale also had a view on the problems inherent in translating Thomas's poetry: "Per comprendere Thomas, e per tradurlo, occorrerebbe il lavoro di un'intera squadra di specialisti; e ancora rimarrebbero non pochi punti oscuri, dubbi e dissensi."[58] Given this qualification and Montale's ambiguous estimation of Thomas's poetry, it may be interesting to see how he approached the business of translating one of Thomas's poems after a brief analysis of the original.

The following is the text of the poem by Dylan Thomas that Montale translated:

> The force that through the green fuse drives the flower
> Drives my green age; that blasts the roots of trees
> Is my destroyer.
> And I am dumb to tell the crooked rose
> My youth is bent by the same wintry fever.
>
> The force that drives the water through the rocks
> Drives my red blood; that drives the mouthing streams
> Turns mine to wax.
> And I am dumb to mouth unto my veins
> How at the mountain spring the same mouth sucks.
>
> The hand that whirls the water in the pool
> Stirs the quicksand; that ropes the blowing wind
> Hauls my shroud sail.
> And I am dumb to tell the hanging man
> How of my clay is made the hangman's lime.
>
> The lips of time leech to the fountain head;
> Love drips and gathers, but the fallen blood
> Shall calm her sores.
> And I am dumb to tell a weather's wind
> How time has ticked a heaven round the stars.
>
> And I am dumb to tell the lover's tomb
> How at my sheet goes the same crooked worm.

The poem is composed of four five-line stanzas and a final couplet. In each stanza the third line is short and the other four are in iambic pentameter. There are, however, frequent *enjambements* and caesuras in each of the stanzas. Several different features characterize the poem. A figure consisting of a definite article + noun + relative pronoun (such as "The force that") opens each of the first three stanzas. This construction corresponds to the Italian construction "il *x* che", which is a favourite Montalian construction.[59] Repetition is a key to the incantatory power of Thomas's poem. The refrain "And I am dumb to tell/mouth" in each stanza, including the couplet, adds to this effect. The repetition of /t/, /th/ and /d/ sounds throughout the poem is another aspect of its auditory appeal. Thomas used alliteration unsparingly, as in "force" → "fuse" → "flower" or "whirls" → "water" → "blowing" → "wind". The vowels characteristic of Welsh English are used to form a web of assonance in the poem, as for example in the final couplet, where the three words "dumb", "tomb" and "worm" are all connected by assonance. In fact assonance is a more active principle of organization in the poem than rhyme. Thomas seems deliberately to choose words which just avoid rhyming for positions in which readers and listeners accustomed to pre-modern English poetry might expect rhymes, for instance "destroyer":"fever", "rocks":"wax":"sucks" and "tomb":"worm". The feature of the poem most resistant to translation into Italian, however, is the preponderance of monosyllables: there are only sixteen words in the whole poem which are not monosyllabic. Of these sixteen, eight are modifiers.[60]

This poem, together with "Pied Beauty", is one of the most demanding texts which Montale chose to translate, because of the extent to which Dylan Thomas exploited the expressive rather than the rational resources of the English language.

The following is his translation of Thomas's poem, to which the title "Quinta poesia" was given:

La forza che urgendo nel verde calamo guida il fiore,
guida la mia verde età; quell' impeto che squassa le radici
degli alberi
è per me distruzione.
E muto non so dire alla rosa avvizzita
che questa febbre invernale piega anche la mia giovinezza.

La forza che guida l'acqua tra le rocce,
guida il mio rosso sangue; quella stessa che asciuga le sorgenti
che gridano,
le mie raggruma;
e son muto a gridare alle mie vene
che a quell' alpestre polla succhia la stessa bocca.

La mano che mulina l'acqua dentro alla pozza
sommuove il fondo limo; quella che lega i vènti, ora il sudario

della mia vela spinge.
E sono muto a dire all'impiccato
quant' è della mia argilla in chi lo impicca.

Le labbra del tempo lambiscono dove la fronte fa vena;
goccia l'amore, gonfia, ma il sangue che cade, di lei
addolcirà le pene.
E sono muto a dire al soffio che si leva
che paradiso è scandito dal tempo intorno alle stelle:

muto a dire alla tomba dell'amante
che sul mio letto appare lo stesso verme aggrinzito.[61]

This text is almost unique among Montale's translations in that there are no surviving variants. It follows the form of Thomas's poem—four five-line stanzas with a final couplet—but Montale's lines are mostly hypermetric. His translation repeats Thomas's *enjambements* and caesuras—a case both of literal translation and of Montale using his own idiom.

The proliferation of syllables, unusual for Montale, suggests a more literal approach to the translation of "Poem Fifth" than to other poems. The translation of Thomas's repeated "the *x* that" figure is literal ("La forza che" in the first two stanzas and "La mano che" in the third), but it is not clear whether Montale's linguistic choice is based on the criterion of literal translation or on that of a congenial linguistic structure with which he was already very familiar. In other translations he maintained a taut metrical structure by excising adjectives which did not seem essential. To a limited extent he appears to continue this approach in "Quinta poesia"; for example, two adjectives are reduced to one in "the same wintry fever" → "questa febbre invernale". On closer inspection, however, it becomes clear that there is no significant reduction in this sentence. "Questa" is, of course, a demonstrative adjective, but that is a minor point. Montale's reason for removing Thomas's "same" has more to do with syntactic clarity than with reduction.

Given that clarity was Montale's guiding criterion, it is likely that he paid correspondingly less attention to the poem's formal characteristics. His text, like Thomas's, does include some half-rhymes and false rhymes, such as "vena":"pene" (lines 16, 18) and "avvizzita":"aggrinzito" (lines 4, 22). But whereas repetition is the key rhetorical feature of the English poem, Montale avoids Thomas's repetitions of "And I am dumb to" by varying his translation of the refrain: "E muto non so dire" (line 4), "e son muto a gridare" (line 9), "E sono muto a dire" (lines 14, 19), "muto a dire" (line 21). This variation procedure is common to virtually all Montale's translations.

Montale's concern with literal interpretation was, however, selective. His "calamo" ("reed" or "stalk") in the opening line makes sense in Italian but it is not a literal translation of "fuse". Lonardi has suggested that Montale's "squassa" for "blasts" (line 2) is inaccurate and has offered two further possibilities, *dissecca* and *distrugge*.[62] In fact, however, Montale's choice of verb is more apt than either of Lonardi's suggestions, though Lonardi does have a point when he draws attention to the linguistic connections with "Tramontana" (1922). The verb ("squassa") and the noun which accompanies it ("radici") both appear in that relatively early poem dedicated to the wind:

> Ogni forma si *squassa* nel subbuglio
> degli elementi; [...],
> mia vita sottile, e come ami
> oggi le tue *radici*.[63]

There is certainly an echo here, and another is heard when the following lines from "Mia vita, a te non chiedo lineamenti" (1924) are recalled:

> Il cuore che ogni moto tiene a vile
> raro è *squassato* da trasalimenti.[64]

The connection between the three poems is the power of the wind. Montale reiterates that power in his translation of "Poem Fifth" where Dylan Thomas does not:

> The force that through the green fuse drives the flower
> Drives my green age; that blasts the roots of trees
> Is my destroyer.

> La *forza* che urgendo nel verde calamo guida il fiore,
> guida la mia verde età; quell' *impeto* che squassa le radici degli alberi
> è per me distruzione.

Montale uses two grammatical subjects, "forza" and "impeto", as against Thomas's one.

There is another subtle shift of meaning. The force, according to Dylan Thomas, "is my destroyer"; for Montale it is "destruction". This is significant because of the echoes of "La bufera", which begins with the same opening figure as "Quinta poesia" ("La bufera che sgronda"); and as in "Quinta poesia" the figure is repeated ("il lampo che candisce").[65] The calamitous term "distruzione" also appears in "La bufera", in a stressed position within the third stanza:

> il lampo che candisce
> alberi e muri e li sorprende in quella
> eternità d'istante—marmo manna
> e distruzione.

Thus Montale's translation of "Poem Fifth" continues motifs which stretch back over twenty years in his own poetry and have as a constant preoccupation the power of the wind and the storm. The wind is both an animating and a lethal agent in Montale's poetry. By the 1940s it has acquired Dantean nuances and become "la bufera".

There is also a subtle shift of meaning in the second stanza. Montale translates "drives" (line 7) as "asciuga" ("dries"), which might suggest a misreading of the English text. On the other hand, "asciuga" is consistent with "raggruma" ("thickens", "coagulates"), which is Montale's translation of "turns mine to wax" (line 8). That image of coagulation of the blood appeared in one of Montale's poems for Volpe thought to have been written in 1949.[66] The other major textual infidelity concerns the verb *lambire* ("to lap" or "to lick"), which Montale used to make sense of Thomas's verb "to leech".[67]

Dylan Thomas's poem, then, would have been congenial to Montale for several reasons. Structurally, its refusal to rhyme in order to gratify the reader's expectations and the prominence of the "the *x* that *y*" figure were both characteristics as much of Montale's own poetry as of Dylan Thomas's. Furthermore, Thomas's mysterious intensity in relation to the animating force in nature would have held attractions for Montale, and translating the poem allowed Montale the opportunity of returning to a theme and motifs which were part of his own poetic past. In 1946 he was looking for an English model for his poetry; he wanted to see and hear how his poetry would feel in English; and in Thomas's poem he could see and hear aspects of his own preoccupations and style.[68]

HOMAGE?

The suggestion that Montale's translations of poems by Blake, Hardy, Joyce, Yeats, Adams and Thomas were acts of homage requires some clarification. The translations were often at least as good as, and in some cases better than, the original poems in English. To improve on something in the process of translating it is an ambiguous kind of homage.

The translations considered in previous chapters were acts of appropriation. They were examples of Montale continuing the work of his elective predecessors but asserting his own difference from them in that act of continuity—a very subtle process.

Montale liked to think of himself as a foreigner or an outsider. He certainly had an interest in seeing how his poetry would work in English. The following example goes against the current of all the translations which have been discussed above, in that it is a translation from Italian into English. Montale remained in Italy working as a translator, outside the English-speaking environment, but by the late 1940s he seems to have been sufficiently confident of his command of English to send his own English translation of "Il gallo cedrone" to Contini.[69] The following is Montale's "Il gallo cedrone" (1949), a poem which shares some of the characteristics of his translations from English into Italian:

> Dove t'abbatti dopo il breve sparo
> (la tua voce ribolle, rossonero
> salmí di cielo e terra a lento fuoco)
> anch' io riparo, brucio anch' io nel fosso.
>
> Chiede aiuto il singulto. Era piú dolce
> vivere che affondare in questo magma,
> piú facile disfarsi al vento che
> qui nel limo, incrostati sulla fiamma.

> Sento nel petto la tua piaga, sotto
> un grumo d'ala; il mio pesante volo
> tenta un muro e di noi solo rimane
> qualche piuma sull'ilice brinata.
>
> Zuffe di rostri, amori, nidi d'uova
> marmorate, divine! Ora la gemma
> delle piante perenni, come il bruco,
> luccica al buio, Giove è sotterrato.

This is a complex post-war poem which has been read as the expression of Montale's disillusionment with the new republic.[70] It is a poem with a number of Montalian characteristics which are also found in his translations from English.[71] It is structurally very tight, consisting of four four-line stanzas of hendecasyllables. There is no rhyme scheme but there are several devices which combine to give the poem an internal coherence. There are internal rhymes and half-rhymes, such as "sparo":"riparo" (lines 1, 4), "grumo":"piuma" (lines 10, 12) and "marmorate":"sotterrato" (lines 14, 16). There is some assonance, as in "affond*are*" → "disf*are*" (lines 6, 7), "brucio" → "bruco" (lines 4, 15) and "dove" → "Giove" (lines 1, 16), and some alliteration, as in the play of voiced and unvoiced plosives in "delle *p*iante *p*erenni, come il *b*ruco / luccica al *b*uio" (lines 15–16). There are many words containing double consonants, such as "abbatti" (line 1), "fiamma" (line 8) and "perenni" (line 15); in fact there is in the poem a definite pattern of words which conform to the following structure: consonant + vowel + double consonant + vowel, for example "fosso" (line 4), "petto", "sotto" (line 9) and "gemma" (line 14). There is only one *parola tronca*, "salmí" (line 3) and there are few *parole sdrucciole*—only "vivere" (line 6), "facile" (line 7), "ilice" (line 12) and "luccica" (line 16).[72] The harsh consonants throughout the poem, such as /z/ and /g/, might suggest the music of English consonants. The composite adjective "rossonero" (line 2) may recall the composite words with which Montale translates descriptions of colour in "La bellezza cangiante" and *La vita della foresta*. Luperini has argued that the technique in the final stanza—the list of concrete and abstract nouns referring to the bird—is the technique used by Hopkins in "The Windhover":

Brute beauty and valour and act, oh, air, pride, plume, here
Buckle![73]

There are also familiar Montalian characteristics in "Il gallo cedrone", such as the wall ("un muro") in the third stanza and the "grub" shining in the dark ("come il bruco,/luccica al buio", lines 15–16), which is part of Montale's *lux-in-tenebra* symbolism.

The following is Montale's own English translation of "Il gallo cedrone":

Where you after the brief shot lower
(your voice seethes, black-red
salmis of sky and earth at slow heat)
also I shelter, I too burn in the gutter.

Your sigh asks for help. 'Twas sweeter
to live than to sink into this jelly,
easier in the wind to undo than
here in the slime, crusted on the flame.

I feel in my chest your sore, beneath
the colt [*sic*] of a wing; my burdened flight
probes a wall and of us only some feathers
upon the hoary ilex remain.

Grapples of rostrums, loves, nests of eggs
marbled, divine! Now the jemmy sprout
of perennial plants, like the grub
sparkles in the gloom, Jupiter is buried.

A first and somewhat trivial point to make about Montale's translation of Italian into English is that it is far more literal than his translations of English into Italian. Sometimes that strategy works quite well, at others it is mildly comical, as in "also I shelter" (line 4) and "the jemmy [*sic*] sprout" (line 14). Montale does not attempt to match his hendecasyllables with iambic pentameter. He does manage to produce some false rhymes, such as "heat": "sweeter":"beneath" (lines 3, 5, 9). The translation is interesting because of Montale's English versions of some of his keywords. "Gloom" is his translation of "buio" (as opposed to "dark", for example). "Gloom" preserves the long vowel of his Italian word.

Montale translates "pesante volo" as "burdened flight", which is probably a better rendering than the very literal "heavy flight" (Pipa and Singh) or the perhaps pejorative "ponderous flight" (Bernard Wall). Montale's translation is the most useful text available for anyone interested in how the poet wished to have his almost untranslatable poetry appear in English.

His translation of "Il gallo cedrone" is, in effect, a further act of homage—not this time to a specific poet but to the tradition of "una certa idea della poesia" in the English language.

NOTES

1 The two Joyce poems are a special case: the translations of them are acts of homage to a recently deceased writer from whom Montale had received much inspiration twenty years earlier.

2 "Dialogo con Montale sulla poesia", in E. Montale, *Sulla poesia*, edited by G. Zampa (Milan, Mondadori, 1976), pp. 577–86 (p. 583).

3 E. Montale, "De Pisis", in his *Sulla poesia*, pp. 287–89 (p. 287). The article was published in *Il corriere della sera*, 28 Apr. 1954, under the rubric "Letture".

4 For example, "Minstrels", "Alla maniera di Filippo De Pisis nell'inviargli questo libro" and "I miraggi"; see E. Montale, *L'opera in versi*, edited by G. Contini and R. Bettarini (Turin, Einaudi, 1980), pp. 14, 128, 623–24.

5 E. Montale, *L'opera in versi*, p. 721. "Alle muse" was first published in the 1948 *Quaderno di traduzioni*.

6 See G. Lonardi, "Fuori e dentro il tradurre montaliano", in his *Il vecchio e il giovane e altri studi su Montale* (Bologna, Zanichelli, 1980), pp. 144–63 (p. 156).

7 The most obvious textual echo (though by no means the only one) is of "commuoversi dell'eterno grembo" in "In limine" (E. Montale, *L'opera in versi*, p. 7).

8 See E. Montale, *L'opera in versi*, pp. 890–92.

9 E. Montale, *L'opera in versi*, p. 625.

10 See E. Montale, "Sulla poesia di Campana" [1942], in his *Sulla poesia*, pp. 248–59: "Nulla ha da temere Campana da una riduzione che salvi il suo dono piú certo: la *diversità* del suo timbro. È vero: il suo messaggio di *voyant* può lasciarci increduli, cosí indefinito com' è; nell'opera sua 'non ci è dato incontrare né il dramma culturale, né l'irrompente ansia religiosa di un Hölderlin' (Solmi); e nemmeno, aggiungiamo noi, lo sfolgorio di un Blake o il sotterraneo e coerente tematismo di un Rimbaud" (p. 259; Montale's italics).

11 E. Montale, "Emily" [1957], in his *Sulla poesia*, pp. 494–99 (p. 497).

12 E. Montale, "Thomas Hardy", in his *Sulla poesia*, pp. 527–29; T. Hardy, *Poesie*, edited and translated by G. Singh (Parma, Guanda, 1968).

13 E. Montale, "Thomas Hardy", p. 527.

14 Singh had written: "Nella poesia di Hardy la prima cosa da constatare è proprio quell'avvicinamento, anzi quell'identificazione, sia sul piano lingui-

stico che su quello tematico, fra ciò che viene tradizionalmente considerato poetico e ciò che è prosastico" (T. Hardy, *Poesie*, p. xxii).

15 E. Montale, "Thomas Hardy", pp. 527–28; Montale's italics.

16 E. Montale, "Della poesia d'oggi" [1931], in his *Sulla poesia*, pp. 557–58 (p. 558); and Montale's article on Ungaretti quoted in G. Lonardi, "Fuori e dentro il tradurre montaliano", p. 153.

17 E. Montale, "Thomas Hardy", pp. 528–29.

18 E. Montale, "Thomas Hardy", p. 529; Montale's italics.

19 E. Montale, "Thomas Hardy", p. 529; Montale's italics.

20 E. Montale, "Thomas Hardy", p. 528.

21 Mosca (Drusilla Tanzi) died in 1963.

22 In the *Quaderno di traduzioni* there is a typographical error in the first line of the third stanza, which reads "With them seat does not break down." In the first edition of the *Quaderno di traduzioni* "of" was twice misprinted as "af", but that misprint was corrected in all subsequent editions.

23 See P. V. Mengaldo, "La panchina e i morti (su una versione di Montale)", in *La poesia di Montale* by various authors (Milan, Librex, 1983), pp. 133–48 (p. 136).

24 P. V. Mengaldo, "La panchina e i morti", p. 136.

25 While the phrase "il ritorno dei morti" has been used in relation to Montale's poetry, its English version, "the return of the dead", carries echoes of Harold Bloom's book *The Anxiety of Influence* (New York, Oxford University Press, 1973), especially pp. 139–55. The echo is unfortunate because Bloom's phrase means something quite different, and no allusion to it is intended here.

26 E. Montale, *L'opera in versi*, p. 726. The translation was first published in the 1948 *Quaderno di traduzioni*.

27 See P. V. Mengaldo, "La panchina e i morti", pp. 135–36. Mengaldo's analysis of "Vecchia panchina" is excellent, and this section of the present chapter draws heavily on it.

28 See G. Lonardi, "Fuori e dentro il tradurre montaliano", p. 154; P. V. Mengaldo "La panchina e i morti", p. 139.

29 See P. V. Mengaldo, "La panchina e i morti", p. 146 n. 15.

30 P. V. Mengaldo, "La panchina e i morti", p. 137.

31 P. V. Mengaldo, "La panchina e i morti", p. 139; Montale's italics.

32 See E. Montale, *L'opera in versi*, pp. 40, 138, 81–82; G. Contini, *Una lunga fedeltà: sulla poesia di Montale* (Turin, Einaudi, 1974), pp. 69–73.

33 Joyce had taught Svevo English in Trieste and the two men had become friends. After Joyce left Trieste they exchanged letters more or less frequently. Svevo's literary debt to Joyce's work has been noted by several critics, including Montale: see Montale's preface to the 1976 reissue of Svevo's *La coscienza di Zeno* (Milan, Dall'Oglio, 1976).

34 The more "common" dictionary meaning of the word is "a knight having vassals under his banner" or "one knighted in the field for valour".

35 E. Montale, *L'opera in versi*, p. 729. This translation was first published in *Il mondo* [Florence], 19 (5 Jan. 1946), 7.

36 In "Tempesta" Montale had translated "wild" as "desolato"; see pp. 97, 99 and 102 above.

37 See, for example, the "Mediterraneo" section of *Ossi di seppia*, "Casa sul mare" or "La casa dei doganieri" (E. Montale, *L'opera in versi*, pp. 51–59, 91–92, 161).

38 See, for example, "Corno inglese", "L'agave su lo scoglio" or "La bufera" (E. Montale, *L'opera in versi*, pp. 11, 68–70, 189).

39 See, for example, "I morti", the *mottetti* or "A mia madre" (E. Montale, *L'opera in versi*, pp. 93–94, 133–52, 203).

40 E. Montale, *L'opera in versi*, p. 730. This translation was first published in *Il mondo*, 19 (5 Jan. 1946), 7, together with "Guardando i canottieri a San Sabba".

41 Musatti has commented on Montale's variation procedure in this translation: "L'aggettivo *frail* ricorre ben quattro volte nel testo inglese di soli otto versi. Nella traduzione è sostituito da tre sinonimi: *gracile*, *frale* (attributivi, nella prima quartina), *fragile* (due volte come predicativo nella seconda quartina)." See M. P. Musatti, "Montale traduttore: la mediazione della poesia", *Strumenti critici*, 41 (Feb. 1980), 122–48 (p. 127).

42 See R. Luperini, *Storia di Montale* (Rome–Bari, Laterza, 1986), p. 178: "Sul piano tematico, sarà utile intanto osservare che le traduzioni poetiche montaliane non nascono tanto dall'interesse per l'opera complessiva di un autore straniero, quanto dall'accensione esistenziale e/o dallo stimolo formale che un singolo testo gli offre, presentandosi a lui, dunque come 'occasione' individuale."

43 E. Montale, "Ricordo di T. S. Eliot" [1965], in his *Sulla poesia*, pp. 516–20 (p. 520); Montale's italics.

44 E. Montale, "Resta la vena della satira" [1969], in his *Sulla poesia*, pp. 152–53 (p. 152).

45 E. Montale, "W. H. Auden" [1952], in his *Sulla poesia*, pp. 474–80 (p. 476).

46 E. Montale, "Il cammino della nuova poesia" [1951], in his *Sulla poesia*, pp. 465–71 (p. 469).

47 E. Montale, "Un poeta alessandrino" [1955], in his *Sulla poesia*, pp. 540–44 (p. 541).

48 Montale's translation was first published in the 1948 *Quaderno di traduzioni*. There are no significant variants.

49 Strangely, Montale did not translate "to dart" as *guizzare* but used instead the much more recherché *razzare*.

50 "Ninna nanna" was first published in *Circoli* [Genoa], 3, vi (Nov–Dec. 1933), 102–03.

51 *Contemporary Poets*, edited by J. Vinson and D. L. Kirkpatrick (London–New York, St James Press, 1975), pp. 17–19 (p. 18). This is the source of my biographical information on Léonie Adams.

52 *Those Not Elect* (New York, McBride, 1925); *High Falcon and Other Poems* (New York, Day, 1929). Montale may have been attracted by the title of Adams's first collection, but it is unlikely that he had much interest in the poem with the same title. The following is the text of Léonie Adams's "Those Not Elect": "Never, being damned, see paradise,/The heart will sweeten at its look;/Nor hell was known, till paradise/Our senses shook.//Never hear angels at laughter,/For how comports with grief to know/Wisdom in heaven bends to laughter, laughter,/Laughter upon woe?//Never fall dreaming on celestials,/Lest, bound in a ruinous place,/You turn to wander with celestials/Down holy space.//Never taste that fruit with the soul/Whereof the body may not eat,/Lest flesh at length lay waste the soul/In its sick heat."

53 Essays on Adams's poetry include a review by Eda Low Walton in *The Nation* [New York], 1930 and "Three Younger Poets" by Louis Untermeyer in *The English Journal* (Champaign, Illinois), 1932.

54 There is only one substantial variant between the versions of 1933 and the *Quaderno di traduzioni*: the 1933 version began "Taci ninna nanna" rather than "Smettila ninna nanna".
55 E. Montale, *L'opera in versi*, p. 48.
56 E. Montale, *L'opera in versi*, p. 140.
57 See E. Montale, "Thomas" [1954], in his *Sulla poesia*, pp. 487–88. The essay was nominally a review of Roberto Sanesi's edition and translation of Dylan Thomas's *Poesie* (Parma, Guanda, 1954).
58 All the foregoing quotations concerning Dylan Thomas are from E. Montale, "Thomas", p. 488.
59 Montale used this construction in his adaptation of Léonie Adams's "Lullaby" as a means of avoiding an adjective + noun construction. He also used it in his own poems, e.g. at the beginning of "Corno inglese" ("Il vento che"), "Il fuoco che scoppietta" and the *mottetto* "Il fiore che ripete" (E. Montale, *L'opera in versi*, pp. 11, 21, 148).
60 They are: "crooked" (ll. 4, 22), "wintry" (l. 5), "mouthing" (l. 7), "mountain" (l. 10), "blowing" (l. 12), "hanging" (l. 14), "hangman's" (l. 15) and "lover's" (l. 21).
61 Montale's translation was first published in *Il mondo*, 23 (2 Mar. 1946), 6, under the editor's title "La 'Quinta poesia' di Dylan Thomas", presumably because the poem is the one printed fifth in the edition of Thomas's poems used by Montale. "The force that through the green fuse drives the flower" is the fifth poem in Thomas's *18 Poems* (London, Sunday Referee and Sarton Bookshop, 1934; second edition 1936).
62 See G. Lonardi, "Fuori e dentro il tradurre montaliano", pp. 147–48.
63 E. Montale, *L'opera in versi*, p. 69.
64 E. Montale, *L'opera in versi*, p. 31.
65 E. Montale, *L'opera in versi*, p. 189.
66 The poem in question is "Anniversario" (E. Montale, *L'opera in versi*, p. 264), the final stanza of which reads as follows: "Resto in ginocchio: il dono che sognavo/non per me ma per tutti/appartiene a me solo, Dio diviso/dagli uomini, dal sangue raggrumato/sui rami alti, sui frutti." This poem is the final component of the "Madrigali privati" section (i.e. the poems for Volpe) of *La bufera e altro*. It is, in a way, an epilogue to the Clizia poems concerned with the theme of sacrifice. In it the poem's "io" feels his faults expiated; the gift he had wished on others has become his own and he kneels before a tree whose fruit is coagulated blood. The tree whose fruit is coagulated blood suggests the Passion, sacrifice, and atonement for Adam's sin, but Montale offered no gloss on the poem.
67 Montale had used *lambire* in two of his "coastline" poems, "Portovenere" and "Punta del Mesco" (*L'opera in versi*, pp. 35, 166).
68 This seems the most likely interpretation of Montale's interest in translating his own poetry into English (see below).
69 For "Il gallo cedrone" see E. Montale, *L'opera in versi*, p. 253, and for Montale's (untitled) English translation of it see pp. 967–68 of the same volume. Arshi Pipa's (untitled) translation of the poem appears in his *Montale and Dante* (Minnesota, University of Minnesota Press, 1968), p. 101. Bernard Wall's translation ("The Wood Grouse") is included in *Twentieth-century Italian Poetry: A Bilingual Anthology*, edited by L. R. Lind (Indianapolis–New York, Bobbs–Merrill, 1974), p. 219. Ghanshyam Singh's translation is to be found in

his *Eugenio Montale: A Critical Study of His Poetry, Prose and Criticism* (New Haven–London, Yale University Press, 1973), pp. 180–81.

70 G. Singh, *Eugenio Montale,* for example, reads it in this way (pp. 180–81). R. Luperini, *Montale o l'identità negata* (Naples, Liguori, 1984), on the other hand, reads "Il gallo cedrone" as a poem of hope (pp. 135–40).

71 It is possible that Montale wrote the poem in English and then translated it into Italian, but, as we shall see, it is unlikely.

72 "Salmí" is an unusual word in Italian, and its English equivalent, "salmi" or "salmis", is no more usual. The *Vocabolario della lingua italiana di Nicola Zingarelli,* edited by M. Dogliotti and L. Rosiello, eleventh edition (Bologna, Zanichelli, 1989) offers the following definition: "[dal fr. *salmis,* abbr. di *salmagondis,* dall'it. *salami conditi*] s. m. Intingolo preparato con pezzi di selvaggina macerati in vino e poi cotti in un sugo piccante e aromatico: *lepre in —; — di pernice.*"

73 See R. Luperini, *Montale o l'identità negata,* p. 177.

Conclusion

MONTALE, TRANSLATION AND ORIGINALITY

Intertextuality and Translation

At the very end of the 1940s Montale wrote: "Si traduce molto, in Italia, sebbene meno che altrove—leggiamo ancora, ma come si traduce? Tradurre è difficile, in certo senso piú difficile che scrivere opere originali. Si può diventare un grande scrittore in proprio usando poche centinaia di parole; ma per tradurre occorre una vasta tastiera."[1] His most intensive period as a translator was over at that point. There is obviously much truth in what he says about translators needing to use many more words than "creative" writers, but there is also, as usual, an element of irony, as we shall see.

In many of the texts Montale translated there was something already in the English text which he read in a personal way and took as a pretext for appropriating that text as his own. He also stated that "sarebbe un errore leggere una sola poesia e cercare di anatomizzarla, perché c'è sempre un richiamo da un suono all'altro, ma anche da una poesia all'altra."[2] He translated individual texts, but each text was a part of a whole, a tradition which was greater than the sum of the component parts. He took Shakespeare as a point of reference, using Shakespeare's sonnets as an opportunity to experiment with strict traditional forms (something against which he had rebelled in his early poetry). From the other poets, and from the specific poems translated, he took the opportunity of developing individual themes; but from a broader view of these writers it is clear that Montale intended to bring into Italian, by means of translation, a tradition of poetry that was not represented in Italy, an alternative tradition which he referred to as "una certa idea della poesia". He made this clear himself in "Eliot e noi" (1947):

> Volgiamoci indietro, risaliamo a ritroso la corrente, anche se su questo filo piú di una grande tradizione poetica scomparirà per un momento dal nostro sguardo. Eliot, Valéry, poco piú addietro nel tempo due altri: Yeats (piú anziano ma ringiovanito al contatto dei giovani) e Apollinaire, che non si possono esaurire nel dono della loro apparente spontaneità; e piú addietro ancora i simbolisti della prima generazione, i "maledetti", e il loro quasi contemporaneo Hopkins, e in fondo—non già iniziatrice della serie—Emily Dickinson, sospesa tra la sublimità e i *nonsenses*... In meno di cent' anni, quali voci può lasciare *una certa idea* (un'idea sbagliata, secondo alcuni) della poesia, al mondo di domani, se il mondo d'oggi potrà avere ancora una storia![3]

Having come into contact with Modernism, Montale cultivated a foreign sensibility in his own work. That may account, in part at least, for the harsh, un-Petrarchan sounds which feature in much of his poetry. The Modernists, however, had English or French as their *lingua franca* while he wrote in Italian.

A Sense of Place

In the later 1920s and the 1930s, having left Liguria, Montale tried to live in Florence as a foreigner, as Browning had done in the previous century, doing his best to ignore contemporary Italian politics. Montale's was, however, an untenable position because, try as he might to ignore Italian politics, Italian politics did not ignore him. In 1929 he had been appointed director of the Gabinetto Vieusseux because he was an anti-Fascist; nine years later he found himself dismissed for precisely the same reason. He could have left Italy in 1938 or 1939—there is little doubt that an American university would have employed him, again because of his status, this time as an established poet and a dissident exile. But he could not bring himself to go.[4]

Instead he remained in Italy working as a translator, a job he claimed to despise, and set about developing a Petrarchan disdain for his contemporaries and apparently idealizing England, perhaps as a place of tolerance and freedom. He had already travelled to England in the 1930s, and the visit had left its mark in his poetry in the shape of his poem "Eastbourne". Rebay and Becker both read "Eastbourne" as a poem concerned with impending war. Certainly the "wheel of fate" symbolism in the poem is very suggestive of disaster; for example:

> Vanno su sedie a ruote i mutilati,
> li accompagnano cani dagli orecchi
> lunghi, bimbi in silenzio o vecchi. (Forse
> domani tutto parrà un sogno). [...]
>
> Come lucente muove sui suoi spicchi
> la porta di un albergo
> —risponde un'altra e le rivolge un raggio—
> m'agita un carosello che travolge
> tutto dentro il suo giro [...].
>
> Vince il male... La ruota non s'arresta.[5]

The image of the war veterans in wheelchairs seems, in itself, to be Montale's commentary on the legacy and prospect of war, but the place of patriotism in the poem ("Dio salvi il re", "mia patria!", for instance), intimately connected with the notion of going to war, is not so easy to interpret as a homage to the English way of life. Living in Italy in the 1930s Montale had good reason to be suspicious of such forms of patriotism. In Mario Praz he had an important and influential friend in England, and had he wished to leave Italy for England it is quite likely that Praz would have assisted him. But, as with the opportunity of going to America, Montale did not pursue the matter. He had been prepared to live in Florence as a foreigner, but despite his carefully expressed respect for England and explicit invitations to America, he was not prepared to live abroad as an Italian. He wished to claim American, English, Irish and Welsh writers as his literary predecessors but that did not mean he was prepared to go away to live in the English-speaking world. He was content to absorb the international Modernist tradition while remaining at home. Despite his elective affinity with English, then, Montale remained "inguaribilmente italiano: e senza rimpianto".[6] In other words, he absorbed the tradition of international Modernism, and translated that tradition into Italian, without losing his own identity.

How can a translator maintain his own identity when he is working in the shadow of foreign texts?

Metre, Variation, Identity and Difference

A characteristic common to all Montale's translations from English is his variation procedure. This procedure assumes several different forms. He deliberately mistranslated the titles of *Green Mansions* and of several of the poems he translated ("A Song for Simeon", for instance, became "Canto di Simeone"). The deliberate mistranslation of titles is the most superficial manner in which Montale asserted the difference between his translation and the original work out of which it developed.

He consistently eschewed repetition, both in the poems and in the descriptive passages of *La vita della foresta*. This procedure has already been noted by critics, and attention has been drawn to Montale's refusal to repeat himself in the foregoing chapters. Hardy's ballad "The Garden Seat" provides probably the most extreme example of such a refusal. The refrains in Hardy's poem—the third and fourth lines of each stanza—are practically identical, word for word. Montale, who tended to avoid repetition in his own poetry, varies the lines of each refrain in "Vecchia panchina".

In the translations he also excised what he presumably regarded as redundant or unnecessary adjectives, substituting either one adjective or a precise noun for several adjectives. That procedure is at its clearest in the descriptive passages of *La vita della foresta* and in "Billy in catene", possibly Montale's freest translation, or the one in which he took the greatest liberties with the diction. He read the ballad as narrative poetry, and narrative poetry, he argued in 1957, is quite unlike lyric poetry.[7] Consequently, he translated Melville's sometimes florid and usually literary language into the standard descriptive language of prose.

Part of his motivation for the reduction of adjectives and his use of *enjambement* (as a way of accelerating his Italian lines) concerns the relative speeds of English and Italian. English is a much faster language, and Montale's decision to match English forms in his Italian translations imposed on him the necessity of refining his native means of expression. He did make some use of Italian monosyllables to convey the effect of English monosyllables, but he did not use them extensively, for the very good reason that the Italian monosyllable is a minority species. He used other devices to dislocate the normal rhythm of Italian poetry (such as the significant number of *parole sdrucciole* in "Ninna nanna") and to shorten the length of Italian vowels (such as the pattern of words in "La bellezza cangiante" containing double consonants). He claimed that his activity as a translator may have helped him to "scavare un'altra dimensione" in his own heavy polysyllabic language, and there is indeed some evidence to support that claim, as we have seen in the case of "Il gallo cedrone".

But the most original way in which Montale as a translator managed to express his own identity was his deliberate assimilation of aspects of his own work into the foreign texts, a process referred to above as intertextuality. Reading Montale's translations in terms of his original work can be an illuminating exercise, both linguistically and thematically. His great theme of the 1940s, the period of his most intense activity as a translator, was the sacrifice theme, and this attracted him to the work of Hudson, Melville and Hopkins.

Hopkins and Montale share a predilection for music which manifests itself quite independently in their poetry, in alliteration and rhyme, but perhaps more fundamentally in their approach to rhythm. It is clear from Hopkins's preface to his mature poems that he felt metre in musical rather than in traditional visual terms.[8] His musical sensibility and a lack of received terminology for the description of his sprung rhythm inspired terms such as "outrides". Hopkins intended his poems to be read aloud, the reader stressing the important words in *rubato* fashion and allowing less important ones to occupy less space in compensation.

It is very unlikely that Montale was acquainted with Hopkins's work before the 1930s. Yet in *Ossi di seppia* he had already attempted to break with the traditional rhetoric of Italian poetry by replacing syllabic lines with tonic-syllabic lines, in order to capture the rhythms of speech.[9] Thus Montale's discovery of Hopkins suggests a process of vindication rather than of conversion. Barile has traced an interesting correspondence between Croce's article on Hopkins and a passage in Montale's "Intervista immaginaria".[10] Croce wrote of the necessity for rhetoric in poetry, maintaining that rhetoric was "l'elemento della letteratura, pari alla grammatica per la lingua, al basso continuo per la musica". Montale takes up the analogy of the *basso continuo*, contending that "*Le occasioni* erano un'arancia, o meglio un limone a cui mancava uno spicchio: non proprio quello della poesia pura nel senso che ho indicato prima, ma in quello del *pedale*, della musica profonda e della contemplazione."[11] Barile pursues the "musica profonda" ascribed by Montale to *Le occasioni* and finds recurrences of phoneme-combinations such as /nt/, /nd/, /nts/, /mp/ and /mb/ in his 1940s poetry.[12] Montale was there adopting, as Hopkins had done, a conception of poetic organization different from that of the received tradition, one in which words or even phoneme-combinations were treated as objects.

The important point to bear in mind is that Montale already had a refined poetics and a collection of poems published before he discovered Hopkins's poetry. *Ossi di seppia* therefore lies outside the range of speculation about literary influence. Any influence of Hopkins on Montale begins quite firmly in the 1930s, which, as we know, saw the start of his period of translations.

Montale's major infidelity in the case of "La bellezza cangiante" lies in the image of the "tonfar delle castagnette/—crollo di tizzi giovani nel fuoco", which is a substantial elaboration of a relatively small item in Hopkins's text ("fresh-firecoal chestnut-falls"). Montale's tendency to reduce rather than to elaborate in his translation practice has already been noted. So when we find deliberate elaboration in one of his translations we may expect that something significant is happening.

Linguistic echoes in these two lines of "La bellezza cangiante" lead back to several earlier poems, and to two in particular, "Scendiamo la via che divalla" and "Arsenio". Those two poems share the structural feature of a downward trajectory. Arsenio goes down to the sea, and, as we have seen, Montale read that descent (in relation to Billy Budd, at least) as a sacrificial journey. There is a similar downward trajectory in "La bellezza cangiante" but in that poem the descent is a fall not into water but into fire. In "La bellezza cangiante" there is no trace of Arsenio, but Clizia is there, connoted by the "*tizzi* giovani", a play on the surname (Brandeis) of the real woman who became Clizia in Montale's poetry. Montale made the translation in the 1940s, the period in which Clizia consummated her sacrificial destiny. As Barile has shown, the image of "tizzi giovani nel fuoco" in "La bellezza cangiante" has a cognate in the first stanza of "Iride" (1943), the poem which makes Clizia's sacrificial destiny explicit:

Quando di colpo San Martino smotta
le sue braci e le attizza in fondo al cupo
fornello dell'Ontario,
schiocchi di pigne verdi fra la cenere
o il fumo d'un infuso di papaveri
e il Volto insanguinato sul sudario
che mi divide da te [...].[13]

"La bellezza cangiante" may represent an important development in Montale's poetry, and it may be argued that there is a case for seeing an influence of Hopkins on Montale's development. That, however, is not really so. Montale appropriated "Pied Beauty" as his own, and the Montalian development consists in the replacement of water by fire as the element associated with sacrifice. The descent into the sea has been replaced by the almost metaphysical fall into fire, which may strike the reader as fulfilment of the prophecy in the first *mottetto* that "l'inferno è certo".[14]

The main argument against Barile's position, according to which Hopkins is the primary influence on Montale's metaphysical development in the 1940s, is that the fall into fire is more explicitly related to sacrifice in another text which Montale translated, W. H. Hudson's *Green Mansions*. The imagery used by Hudson to describe Rima has more in common with Montale's Clizia imagery than anything Montale could have found in Hopkins's poetry. The connection of Rima and Clizia is so close as to be uncanny: Rima's name is actually an anagram of Irma, the first name of the "real" Clizia. Rima's death, at the hands of the frenzied and superstitious Parahuari, is the ritual *auto da fé*. Having taken refuge in a tree, Rima finds herself imprisoned on her own pyre as the Parahuari set light to the scrub which they have piled around the trunk. As the tree blazes she falls into the fire, where she dies. The structure of the *auto da fé* is repeated later in the novel when the moth, circling around Abel's room, falls into the flames of the hearth.

It does not seem reasonable to contend that Montale's debt to Hopkins *vis-à-vis* the sacrifice theme is any more profound than his debt to Melville or Hudson. The translations are as much landmarks in Montale's own development as they are examples of influence. The shift of emphasis from water to fire is also significant in that regard. "Mediterraneo", Montale's suite dedicated to the power of the sea and its influence on his adolescence and youth, ends with a statement of his own difference from the sea, a statement in which his identity is posited as the very opposite of water:

> Presa la mia lezione
> piú che dalla tua gloria
> aperta, dall'ansare
> che quasi non dà suono
> di qualche tuo meriggio desolato,
> a te mi rendo in umiltà. *Non sono*
> *che favilla d'un tirso. Bene lo so: bruciare,*
> *questo, non altro, è il mio significato.*[15]

That is quite a good metaphor for his work as a translator.

In translating, Montale did create his own tradition but he did not submit to the individual influences of particular poets. Both *Green Mansions* and the poems he translated stimulated him to originality even within the apparently confined space of a translation. The concept of intertextuality may be the key to the paradox of his being original while translating a poem by another poet, and it provides the opportunity of developing the argument that the subtle interaction between Montale's own poems and his translations, to the point where the translations became Montalian originals, is an example of creative genius.

Translation and a Poet's Memory

Montale has been eulogized as "un profondo conoscitore della letteratura anglosassone", which might give the impression that he was an important and original *anglista*.[16] Montale was not, however, an expert English scholar. His critical essays, when he actually wrote them himself, were generally derived from the received critical position regarding the writer in question. (There is no shame in that: the columns of the *Corriere della sera* were probably not the place for new advances in the appreciation of Anglo-American literature.) Many of his prose "translations" were in fact revisions of intermediary renderings, and a substantial number of the poems which he translated had already been translated into Italian, so that he had access to other versions.

The foregoing analyses of Montale's translations have revealed significant instances of developments in his own poetry. He appropriated the foreign texts, rewrote them, and in that process what had begun as a translation became an autonomous and original work. It may be interesting to re-read the famous lament in "Crisalide" (1924) from this standpoint:

> Ah crisalide, com' è amara questa
> tortura senza nome che ci volve
> e ci porta lontani—e poi non restano
> neppure le nostre orme sulla polvere;
> e noi andremo innanzi senza smuovere
> un sasso solo della gran muraglia;
> e *forse tutto è fisso, tutto è scritto,*
> e non vedremo sorgere per via
> la libertà, il miracolo,
> il fatto che non era necessario![17]

Montale's fear that "forse tutto è fisso, tutto è scritto" may not be an uncommon or an unnatural fear for a young writer coming into contact with the weight of a tradition. Montale was an obsessive reader who read his own concerns in other people's work. He translated his elective tradition not just into Italian but into his own Montalian Italian, his idiolect—hence the irony in the quotation with which this Conclusion began. He created his predecessors in his own words, which means that his own poetic development became identified with continuing that alternative tradition. His translations of foreign poems and of *Green Mansions* into his own idiom were not gratuitous acts or merely literary exercises: he treated a foreign text as a resource for his own poetry. Intertextuality, or wilful repetition, was an essential part of Montale's technique of composition. He provides a good example of Edward Said's Modernist writer:

> The best way to consider originality is to look not for the first instances of a phenomenon, but rather to see duplication, parallelism, parody, repetition, echoes of it—the way, for example, literature has made itself into a topos of writing. What the modern [...] imagination thinks of is less the confining of something to a book, and more the release of something from a book in writing [...]. The writer thinks less of writing originally, and more of rewriting. The image for writing changes from original inscription to parallel script, from tumbled-out confidence to deliberately fathering-forth (in which Hopkins's alliteration signifies parallel), from melody to fugue.[18]

Said's characterization of a Modernist's originality does justice to Montale's idea of his task as a translator. Strictly speaking, Montale's translations are "creative transpositions", reworkings of an existing text into another context.

Montale did not leave a written discussion of the nature of translation. If we were to construct a theory on the evidence of his practice, it might run as follows: A word in isolation refers to nothing outside the framework of a system of language. Words acquire their meaning from our memory of their use in previous contexts and their difference from other words. Words without memory are empty signs, signifying nothing. That is why the Futurist notion of originality in poetry, new words for every occasion, is an illusion.

Montale uses the vocabulary of Italian, a system shared by a linguistic community and consisting, for its meaning, in organized memory, an organized memory which makes no significant distinction between living speech and the written texts of those long dead. Planted within that shared language there is what we have been calling Montale's idiolect, his characteristic use of language, which defines itself in terms of lexical choice, in difference from other words which might denote particular objects in the external world just as well as the ones he uses. In the course of this study we have seen numerous occasions on which Montale uses a particular word in a translation because of its echo in his poetic memory rather than because of its propriety in a given context. Our perception of the world is cloaked in language, and language makes sense only in the context of memory. In his translations Montale does not attempt an illusory originality: he takes what is there already and changes it almost imperceptibly—a subtle process of inserting his texts into the memory of the living and the dead.

NOTES

1 E. Montale, "Buon anno senza perle ai traduttori mal pagati!", *Corriere d'informazione*, 28–29 Dec. 1949, 1.

2 Quoted in M. Corti, "*Satura* di Eugenio Montale", *L'approdo letterario*, 53 (1971), 107–16 (p. 115).

3 E. Montale, "Eliot e noi" [1947], in his *Sulla poesia*, edited by G. Zampa (Milan, Mondadori, 1976), pp. 441–46 (pp. 445–46); Montale's italics.

4 See L. Rebay, "Montale, Clizia e l'America", *Forum Italicum*, 16, iii (Winter 1982), 171–202 (pp. 174 and 177); D. Isella, "La fontana delle ultime *Occasioni*", *Strumenti critici*, 57 (1988), 179–208 (pp. 180 and 198). Montale was quite scathing on the subject of those who did go, e.g.: "Ci sono uomini che s'incontrano tutti i giorni senza che con essi si possa entrar mai in rapporti d'amicizia; altri, appena sfiorati o intravveduti, con i quali ci si sente in immediata intimità. Come Valéry, T. S. Eliot appartiene a questo tipo di uomini: poeta, ha una voce che non si dimentica e che si riconosce anche dopo una lunga desuetudine. Uomo e poeta non chiede aggiornamenti a chi lo avvicina, non è soggetto alle mutazioni delle molteplici crisi alle quali ci hanno abituati i poeti dei *thirties* che lo hanno seguito. (E non per nulla, visto che superarlo nell'ordine della fecondità era troppo facile e inconcludente, qualcuno d'essi, come Auden, percorre il viaggio a ritroso e tenta la riconquista del Nuovo Mondo.)" ("Eliot e noi", p. 442). The implication seems to be that flight to America was tantamount to failure.

5 E. Montale, *L'opera in versi*, edited by G. Contini and R. Bettarini (Turin, Einaudi, 1980), pp. 170–71.

6 E. Montale, "Intenzioni (intervista immaginaria)", in his *Sulla poesia*, pp. 561–69 (p. 567).

7 See E. Montale, "Parliamo della poesia" [1957], in his *Sulla poesia*, pp. 126–28 (p. 126).

8 See *Gerard Manley Hopkins*, edited by C. Phillips (Oxford, Oxford University Press,1986), pp. 106–09.

9 See A. Pinchera, "La versificazione tonico-sillabica nella poesia di Montale", *Quaderni urbinati*, 7 (1969), 155–84 (p. 160); G. Marucelli, "La metrica di Montale: isosillabismo ed equivalenza ritmica dagli *Ossi* alle *Occasioni*", in *Contributi per Montale*, edited by G. Cillo (Lecce, Milella, 1976), pp. 91–108; L. Barile, "Sparviero o procellaria? Una versione di Montale da Hopkins", in her *Adorate mie larve: Montale e la poesia anglosassone* (Bologna, Mulino, 1990), pp. 15–50 (pp. 15 and 18).

10 See L. Barile, "Sparviero o procellaria?", p. 21.

11 E. Montale, "Intenzioni", p. 567; Montale's italics.

12 See L. Barile, "Sparviero o procellaria?", p. 21.

13 E. Montale, *L'opera in versi*, pp. 239–40.

14 E. Montale, *L'opera in versi*, p. 133.

15 E. Montale, *L'opera in versi*, p. 59; my italics.

16 See the publisher's note on the dust-jacket of Montale's *Sulla poesia*.

17 E. Montale, *L'opera in versi*, p. 86; my italics.

18 E. W. Said, "On Originality", in his *The World, the Text and the Critic* (Cambridge, Mass., Harvard University Press, 1983; London, Faber, 1984), pp. 126–39 (p. 135).

BIBLIOGRAPHY

The following are the works referred to in the course of this book. For more complete bibliographies of secondary sources, see L. Barile, *Bibliografia montaliana* (Milan, Mondadori, 1977), G. Zampa, *Eugenio Montale: tutte le poesie* (Milan, Mondadori, 1984) and M. Forti, *Eugenio Montale: poesie scelte* (Milan, Mondadori, 1987).

Montale's Works

Ossi di seppia (Turin, Gobetti, 1925; second edition Turin, Ribet, 1928)

Le occasioni (Turin, Einaudi, 1939; second edition Turin, Einaudi, 1940)

La bufera e altro (Vicenza, Neri Pozza, 1956)

Farfalla di Dinard (Vicenza, Neri Pozza, 1956; second edition Milan, Mondadori, 1960)

Auto da fé: cronache in due tempi, edited by G. Zampa (Milan, Saggiatore, 1966; second edition 1972)

Fuori di casa (Milan–Naples, Ricciardi, 1969)

Satura (Milan, Mondadori, 1971)

Diario del '71 e del '72 (Milan, Mondadori, 1973)

Nel nostro tempo (Milan, Rizzoli, 1973)

Sulla poesia, edited by G. Zampa (Milan, Mondadori, 1976)

Carteggio Svevo–Montale, edited by G. Zampa (Milan, Mondadori, 1976)

Autografi di Montale: Fondo dell'Università di Pavia, edited by M. Corti and M. A. Grignani (Turin, Einaudi, 1976)

Quaderno di quattro anni (Milan, Mondadori, 1978)

L'opera in versi, edited by G. Contini and R. Bettarini (Turin, Einaudi, 1980)

Prime alla Scala (Milan, Mondadori, 1981)

Lettere a Salvatore Quasimodo (Milan, Mondadori, 1981)

Quaderno genovese, edited by L. Barile (Milan, Mondadori, 1983)

Tutte le poesie, edited by G. Zampa (Milan, Mondadori, 1984)

Diario postumo, edited by A. Cima (Milan, Fondazione Schlesinger, 1991)

Montale's Translations

John Steinbeck, *La battaglia* [*In Dubious Battle*] (Milan, Bompiani, 1940)

Narratori spagnoli, edited by C. Bo (Milan, Bompiani, 1941): includes translations by Montale of *Il matrimonio truffaldino*, *Colloquio dei cani*, *Colloquio di Scipione e Bergonza* by Miguel de Cervantes, *Il raggio di luna* by Gustavo Adolfo Bécquer and *Frottole* by Ramón Gómez de La Serna.

Teatro spagnolo, edited by E. Vittorini (Milan, Bompiani, 1941): includes translations by Montale of *Intermezzo della sentinella all'erta*, *Intermezzo del quadro delle meraviglie* and *Intermezzo del vecchio geloso* by Miguel de Cervantes.

Dorothy Parker, *Il mio mondo è qui* [*My World is Here*] (Milan, Bompiani, 1941)

Americana, edited by E. Vittorini (Milan, Bompiani, 1941 and 1942; second edition 1985): includes translations by Montale of Nathaniel Hawthorne, "Wakefield" ["Wakefield"], "Il velo nero del pastore" ["The Minister's Black Veil"] and "Il volto di pietra" ["The Great Stone Face"]; Herman Melville, *Billy Budd* (extract); Mark Twain, "L'uomo che corruppe Hadleyburg" ["The Man Who Corrupted Hadleyburg"]; Francis Bret Harte, "La fortuna di Roaring Camp" ["The Luck of Roaring Camp"]; Evelyn Scott, "Pagine di diario" ["Escapade"]; F. Scott Fitzgerald, "Il giovin signore" ["The Rich Boy"]; Kay Boyle, "Cura di riposo" ["Rest Cure"]; William Faulkner, "Il sole della sera" ["That Evening Sun"].

Herman Melville, *La storia di Billy Budd* (Milan, Bompiani, 1942)

Eugene O'Neill, *Strano interludio* [*Strange Interlude*] (Rome, Edizioni del Teatro dell'Università, 1943)

John Steinbeck, *Al dio sconosciuto* [*To a God Unknown*] (Milan, Bompiani, 1946)

Il volto di pietra ed altri racconti, edited by E. Montale (Milan, Bompiani, 1947): contains Montale's translation of Nathaniel Hawthorne's "Il tesoro di Peter Goldthwaite".

Eugenio Montale, *Quaderno di traduzioni* (Milan, Meridiana, 1948; second edition Milan, Mondadori, 1975)

William Shakespeare, *Amleto principe di Danimarca* (Milan, Cederna, 1949); reissued as *Montale traduce Amleto di William Shakespeare* (Milan, Longanesi, 1971)

William Shakespeare, *Teatro*, edited by M. Praz, 3 vols (Florence, Sansoni, 1949): includes translations by Montale of *La commedia degli errori* (I, 411–73), *Timone d'Atene* (III, 635–712) and *Racconto d'inverno* (III, 899–996).

Il cordovano, opera in one act, music by Goffredo Petrassi (Milan, Suvini Zerboni, 1949): Montale's libretto is a translation of an *entremese* by Miguel de Cervantes Saavedra.

Teatro elisabettiano, edited by A. Obertello (Milan, Bompiani, 1951): includes Montale's translation of *La tragica storia del Dottor Faust* [*The Tragicall History of Doctor Faustus*] by Christopher Marlowe.

Omar de Carlo, *Proserpina e lo straniero*, music by Juan José Castro (Milan, Ricordi, 1952): Montale made a translation for performance of the libretto.

Ezra Pound, *Iconografia italiana di Ezra Pound*, edited by V. Scheiwiller (Milan, All'Insegna del Pesce d'Oro, 1956): includes Montale's translation of *Hugh Selwyn Mauberley*, part I, fragment 5 (the translation is also included in the second edition of the *Quaderno di traduzioni*).

Angus Wilson, *La cicuta e dopo* (Milan, Garzanti, 1956)

William Walton and Christopher Hassal, *Troilo e Cressida* (Milan, Carish, 1956): Montale made a translation for performance of the libretto.

Jorge Guillén tradotto da Eugenio Montale (Milan, All'Insegna del Pesce d'Oro, 1958)

T. S. Eliot tradotto da Eugenio Montale (Milan, All'Insegna del Pesce d'Oro, 1958)

Teatro francese del grande secolo (Turin, ERI, 1960): includes Montale's translation of *Il Cid* by Pierre Corneille.

Jacinto Verdaguer and Manuel de Falla, *Atlàntida* (posthumous work completed by Ernesto Halffter; Milan, Ricordi, 1962): Montale made a translation for performance of the libretto.

William Henry Hudson, *La vita della foresta* (Turin, Einaudi, 1987)

Other Primary Sources

Léonie Adams, *Those Not Elect* (New York, McBride, 1925)

Léonie Adams, *High Falcon and Other Poems* (New York, Day, 1929)

Emily Dickinson, *Selected Poems*, edited by C. Aiken (London, Cape, 1924)

Emily Dickinson, *The Complete Poems*, edited by T. H. Johnson (London, Faber, 1970)

The Sermons and Devotional Writings of Gerard Manley Hopkins, edited by C. Devlin, second edition (London, Oxford University Press, 1967)

Gerard Manley Hopkins, *Poems and Prose*, edited by W. H. Gardner (Harmondsworth, Penguin, 1984)

Gerard Manley Hopkins, edited by C. Phillips (Oxford, Oxford University Press, 1987)

William Henry Hudson, *Green Mansions* (London, Duckworth, 1904)

William Henry Hudson, *Verdi dimore*, translated by Angelo Bianco [Aldo Camerino] (Milan, Bompiani, 1945)

William Henry Hudson, *The Land's End: A Naturalist's Impressions in West Cornwall* (London, Hutchinson, 1908; reissue edited by I. Niall, London, Wildwood House, 1980)

William Henry Hudson, *Far Away and Long Ago* (London, Dent, 1918)

Herman Melville, *Billy Budd, Sailor and Other Stories*, edited by H. Beaver (Harmondsworth, Penguin, 1967)

Herman Melville, *Billy Budd*, translated by Mariella Segre (Rome, Casini, 1966)

Herman Melville, *Pierre, Israel Potter, The Confidence Man, Tales and Billy Budd*, edited by H. Hayford (Cambridge, Cambridge University Press, 1984)

Giuseppe Ungaretti, *Tutte le poesie* (Milan, Mondadori, 1969)

Giuseppe Ungaretti, *Saggi e interventi* (Milan, Mondadori, 1974)

Secondary Sources

Agard, F. B., and R. J. Di Pietro, *The Sounds of English and Italian* (Chicago–London, Chicago University Press, 1965; Midway reprint 1973)

Almansi, G., "In Defence of Mistranslating", *Twentieth-century Studies*, Sept. 1974 (special issue on "Translation and Transformation"), pp. 64–75

Almansi, G., and B. Merry, *Eugenio Montale: The Private Language of Poetry* (Edinburgh, Edinburgh University Press, 1977)

Antonello, M., "Tre versioni montaliane da Shakespeare: *La commedia degli errori, Timone d'Atene* e *Il racconto d'inverno*" (unpublished essay)

Apollonio, C., "La crisi esistenziale dell'uomo contemporaneo nelle prime poesie di T. S. Eliot e Eugenio Montale", *Otto/Novecento*, 1 (1977), 77–94

Avalle, D'A. S., *Tre saggi su Montale* (Turin, Einaudi, 1970 and 1972)

Aversano, M., "Per album: la 'Volpe' di Montale e il melodramma", *Lingua e stile*, 23, ii (June 1988), 313–26

Barański, Z. G., "A Note on Montale's Presumed Dantism in 'Meriggiare pallido e assorto'", *Italica*, 56 (1979), 394–402

Barański, Z. G., "Dante and Montale: The Threads of Influence", in *Dante Comparisons*, edited by E. Haywood and B. Jones (Dublin, Irish Academic Press, 1985), pp. 11–48

Bàrberi Squarotti, G., "La metrica e altro" and "L'ironia: scatologia ed escatologia", in his *Gli inferi e il labirinto* (Bologna, Cappelli, 1974), pp. 195–210 and 223–49

Barbuto, A., *Le parole di Montale: glossario del lessico poetico* (Rome, Bulzoni, 1973)

Bardazzi, G., "Schopenhauer tra Montale e Sbarbaro", *Studi novecenteschi*, 35 (June 1988), 63–107

Barfoot, G., "Eugenio Montale and Thomas Hardy", *Italianistica*, 19, i (Jan–Apr. 1990), 131–43

Barile, L., *Adorate mie larve: Montale e la poesia anglosassone* (Bologna, Mulino, 1990)

Becker, J., *Eugenio Montale* (Boston, Twayne, 1986)

Benjamin, W., *Schriften* (Frankfurt-am-Main, Suhrkamp, 1955)

Benjamin, W., *Illuminations*, translated by H. Zohn (London, Fontana, 1973)

Bigongiari, P., *Poesia italiana del Novecento*, 2 vols (Milan, Saggiatore, 1980)

Blasucci, L., "Presenze dantesche nella poesia del Novecento: da D'Annunzio a Montale", *Bollettino della Società letteraria di Verona*, 5–6 (1982), 43–47

Blasucci, L., "Montale, Govoni e l''oggetto povero'", *Rassegna della letteratura italiana*, 94 (1990), 43–63

Bloom, H., *The Anxiety of Influence* (New York, Oxford University Press, 1973)

Bo, R., "Tra cielo e terra: viaggio attraverso i simboli animali della donna nella *Bufera* di Montale", *Studi novecenteschi*, 39 (June 1990), 103–29

Bonfiglioli, P., "Pascoli e Montale", in *Studi per il centenario della nascita di G. Pascoli* (Bologna, Commissione per i testi di lingua, 1962), pp. 219–43

Bonfiglioli, P., "Dante, Pascoli, Montale", in *Nuovi studi pascoliani: atti del Convegno nazionale di studi pascoliani* (Bolzano–Cesena, Società di studi romagnoli, 1963), pp. 35–92

Bonora, E., *La poesia di Montale: Ossi di seppia* (Padova, Liviana, 1982)

Briganti, A., "Comportamenti metrici montaliani: la strofa degli *Ossi di seppia*", in *La poesia di Eugenio Montale*, edited by S. Campailla and C. F. Goffis (Florence, Le Monnier, 1984), pp. 177–94

Bulgheroni, M., "Dickinson/Montale: il passo sull'erba", in *Eugenio Montale: profilo di un autore*, edited by A. Cima and C. Segre (Milan, Rizzoli, 1977), pp. 91–114

Cambon, G., "Montale dantesco e brueghelіano", *Aut-aut*, 35 (1956), 371–91; reprinted as "Montale e l'altro" in his *Lotta con Proteo* (Milan, Bompiani, 1963), pp. 113–37

Cambon, G., *Eugenio Montale's Poetry: A Dream in Reason's Presence* (Princeton, Princeton University Press, 1982)

Cambon, G., "Ancora su 'Iride', frammento di Apocalisse", in *La poesia di Eugenio Montale* by various authors (Milan, Librex, 1983), pp. 227–44

Camon, F., "Incontro con Montale" [1965], in his *Il mestiere del poeta* (Milan, Garzanti, 1965), pp. 79–84

Carducci, N., *Gli intellettuali e l'ideologia americana nell'Italia letteraria degli anni Trenta* (Manduria, Lacaita, 1973)

Caretti, L., *T. S. Eliot in Italia* (Bari, Adriatica, 1968)

Carpi, U., *"La voce": letteratura e primato degli intellettuali* (Bari, De Donato, 1975)

Carpi, U., *Il poeta e la politica* (Naples, Liguori, 1978)

Cecchi, E. and G., *Emily Dickinson* (Brescia, Morcelliana, 1939)

Contemporary Poets, edited by J. Vinson and D. L. Kirkpatrick (London–New York, St James Press, 1975)

Contini, G., *Una lunga fedeltà: sulla poesia di Montale* (Turin, Einaudi, 1974)

Contributi per Montale, edited by G. Cillo (Lecce, Milella, 1976)

Corti, M., "Montale negli Stati uniti", *Autografo*, 12 (1987), 11–28

Croce, B., *Poesia antica e moderna* (Bari, Laterza, 1966)

de Beaugrande, R-A., *Factors in a Theory of Poetic Translating* (Assen, Van Gorcum, 1978)

de Beaugrande, R-A., and W. U. Dressler, *Introduction to Text Linguistics* (London–New York, Longman, 1981)

Dolfi, A., "Dante e i poeti del Novecento", *Studi danteschi*, 58 (1990), 307–42

Empson, W., *Seven Types of Ambiguity* (London, Chatto and Windus, 1930)

Eugenio Montale: profilo di un autore, edited by A. Cima and C. Segre (Milan, Rizzoli, 1977)

Federici, C., "Spatial Conceptualization in Montale's Later Poetry", *Forum Italicum*, 24, ii (Fall 1990), 176–88

Fitts, D., "The Poetic Nuance", in *On Translation*, edited by R. A. Brower (Cambridge, Mass., Harvard University Press, 1959), pp. 32–47

Forti, M., "Esercizio su *I limoni*", in *Eugenio Montale: profilo di un autore*, edited by A. Cima and C. Segre (Milan, Rizzoli, 1977), pp. 21–37

Gargiulo, A., "Introduzione a *Ossi di seppia*" [1928], in his *Letteratura italiana del Novecento* (Florence, Le Monnier, 1940), pp. 453–57

Gathercole, P., "Two Kindred Spirits: Eugenio Montale and T. S. Eliot", *Italica*, 3 (1955), 170–79

Gatt-Rutter, J., *Writers and Politics in Modern Italy* (Sevenoaks, Hodder and Stoughton, 1978)

Gentili, A., "Per una lettura di Eugenio Montale (1896–1981), 'Poiché la vita fugge'; Robert Lowell (1917–1977), 'Epilogue'", *Journal of the Association of Teachers of Italian*, 39 (Summer 1983), 53–65

Giachery, E., "Figure di Montale: l'ossimoro", in *Per la lingua di Montale*, edited by G. Savoca (Florence, Olschki, 1989), pp. 45–52

Grignani, M. A., *Prologhi ed epiloghi: sulla poesia di Montale* (Ravenna, Longo, 1987)

Grignani, M. A., "La firma stilistica di Montale traduttore", *Autografo*, 15 (1988), 3–20

Guzzetta, L. F., *Solaria e la narrativa italiana intorno al 1930* (Ravenna, Longo, 1973)

Hamburger, M., *The Truth of Poetry* (London, Weidenfeld and Nicholson, 1969)

Hopkins: The Critical Heritage, edited by G. Roberts (London, Routledge and Keegan Paul, 1987)

Horne, P., "Further Notes towards a Reading of Montale's 'Arsenio'", *Journal of the Association of Teachers of Italian*, 37 (Autumn 1982), 11–18

Huffman, C. de C. L., *Montale and the Occasions of Poetry* (Princeton, Princeton University Press, 1983)

Isella, D., "La fontana delle ultime 'Occasioni'", *Strumenti critici*, 57 (1988), 179–208

Jacomuzzi, A., *La poesia di Montale*, second edition (Turin, Einaudi, 1978)

Jakobson, R., *Language in Literature*, edited by K. Pomorska and S. Rudy (Cambridge, Mass., Harvard University Press, 1987)

Jones, F. J., *Ungaretti: Poet and Critic* (Edinburgh, Edinburgh University Press, 1977)

Jones, F. J., "The Mythological Status of Arsenio in Montale's Ideology", *Journal of the Association of Teachers of Italian*, 38 (Spring 1983), 73–78

Jones, F. J., *The Modern Italian Lyric* (Cardiff, University of Wales Press, 1986)

Kristeva, J., "L'intertextualité", in her *Le Texte du roman* (The Hague, Mouton, 1970), pp. 139–76

Leavis, F. R., *New Bearings in English Poetry* (London, Chatto and Windus, 1932)

Letteratura e cultura del periodo fascista, edited by G. Manacorda (Milan, Principato, 1974)

Lonardi, G., *Leopardismo* (Florence, Sansoni, 1974)

Lonardi, G., *Il vecchio e il giovane e altri studi su Montale* (Bologna, Zanichelli, 1980)

Lonardi, G., "Piccolo, Montale e l'agone", *Studi novecenteschi*, 35 (1988), 125–42

Loyola, I., *Spiritual Exercises*, translated by T. Corbishley, SJ (London, Burns and Oates, 1963)

Luperini, R., "Appunti su *Mediterraneo*: Montale tra Svevo e Lautréamont", in *La poesia di Eugenio Montale*, edited by S. Campailla and C. F. Goffis (Florence, Le Monnier, 1984), pp. 131–40

Luperini, R., *Montale o l'identità negata* (Naples, Liguori, 1984)

Luperini, R., *Storia di Montale* (Rome–Bari, Laterza, 1986)

Lupo, C., "Eugenio Montale e la letterature inglese", *ACME*, 20, i-iii (Jan–Aug. 1962), 45–56

Lupo, C., "Eugenio Montale e la letteratura americana", *Studi americani* [Milan], 1 (1963), 467–88

Mahler-Schächter, E., "Notes towards a Reading of Montale's 'Arsenio'", *Journal of the Association of Teachers of Italian*, 36 (Summer 1982), 42–55

Mahler-Schächter, E., "A Postscript to Montale's 'Arsenio'", *Journal of the Association of Teachers of Italian*, 38 (Spring 1983), 79–81

Mantova per Montale: immagini e documenti, edited by V. Scheiwiller (Milan, All'Insegna del Pesce d'Oro, 1983)

Martini, A., "Occasioni musicali nella poesia del primo Montale", *Versants*, 11 (1987), 105–22

Marucelli, G., "La metrica di Montale: isosillabismo ed equivalenza ritmica dagli *Ossi* alle *Occasioni*", in *Contributi per Montale*, edited by G. Cillo (Lecce, Milella, 1976), pp. 91–108

Matthews, J., "Third Thoughts on Translating Poetry", in *On Translation*, edited by R. A. Brower (Cambridge, Mass., Harvard University Press, 1959), pp. 67–77

Mengaldo, P. V., "Da D'Annunzio a Montale", in his *Tradizione del Novecento* (Milan, Feltrinelli, 1975), pp. 13–106

Mengaldo, P. V., "La panchina e i morti (su una versione di Montale)", in *La poesia di Eugenio Montale* by various authors (Milan, Librex, 1983), pp. 133–48

Mengaldo, P. V., "Ah! Mah!" [review of G. Savoca, *Concordanza di tutte le poesie di Montale* (Florence, Olschki, 1987)], *L'indice*, 5, iv (Apr. 1988), 8–9

Meoli Toulmin, R., "Shakespeare ed Eliot nelle versioni di Eugenio Montale", *Belfagor*, 26 (1971), 453–71

Milano, P., "Il traduttore Montale", *L'espresso*, 23 Nov. 1975, 81–82

"Montale e il *Corriere*", edited by F. Roncoroni (Milan, supplement to *Corriere della sera*, 27 June 1986)

Montesperelli, F., "Montale e Browning: poesia dell'oggetto", *Paragone*, 326 (Apr. 1977), 55–81

Musatti, M. P., "Montale traduttore: la mediazione della poesia", *Strumenti critici*, 41 (Feb. 1980), 76–98

Nascimbeni, G., *Eugenio Montale*, fourth edition (Milan, Longanesi, 1986)

Newmark, P., *A Textbook of Translation* (Hemel Hempstead, Prentice Hall, 1988)

Nida, E., "A Framework for the Analysis and Evaluation of Theories of Translation", in *Translation: Applications and Research*, edited by R. W. Brislin (New York, Gardner, 1976), pp. 47–91

O'Neill, T., "Montale's Fishy Petrarchism", *MLN*, 106 (1991), 78–116

On Translation, edited by R. A. Brower (Cambridge, Mass., Harvard University Press, 1959)

Orelli, G., *Accertamenti montaliani* (Bologna, Mulino, 1984)

Orlando, R., "Il tema del prigioniero in Montale: note sulla traduzione della 'Storia di Billy Budd'", *Italianistica*, 21 (1992), 107–14

Pancrazi, P., "Eugenio Montale: poeta fisico e metafisico", in his *Scrittori italiani del Novecento* (Bari, Laterza, 1934), pp. 248–58

Pannella, S., "E. Montale e T. S. Eliot", *Galleria*, 4, v–vi (Dec. 1954), 244–56

Passannante, A., "'The Indian to his Love'—'L'indiano all'amata'", in *Quaderno montaliano*, edited by P. V. Mengaldo (Padua, Liviana, 1989), pp. 119–29

Pavese, C., "Ieri e oggi" [1947], in *Letteratura e cultura del periodo fascista*, edited by G. Manacorda (Milan, Principato, 1974), pp. 228–30

Pavese, C., *La letteratura americana e altri saggi*, edited by I. Calvino (Turin, Einaudi, 1962)

Pavese, C., *Lettere*, edited by L. Mondo and I. Calvino, 2 vols (Turin, Einaudi, 1966)

The Penguin Book of Italian Verse, edited and translated by G. Kay (London, Penguin, 1958)

Per la lingua di Montale, edited by G. Savoca (Florence, Olschki, 1989)

Pertile, L., "Fascism and Literature", in *Rethinking Italian Fascism*, edited by D. Forgacs (London, Lawrence and Wishart, 1986), pp. 162–84

Pietralunga, M., *Beppe Fenoglio and English Literature* (California–London, University of California Press, 1987)

Pinchera, A., "La versificazione tonico-sillabico nella poesia di Montale", *Quaderni urbinati*, 7 (1969), 155–84

Pipa, A., *Montale and Dante* (Minnesota, University of Minnesota Press, 1968)

La poesia di Eugenio Montale: atti del Convegno internazionale [12–18 Sept. 1982] (Milan, Librex, 1983)

Poeti antichi e moderni tradotti dai lirici nuovi, edited by L. Anceschi and D. Porzio (Milan, Hoepli, 1945)

Poeti italiani del Novecento, edited by P. V. Mengaldo (Milan, Mondadori, 1978)

Powell, R. C., "Vittorini and America", *Journal of the Association of Teachers of Italian*, 22 (Summer 1977), 22–31

Praz, M., "T. S. Eliot and Eugenio Montale", in *T. S. Eliot: A Symposium*, edited by R. March and M. J. Tambimuttu (London, Poetry Editions, 1948), pp. 244–48

Praz, M., *The Flaming Heart* (Gloucester, Mass., Smith, 1966)

Quaderno montaliano, edited by P. V. Mengaldo (Padua, Liviana, 1989)

Ramat, S., *L'acacia ferita e altri saggi su Montale* (Venice, Marsilio, 1986)

Rebay, L., "Montale, Clizia e l'America", *Forum Italicum*, 16 (Winter 1982), 171–202; also in *La poesia di Montale* by various authors (Milan, Librex, 1983), pp. 281–308

Rethinking Italian Fascism, edited by D. Forgacs (London, Lawrence and Wishart, 1986)

Rosiello, L., "Consistenza e distribuzione statistica del lessico poetico di Montale", *Rendiconti*, 11–12 (Sept. 1965), 397–421

Said, E. W., *The World, the Text and the Critic* (Cambridge, Mass., Harvard University Press, 1983; London, Faber, 1984)

Sanguineti, E., "Da Gozzano a Montale" [1954], in his *Tra liberty e crepuscolarismo*, second edition (Milan, Mursia, 1977), pp. 40–79

Savoca, G., *Concordanza di tutte le poesie di Eugenio Montale* (Florence, Olschki, 1987)

Shrubsall, D., "W. H. Hudson's English Country Rambles", *English Literature in Transition, 1880–1920*, 33 (1990), 64–83

Siciliano, E., "La memoria di Montale", *Corriere della sera*, 25 Oct. 1989, 3

Singh, G., *Eugenio Montale: A Critical Study of His Poetry, Prose and Criticism* (New Haven–London, Yale University Press, 1973)

Siti, W., "'Iride'", *Rivista di letteratura italiana*, 1 (1983), 97–138

Solmi, S., *Scrittori negli anni: saggi e note sulla letteratura italiana del Novecento* (Milan, Saggiatore, 1963)

Sotis, G., "Montale traduttore e interprete del *Billy Budd* di Melville", *Forum Italicum*, 23 (1989), 195–211

Steiner, G., *After Babel* (Oxford, Oxford University Press, 1975)

T. S. Eliot: A Symposium, edited by R. March and M. J. Tambimuttu (London, Poetry Editions, 1948)

Tomalin, R., *W. H. Hudson: A Biography* (London, Oxford University Press, 1982; Oxford paperback 1984)

Valli, D., "Montale, Saba e la poetica dell'oggetto", *Letteratura*, 79–81 (Jan–June 1966), 23–38

Warren, R., "Montale: Translator, or Translated", in her *The Art of Translation* (Boston, Northeastern University Press, 1989), pp. 217–21

West, R. J., *Eugenio Montale: Poet on the Edge* (Cambridge, Mass., Harvard University Press, 1981)

Wiskeman, E., *Fascism in Italy: Its Development and Influence* (London, Oxford University Press, 1969)

Woolf, V., *The Common Reader* (London, Hogarth Press, 1925)

INDEX OF REFERENCES TO MONTALE'S WORKS

INDEX OF NAMES